CONTEXTS

Series Editor:

Steven Matthews
Oxford Brookes University, UK

Other titles in the series

Victorian Fiction Gail Marshall, University of Leeds, UK
Modernism Steven Matthews, Oxford Brookes University, UK
Renaissance Drama Andrew McRae, University of Exeter, UK
Renaissance Poetry James Loxley, University of Edinburgh, UK

ROMANTIC LITERATURE

JENNIFER BREEN

School of Arts and Humanities, University of North London, UK

and

MARY NOBLE

English Department, Princeton University, USA

BLOOMSBURY

NEW DELHI • LONDON • OXFORD • NEW YORK • SYDNEY

BLOOMSBURY INDIA
Bloomsbury Publishing India Pvt. Ltd
Second Floor, Building No. 4
DDA Complex LSC, Pocket C – 6 & 7
Vasant Kunj, New Delhi 110070
www.bloomsbury.com

BLOOMSBURY, Bloomsbury Academic India and the Diana
logo are trademarks of Bloomsbury Publishing Plc

First published in India 2020
First published in Great Britain in 2002 by
Hodder Arnold, an imprint of Hodder Education and
a member of the Hodder Headline Group,
an Hachette Livre UK Company,
338 Euston Road, London NW! 3BH

www.hoddereducation.com

British Library Cataloguing-in-Publication Data
A catalogue record for this book is available from the British Library.

Library of Congress Cataloging-in-Publication Data
A catalog record for this book is available from the Library of Congress

ISBN: 978-93-89449-69-3
10 9 8 7 6 5 4 3 2 1

For Sale in the Indian subcontinent only

Exclusively distributed in the Indian subcontinent by
Manohar Publishers & Distributors
4753/23, Ansari Road
Darya Ganj, New Delhi 110002
Tel.: 23284848, 23289100
Email: sales@manoharbooks.com, manoharbooks@gmail.com

Production Editor: Rada Radojicic
Production Controller: Martin Kerans
Cover Design: Terry Griffiths

Typeset in 10 on 12 pt Sabon by Phoenix Photosetting, Chatham, Kent.
Printed and bound in India by Replika Press Pvt. Ltd.

Contents

Series editor's preface

The plural in the title of this series, *Contexts*, is intentional. Literature, while it emerges from, and responds to, historical, social and cultural moments, also to a large extent establishes its own contexts, through the particular inflection it puts upon its ostensible 'materials', themes and preoccupations. Therefore, rather than offering a traditional 'major works/historical background' parallel discussion, each *Contexts* volume takes its instigation from the ways in which literary texts have defined their areas of reference, and in which they are in active dialogue with key cultural ideas and events of their time. What aspects of a period most concerned writers? What effect upon literary form have various social and cultural trends had? How have different texts responded to single historical events? How do different texts, ultimately, 'speak back' to their period?

Historical background is made readily available in each volume, but is always closely integrated within discussion of literary texts. As such, the narrative woven around each literary historical period in the individual volumes follows no uniform pattern, but reflects their particular author's sense of the ways in which the contexts of their period establish themselves – generically, thematically, or involving debates about language, gender, religion or social change, for example. While each volume provides detailed discussion of its period's most studied literary works, it also asks informed questions about the canon and periodization itself. Each volume also contains a timeline, full bibliography, and several contemporary literary, cultural, or historical documents which provide material for further reflection and discussion.

Steven Matthews

Acknowledgements

The aim of this book is to help readers and students explore some of the important aspects of the Romantic age that are manifested in British literature of the period 1785–1832. Selected texts, including well-established as well as neglected works, are discussed in order to focus attention on elements in the Romantic age that are central to understanding the ways in which imagery and ideas from this period have permeated later British literary culture. A consideration of possible revisions to the canon of British Romantic literary works comprises the conclusion of this book. Mary Noble wrote Chapter 2, 'Novels of the Romantic age' and contributed some of the material on fiction in Chapter 6, 'Satire in Romantic literature'.

The authors are grateful to Dr Steven Matthews (Series Editor), Ms Elena Seymenliyska (Publisher), Dr Eva Martinez (Editor), and Edward Arnold's two academic readers, for their helpful advice. Acknowledgements are also made to R.W. Noble for his literary advice; to Dan Davison for editorial assistance with Chapter 2; and to Katherine Noble for her help with the chronology of the Romantic age.

Jennifer Breen and Mary Noble

1
Introduction

The background to Romanticism in British literature

The history of British Romantic literature has frequently been dominated by an assumption that a small group of poets is representative of 40 diverse years of literary creativity. Often in university undergraduate courses only five poets comprise 'the Romantic canon' of works that have been chosen for serious reading and study: William Wordsworth, Samuel Taylor Coleridge, Lord Byron, Percy Bysshe Shelley, and John Keats. Sometimes earlier poets, such as William Blake and Robert Burns, have been included. Only occasionally has the undergraduate 'canon' been stretched to include an essayist such as William Hazlitt, or a novelist such as Mary Godwin Shelley with her work of science fiction, *Frankenstein.*

Our book is an attempt to provide undergraduate and general readers with a straightforward introduction not only to the brief 'old' canon but also to a broader 'new' canon. In British literary studies, definitions of Romanticism tend to be of two kinds: first, many attempts have been made to determine the characteristic qualities of the work of the 'big five' poets, qualities that are then subsumed under the heading of 'Romanticism'. This definition of 'Romanticism' is circular in that what is assumed to be 'Romantic' must be found in the attributes of these chosen poets. Moreover, in earlier years, even Lord Byron was omitted from the 'core canon' because his most significant work is satire, which was at one time seen as not suitably 'Romantic'. Second, 'Romanticism' has sometimes been defined in terms of ideological world-views that are identifiable in a few works – whether in literature, pictorial art, or music – that purportedly typify the Romantic age, which in literary studies is usually seen as between approximately 1785 and 1832.

Definitions of Romanticism

'Romanticism' has been defined by some critics as a school of thought that arose in opposition to the kind of art produced in the period that immediately preceded it, that of 'neo-Classicism'. Romanticism has also been posited as a school of thought that conflicted with what is considered as part of the 'Enlightenment' – that is, scientific and rational philosophies of some of the new thinkers of the eighteenth century, such as David Hume, Adam Smith, and Edmund Burke. In *Romantics, Rebels and Reactionaries: English Literature and its Background 1760–1830* (1981), Marilyn Butler discounts such received views in favour of a more 'inchoate' Romanticism:

> We began with the received view that at some time at the end of the eighteenth century a Romantic Revolution occurred, which worked a permanent change in literature and in the other arts, and scored a decisive victory over the classicism which was there before. In reality there would seem to have been no one battle and no complete victory.[1]

Indeed, for some major writers of the Romantic age, there was no 'battle' at all, but an evolution of tradition.

Marshall Brown, in the more recent *Cambridge Companion to British Romanticism* (1993), however, goes somewhat further than most earlier critics, in that he has rejected entirely the supposed opposition between 'Enlightenment' and 'Romanticism': 'Far from being a repudiation of Enlightenment, Romanticism was its fulfilling summation.' Brown cites William Hazlitt, among others, as an example of how writers in the Romantic era extended the scope of the Enlightenment: 'The best of the Enlightenment, as Hazlitt saw it, was striving toward a Romantic potential.' In conclusion, Brown asserts that the so-called Romantic 'revolution' is based on a misunderstanding of that word. He claims that in the eighteenth and nineteenth centuries:

> The word [revolution] meant a turning back before it meant a turning away. . . . It had its moments of rebellion, yet it was not fundamentally a rebellion against its predecessors. Rather, it was revolutionary in that older and more encompassing sense in which a revolution gathers up and recollects, as it sweeps all with it toward the future.[2]

A.C. Goodson takes a similar view to Marshall Brown in that he envisages a continuous line of thought about language from the beginnings of the Enlightenment with Francis Bacon to the twentieth century. Goodson links Wordsworth's 'Preface' to the 1800 *Lyrical Ballads* with the past and future:

> [Wordsworth's] critique of language, as I propose to call this long conversation about words, is an engine of Enlightenment thinking, an essential means of social and epistemological observation that reaches from Bacon and Locke through to logical positivism and the language revolution of literary modernism.[3]

Goodson thus argues that enlightened thinkers of the eighteenth century such as David Hume began to question the nature of rational thought; and that Wordsworth and others developed this process in the Romantic age. Creative artists of the modernist movement in the early twentieth century began to recognize the fact that the language of human thought processes is often illogical in that the mind jumps unsystematically from one image or symbol to another in a seemingly irrational manner. Romanticism can thus be viewed as a forerunner of twentieth-century modernism, rather than as a reaction to the 'Enlightenment'.

Romanticism might be more usefully defined by means of its traditional historical dates, from 1785 to 1832. David Simpson, for example, uses the term 'Romanticism' to 'mean, very roughly, the writings of the late eighteenth and nineteenth centuries, sharing a general historical situation but not necessarily held together by any essential or prescriptive characteristics'. Thus Simpson avoids the inconsistencies of critics who would label one particular work 'Romantic' and another not, even when written in the same period: 'Literary critics and historians have traditionally posited such characteristics in a manner allowing them to distinguish between what is more or less "romantic", early and late romantic, pre- and post-romantic, highly or anti-romantic. Such usages are seldom consistent, and have mostly been employed to justify one set of preferences over others according to some standard or other of exemplary historicality.'[4] Simpson's observations should be augmented with certain additions, because, as mentioned earlier, until recently the term 'Romanticism' has primarily been used to describe men's writing especially in relation to poetry with its visionary and symbolic qualities. The main problem with devising a definition of 'Romanticism' which is based on the work of such a few poets – William Wordsworth, Samuel Taylor Coleridge, Lord Byron, John Keats and Percy Bysshe Shelley – is that a considerably wider range of writings from the years 1785–1832 is required in order to devise an adequate definition. Until about 10 years ago, for instance, critics and readers overlooked women poets of the period 1785–1832. It has only been since the 1970s, with the resurgence of interest in women's literature, that women's Romantic poetry has been brought back into print. Some editors and critics, including myself, began to wonder if all of those women poets were indeed so little worth consideration as had long been silently maintained.

A way round the dilemma of how to include women writers in the 'Romantic' canon when these women writers do not seem to be particularly 'Romantic' – according to the traditional definition of this term – is merely to state that any work written during the period 1785–1832 is necessarily 'Romantic'. Then it is up to editors and critics to establish whether a particular work is worth reading. Anthologies of women poets who published their work during the 'Romantic' period have appeared steadily since the publication of my *Women Romantic Poets* in 1992, and a few women poets of the 'Romantic' period have had their collected poetry, or large selections of their poetry, reprinted. The poems of Charlotte Smith, Anna Barbauld, Mary Robinson, and Joanna Baillie have recently appeared in individual annotated editions. I have made a case for the inclusion of some of Joanna Baillie's lyric poetry in the canon,[5] and other critics have argued the case for the inclusion of one or other of these women poets. What is important here, however, is that the works of these poets have been reprinted in a scholarly manner that allows informed judgements to be made about their work.

Stuart Curran was one of the first critics to take an interest in women poets of the 'Romantic' period. He argues, in his survey 'Romantic Poetry: The I Altered', that, although women poets might not be 'visionary' in the manner of Keats and Shelley, they have 'vision': 'The actual vision might be said to be the province – even the exclusive province – of women poets, whose fine eyes are occupied continually in discriminating minute objects or assembling a world out of its disjointed particulars.'[6] Curran emphasizes that the 'quotidian' or commonplace in women's poetry is one of the aspects of Romanticism that is important, but not every reader would agree with him. Yet an important step has thus been taken towards a more comprehensive definition that includes more major aspects of Romantic literature.

Poets of the Romantic age can often be seen to have followed the diction, forms, and subject matter of eighteenth-century neo-Classical poetry in a trite and attenuated way, or, sometimes, in the accomplished and original manner of poets such as Anna Barbauld and Elizabeth Moody. Other poets, ranging from Joanna Baillie to John Keats, have adapted, if not re-invented, poetic language for a wider spectrum of subjects.

Changes in poetic diction and poetic subjects in the Romantic period

Joanna Baillie, in her 1798 statement of intent, theorized about her own approach to writing poetry:

> I will venture to say, however, that amidst all this decoration and ornament, all this loftiness and refinement, let one simple trait of the human heart, one expression of passion genuine and true to nature, be introduced, and it will stand forth alone in the boldness of reality, whilst the false and unnatural around it, fades away upon every side, like the rising exhalations of the morning. . . . The highest pleasures we receive from poetry, as well as from the real objects which surround us in the world, are derived from the sympathetic interest we all take in beings like ourselves. . . .[7]

Baillie implies here that the 'decoration and ornament' of poetic diction found in eighteenth-century poetry should be substituted with the 'expression' of 'passion genuine and true to nature'. She shows here a departure from artifice in writing towards the representation of feelings of ordinary men and women as the basis of poetry and verse drama.

Subsequently, in his 'Preface' of 1800 to the second edition of *Lyrical Ballads*, Wordsworth specified something similar as one of his aims:

> I have wanted to keep the Reader in the company of flesh and blood, persuaded that by so doing I shall interest him. . . . There will also be found in these volumes little of what is usually called poetic diction; as much pains has been taken to avoid it as is ordinarily taken to produce it; this I have done for the reason already alleged, to bring my language near to the language of men, and further, because the pleasure I have proposed to myself to impart is of a kind very different from that which is supposed by many persons to be the proper object of poetry.[8]

Wordsworth is also interested in the effects of metre and rhyme on the reader, as well as the benefits of expressing himself in a language that is less poeticized than the language of eighteenth-century neo-Classical poetry generally.

Both Baillie and Wordsworth had been influenced by the publication of various editions of songs and ballads, which formed part of a revival of interest in oral balladry of the past. Baillie's career as an author began in her late adolescence in 1779 at her mother's home in Scotland, when, as her biographer, Margaret Carhart, states: 'during the years at Long Calderwood, she [Baillie] had begun to write clever Scotch ballads and adaptations of old songs, which were sung round the ingle hearths of the neighbourhood.'[9] Baillie was thus part of that resurgence of interest in Scottish oral culture, which began with Allan Ramsay's *Tea-Table Miscellany* (1724) and progressed to the years when Herd's *Ancient and Modern Scottish Songs*[10] and Robert Burns' *Poems* (1786) appeared. Joanna Baillie, and Wordsworth and Coleridge, and even Robert Burns, are therefore not the innovators of a new way of writing poetry, but part of a general movement towards the use of ordinary language in serious poetry about individual men and women.

Burns was also the landmark poet in, first, adapting from oral tradition a wider range of subjects, including physical work pursuits, and, second, adopting ideas of freedom and individuality from the eighteenth-century Enlightenment. Yet, where Burns's satiric style reached an apotheosis in 'Tam o' Shanter' (1790), he mocked, through the eyes of his drunken, anti-hero, the characteristic 'Romantic' interest in the supernatural, as well as those who welcomed *de rigueur* Enlightenment ideas brewing in the French Revolution of 1789:

> And vow! *Tam* saw an unco sight!
> Warlocks and witches in a dance;
> Nae cotillion brent new frae *France*,
> But hornpipes, jigs, strathspeys, and reels,
> Put life and mettle in their heels.[11]

Burns here also makes an ironic allusion to the burgeoning Scottish nationalism of the second half of the eighteenth century. Thus, he is an early exemplary 'Romantic' – sending up while also embracing the spirit of the age.

Roy Porter, in *English Society in the Eighteenth Century*, describes a new climate of opinion that was being formed in both Scotland – where Burns adopted as well as mocked the new thinking – and England:

> The thinkers of the Enlightenment championed individual affirmation and liberty. Liberal thinkers, from abstruse philosophers such as Locke to popularisers such as Addison and Goldsmith, spurned blind traditionalism, rejecting their Calvinist theology of original sin and the depravity of man, but equally despising 'Romish' irrationalism. . . .[12]

Burns, in poems such as 'Holy Willie's Prayer' (1785) and 'For a' that and a' that' (1794), can be seen to have ridiculed illiberal religionists as well as those who subscribe to a belief in inherited social rank. Baillie, Wordsworth and Coleridge were also part of the march of new thinking about freedom and the individual in society, in that they attempted to represent in their poems the marginalized individual who has a right, so they thought, to a dignified place in readers' imaginations and in society.[13]

Wordsworth and Coleridge can be shown to have responded to a number of other specific notions that were current at the close of the eighteenth century. Roy Porter describes one of these 'Enlightenment' ideas in relation to the subject of insanity and other mental disabilities:

> Enlightened physicians came to see madness as a *disease* of the body and later one of the mind. The mad were neither brutes nor possessed by devils, but were sick and therefore amenable to treatment and cure. But the right environment would be needed – preferably asylums in rural surroundings, set apart from hubbub and anxiety. Privately run madhouses were founded for those who could afford it (the mad poor either remained at large or were cooped in houses of correction and poor-houses). Instead of confinement, punishment, terror, or sedative medicine, psychological management was championed. Late in the century, 'kindness' became the watchword for a new 'moral therapy'. Rational approaches to madness certainly led to a more considerate treatment for patients.[14]

This process of understanding of the mentally ill had occurred considerably earlier in imaginative writing, however, because dramatists such as Shakespeare and Marlow, and religious visionaries among the Quakers, had shown empathy towards those with emotional problems or 'madness'. Sympathetic literary representations of 'madness', as well as benign treatment in institutions, could be said to have originated at least 200 years earlier, so that empathetic writers in the latter part of the eighteenth century were reflecting a gradual change in attitudes towards what was regarded as 'madness'. Charlotte Smith's sonnet 'On Being Cautioned against Walking on a Headland Overlooking the Sea, Because It Was Frequented by a Lunatic', for example, ironically implies that insanity brings relief from cognisance of the 'depth' and 'duration' of 'woe'. In other words, an excess of sensitivity has led to the 'lunatic's' irrational behaviour, but perhaps he is thus shielded from the worst of life's horrors.

Such literary representations of mental illness, in which 'reason' is contrasted with 'sensibility', sometimes verge on the sentimental and romanticized, as a few of William Wordsworth's and S.T. Coleridge's *Lyrical Ballads* (1798) illustrate. Wordsworth claimed that, although 'The Idiot Boy' might seem an odd choice for the subject of a poem, he is trying to represent the nature of maternal love: 'I have indeed often looked upon the conduct of mothers and fathers of the lower classes of society towards Idiots as the great triumph of the human heart.' Moreover, he feels veneration towards 'idiots': 'I have often applied to Idiots, in my own mind, that sublime expression of Scripture that, *their life is hidden with God*'.[15] Such an attitude to mental disability seems, in the twenty-first century, to overlook the specific disorder of such lives.

In 'Goody Blake and Harry Gill', the narrative pivots on a recognition of the nature of psychosomatic disorders, a subject that Wordsworth would have become familiar with through the aegis of Coleridge, who coined the word 'Psycho-somatic'.[16] Harry Gill is taken in by the supernatural curse that Goody Blake places on him and he believes it:

> Young Harry heard what she had said
> And icy-cold he turned away.
>
> He went complaining all the morrow
> That he was cold and very chill:
> His face was gloom, his heart was sorrow,
> Alas! that day for Harry Gill!
> That day he wore a riding-coat,
> But not a whit the warmer he:
> Another was on Thursday brought,
> And ere the Sabbath he had three.

But Harry Gill is psychologically convinced that Goody Blake's curse is effective, so that his physiology is affected by this belief, and 'He never will be warm again'.[17]

As a study in the compulsive nature of obsession brought on by psychic guilt, Coleridge's ballad 'The Ancient Mariner' has not been surpassed. Because the 'ancient mariner' is influenced by his feeling of guilt at shooting an albatross that he believes might have brought luck to the ship in which he was sailing – instead of the deaths of all the sailors on board – his guilt induces him to tell his story obsessively to chosen listeners. The major difference between these two ballads by Wordsworth and Coleridge and other 'supernatural' ballads of the period is the fact that Wordsworth and Coleridge deconstruct the nature of guilt in relation to what appear to be supernatural events. They bring in mature Enlightenment ideas about the causes and nature of psychological disorders, and they transmute those ideas into poetry. This creative process, drawing upon a variety of new ideas as subject-matter, can also be seen in much of the other major literature of the Romantic age.

Romanticism and the Gothic

'Gothic' images and myths – such as the doomed quest, the cursed wanderer, the medieval haunted castle, the solitary outcast, supposedly supernatural events, the evil villain – represent features that are apparently contrary to the Enlightenment ideas that also characterize much of Romantic literature. Yet, as I indicate above, Coleridge's 'ancient mariner', who can be seen as a version of the cursed and outcast wanderer, also represents the poet's enlightened understanding of guilt and obsession. Coleridge shows awareness of his character's disordered mentality when his mariner describes hearing supernatural voices after falling into a 'fit':

> How long in that same fit I lay
>   I have not to declare;
> But ere my living life return'd,
> I heard and in my soul discern'd
>   Two voices in the air . . .
>
> ('The Ancient Mariner', ll. 398–402)

In Coleridge's allegorical tale, these 'voices' in the mariner's fantasy explain the mariner's guilt as well as his need to expiate, by obsessively repeating his tale, his crime of killing the 'harmless Albatross': 'That anguish comes and makes me tell/My ghastly aventure. . . .'[18] Thus Coleridge combines Enlightenment notions with Gothic imagery in a mesmerizing ballad.

Byron also used Gothic images of the villainous wanderer, but perhaps not so obviously as Coleridge. Fred Botting states that 'Byron's heroes, and his own impersonation of the Byronic hero, possess the defiant energy of a Gothic villain'.[19] Byron, however, satirizes the 'Gothic villain' by means of his characterization of the semi-autobiographical Childe Harold and Don Juan, rather than sensationalizing this mythic figure. Don Juan, in his womanizing and other anti-heroic feats, is portrayed more as a comic villain among villains, as in the episode of cannibalism in Canto II; Byron humorously undercuts the horror of this act as well as showing how Juan behaves morally despite himself when he refuses to eat a portion of the murdered Pedrillo, his tutor. The sailors who consume Pedrillo are punished by madness or death.

Byron explodes several romantic shibboleths in his descriptions of why the mate escaped the fate of becoming one of their next victims:

> He had been rather indisposed of late,
> And that which chiefly proved his saving clause
> Was a small present made to him at Cadiz,
> By general subscription of the ladies.[20]

Romantic love, romantic heroines, romantic heroism – all are ridiculed in this description of the result of the mate's experience in Cadiz brothels, which implies his venereal disease and the other sailors' hypochondria about eating him. Byron's humorous deconstruction of moral taboos against cannibalism also satirizes readers who seek sensations of horror from Gothic fiction as well as those who cultivate a sensibility that only responds to extremes in human behaviour. The cruder representations of the extreme in 'Gothic' novels have little of life or art, whereas Coleridge and Byron, in their individual styles, transmute 'Gothic' imagery into revelatory literature. Further discussion of the 'Gothic' in the genre of the novel can be found in the next chapter.

Sentiment and sensibility

The critics' label 'the cult of sensibility' is an important aspect of Romantic literature. Goethe's sensationalist *The Sorrows of Young Werther* (1774), for example, set the tone for many subsequent works in English, such as Charlotte Smith's best-selling *Elegiac Sonnets* (1784), which ran into seven editions and to which she added a few more new sonnets each time they were reprinted. Her sonnets invariably portray a gloomy, often suicidal protagonist who seeks solace in nature. Five sonnets are constructed as having been written by Werther, Goethe's protagonist.

G. Barker-Benfield defines social and cultural assumptions about the 'sentimental' and 'sensibility' and identifies a 'Werther cult' as one part of that cultivation of sensibility:

> Literary critics and historians, from the earliest to the most recent, have characterized the relationship between writers and readers of sentimental literature (it included poetry and plays as well as fiction) as 'the cult of sensibility'. This cult . . . was coterminous with others: a cult of feeling, a cult of melancholy, a cult of distress, a cult of refined emotionalism, a cult of benevolence, and cults of individual writers (Rousseau's the most famous), and of some of their characters, a 'Werther cult', for example. All may be grouped with the cult of sensibility. . . . The tendency toward the aggrandizement of feeling and its investment with moral value was furthered by preachers and congregants, parents and children, and manufacturers and customers

> as well as writers and readers, all making or coming to terms with the rise of a consumer society.[21]

If sentiment and sensibility have been assigned a 'moral value', as Barker-Benfield claims, and are therefore associated with the consumption of objects in the 'rise of a consumer society', literary art has tended towards debunking consumerism, which for some artists is connected with philistinism.

Moreover, twenty-first-century readers, who are accustomed to the ironic modes of modernism and post-modernism, are not geared towards the appreciation of sentimentalism and sensibility in late eighteenth- and nineteenth-century writings. Such readers probably prefer more satiric Romantic authors ranging from Jane Austen to Lord Byron who even then were already sending up and debunking the cult of sensibility. By the twentieth century, Wilfred Owen's ironic title to his war ode, 'Insensibility' (1917–18), adapted his technique from these earlier satirists by inverting meaning so as to reveal to the reader the incongruence of stock literary responses to occasions that formerly demanded 'sensibility'. Thus, in his use of the abstract noun 'insensibility', with its dual meaning, Owen demonstrates how sentimental feelings that are called out in social situations are often exaggerated or even false, if applied to warfare and bloodshed. Not even the poet is immune to falsity of feeling: 'we wise, who with a thought besmirch/Blood over all our soul. . . .' These lines contrast directly with some of the more sentimental ideas of Keats and Wordsworth about the poet's role. In the extreme situation of warfare, absence of feeling is preferable to experiencing the fear of being killed: 'And some cease feeling/Even themselves or for themselves./Dullness best solves the tease and doubt of shelling. . . .'[22] Owen can be seen as the direct inheritor of Byron's ironic treatment, in *Don Juan* (1819–24), of warfare:

> The groan, the roll in dust, the all-white eye
> Turned back within its socket – these reward
> Your rank and file by thousands, while the rest
> May win perhaps a ribbon at the breast.[23]

Byron's narrator de-sentimentalizes ideals of winning glory through warfare, contrasting the bauble of a military award with war's reality of risking death on the battlefield.

One of the main difficulties for women authors in the period 1785–1832 is that society expected women to express feelings of sentimentality and sensibility in order to appear to be womanly. Authors such as Mary Wollstonecraft and Jane Austen might try to expose the folly of an excess of sentimentality, but other women authors were engaged in writing sentimental verse and fiction in order to attract an audience. In her reviews of poetry and novels for *The Analytical Review*, Mary Wollstonecraft shows a balance between acceptance of women's attraction to the sentimental and of the need for rationality in affairs of the heart. In reference to *Julia, a Novel: interspersed with some poetical Pieces* (1790), by Helen Maria Williams, for example, Wollstonecraft writes:

> There is such feminine sweetness in her style and observations – such modesty and indulgence in her satire – such genuine unaffected piety in her effusions and remarks, that we warmly recommend her novel to our young female readers, who will here meet with refinement of sentiment, without a very great alloy of romantic notions: if the conclusion, that love is not to be conquered by reason, had been omitted, this would be an unexceptionable book for young people.[24]

In her *Thoughts on the Education of Daughters* (1787), Wollstonecraft had already criticized trenchantly what she saw as the corrupting quality of an excess of sensibility in novels for young women:

> Sensibility is described and praised, and the effects of it represented in a way so different from nature, that those who imitate it must make themselves very ridiculous. A false taste is acquired, and sensible books appear dull and insipid after those superficial performances, which obtain their full end if they can keep the mind in a continual ferment. Gallantry is made the only interesting subject with the novelist; reading, therefore, will often co-operate to make his fair admirers insignificant.[25]

A 'sensibility' that is true to 'natural' feeling is acceptable to Mary Wollstonecraft, but she scorns works that play on women's susceptibility to fantasies of a pervasive sexual love.

Hannah More even went so far as to question the lack of censorship of novels read by young women. She suggested that a work such as Rousseau's *La Nouvelle Heloise* (1761), which adds sensuality to sentimentality, was bound to corrupt young women's minds with its implication that freedom from the restraints of civilized behaviour and the full expression of desire should become the norm for young women of that day. Whether novels affect the views of their young women readers is a moot point, but More advocates voluntary or even compulsory censorship of such novels:

> Many instances might be adduced to prove, that the age is gradually grown less scrupulous. We will give only one. Another young lady, independent and rich, about the same time was tempted to send for Rousseau's *Heloise*. A very little progress in the work convinced her, that it was neither safe for her to read, nor, having read it, could she either modestly confess it, or conscientiously deny the perusal, if questioned. Her virtue conquered her curiosity; she sent away, unread, a book which may now be seen lying openly on the tables of many who would be shocked at the slightest imputation on the delicacy of their minds, or the scrupulousness of their morals.[26]

Hannah More, a major leader in the anti-slavery and other reform movements, was not the eccentric that the above argument might make her seem now; she had concluded that thought as well as morals might be corrupted by fiction in which an excess of the cult of sensibility is further sensationalized by the addition of a cult of the sensual. Possibly, however, Jane Austen's fictional satire of 'sensibility' is a more palatable and effective way to reveal both the limitations and the positive qualities of sensibility to feeling.

Art in relation to science

The progress of scientific thought during the eighteenth century was a source of anxiety to some writers who feared that utilitarianism – with its emphasis on the useful and scientific – might undermine the value of poetry and other arts. The satirist Thomas Love Peacock, in an essay, *The Four Ages of Poetry* (1820), took a utilitarian view of the arts, which Percy Bysshe Shelley felt he must take up cudgels against. Shelley's *A Defence of Poetry* was written in 1821, but published posthumously in 1840. Shelley implies that a utilitarian man is seeking Mammon rather than the good of mankind: 'The cultivation of those sciences which have enlarged the limits of the empire of man over the external world has, for want of the poetical faculty, proportionally circumscribed those of the internal world; and man, having enslaved the elements, remains himself a slave.'[27] Shelley believed that without a parallel development in man's imagination the development of the sciences could lead to technologies that might enslave humankind as much as enslaving the earth. Yet Shelley was also knowledgeable in the fields of science and technology. Timothy Webb concludes that Shelley 'was well informed on theories of light, electricity, the nature of matter and the behaviour of volcanoes.'[28] He acquired this knowledge at the schools Syon House and Eton, and from the scientist Dr James Lind (1736–1812).

Peacock's argument against the supremacy of poets had been provoked as much by Wordsworth's exaggerated claims as by Shelley's. In his 'Preface' to the 1802 edition of *Lyrical Ballads* (first edn, 1798), Wordsworth gave a detailed account of his view of the poet's role in society:

> What is a Poet? To whom does he address himself? And what language is to be expected from him? He is a man speaking to men: a man, it is true, endued with more lively sensibility, more enthusiasm and tenderness, who has a greater knowledge of human nature, and a more comprehensive soul, than are supposed to be common among mankind; a man pleased with his own passions and volitions, and who rejoices more than other men in the spirit of life that is in him; delighting to contemplate similar volitions and passions as manifested in the goings-on of the Universe, and habitually impelled to create them where he does not find them. To these qualities he has added a

> disposition to be affected more than other men by absent things as if they were present; an ability of conjuring up in himself passions, which are indeed far from being the same as those produced by real events, yet (especially in those parts of the general sympathy which are pleasing and delightful) do more nearly resemble the passions produced by real events, than anything which, from the motions of their own minds merely, other men are accustomed to feel in themselves; whence, from practice, he has acquired a greater readiness and power in expressing what he thinks and feels, and especially those thoughts and feelings which, by his own choice, or from the structure of his own mind, arise in him without immediate external excitement.[29]

Wordsworth asserts the value of the imaginative life, which the poet possesses more than the non-poetic person. His assertion is made in the face of a society that seems to be turning towards the economic, the practical, and the exploitation of nature as central modes of social operation. Wordsworth insists on the value of the individual's thoughts and feelings at a time when the individual often seemed to be losing rather than gaining various non-material goods.

Conclusion

These introductory points will be developed further in subsequent chapters. In addition, as indicated earlier, this book will, first, discuss – in a historical context – the qualities of a broad selection of poems and prose fiction from the period 1785–1832. Second, literary forms that developed significantly during the Romantic period, particularly those of the sonnet, the ballad, and a kind of 'hybrid' fiction that intertwines romance with realism, will be analysed with regard to their historical development. And, finally, the literary canon of the Romantic period is discussed in relation to changes that might be made or have already been made.

Notes

1 Marilyn Butler, *Romantics, Rebels and Reactionaries: English Literature and its Background 1760–1830* (Oxford, 1981; repr. 1992), p. 184.
2 Marshall Brown, 'Romanticism and Enlightenment', in *The Cambridge Companion to British Romanticism*, ed. Stuart Curran (Cambridge, 1993), pp. 38, 44, 46–7.
3 A.C. Goodson, 'Romantic Theory and the Critique of Language', in *Questioning Romanticism*, ed. John Beer (Baltimore and London, 1995), pp. 4–5.
4 David Simpson, 'Romanticism, Criticism and Theory', in *The Cambridge Companion to Romanticism*, ed. Stuart Curran (Cambridge, 1993), p. 1.
5 'Introduction', *The Selected Poems of Joanna Baillie*, ed. Jennifer Breen (Manchester, 1999), p. 21.

6 Stuart Curran, 'Romantic Poetry: The I Altered', in *Romanticism and Feminism*, ed. Anne K. Mellor (Bloomington, 1988), p. 189.
7 'Introductory Discourse', *The Selected Poems of Joanna Baillie*, ed. Jennifer Breen (Manchester, 1999), p. 191.
8 William Wordsworth and S.T. Coleridge, *Lyrical Ballads*, ed. R.I. Brett and A.R. Jones (London, 1963; 2nd edn, 1991), p. 251.
9 Margaret Carhart, *The Life and Work of Joanna Baillie* (New Haven, USA; London, 1923), p. 168.
10 David Herd, ed., *Ancient and Modern Scottish Songs* (Edinburgh, 1776).
11 *The Poems and Songs of Robert Burns*, ed. James Kinsley, Vol. II (3 vols, London, 1968), pp. 560–1.
12 Roy Porter, *English Society in the Eighteenth Century* (Harmondsworth, 1982; rev. 1990), p. 256.
13 Toby R. Benis argues in *Romanticism on the Road: The Marginal Gains of Wordsworth's Homeless* (Cambridge, 2000) that Wordsworth identified first with the homeless such as the woman portrayed in his poem 'The Female Vagrant', but later came to draw back from such identifications. Wordsworth was perhaps also reflecting shifts of opinion in society itself, since the 'Enlightenment' eventually hardened into a Victorian exploitation of the poor as a labour force for the newly industrialized society (cf. Karl Marx, *Das Kapital*, 1848).
14 Roy Porter, *English Society in the Eighteenth Century*, p. 304.
15 See *Lyrical Ballads*, ed. Brett and Jones, p. xxxi.
16 Walter Jackson Bate, *Coleridge* (Toronto, 1968), p. 103.
17 *Lyrical Ballads*, ed. Brett and Jones, p. 58.
18 *Lyrical Ballads*, ed. Brett and Jones, pp. 21 and 33.
19 Fred Botting, *Gothic* (London and New York, 1996), p. 98.
20 Lord Byron, *Don Juan*, ed. T.G. Steffan, E. Steffan, and W.W. Pratt (Harmondsworth, 1973; rev. T.G. Steffan, 1982), II, Stanza 81, p. 122.
21 G. Barker-Benfield, 'Introduction', *The Culture of Sensibility: Sex and Society in Eighteenth-Century Britain* (Chicago and London, 1992), p. xix.
22 See *Wilfred Owen: Selected Poetry and Prose*, ed. Jennifer Breen (London, 1988), p. 63.
23 Lord Byron, *Don Juan*, VIII, Stanza 13, p. 320.
24 *The Works of Mary Wollstonecraft*, ed. Marilyn Butler and Janet Todd, Vol. 7, *Contributions to the Analytical Review* (London, 1989), p. 252.
25 *The Works of Mary Wollstonecraft*, Vol. 5, *Thoughts on the Education of Daughters*, p. 20.
26 Hannah More, 'Unprofitable Reading', in *Moral Sketches of Prevailing Opinions and Manners* (1819), repr. in *Women Romantics, 1785–1832: Writing in Prose* (London, 1996), p. 116.
27 *A Defence of Poetry*, 1840, repr. in *P.B. Shelley: Selected Poetry and Prose*, ed. Alasdair D.F. Macrae (London, 1991), p. 227.
28 'Introduction', P.B. Shelley, *Selected Poems*, ed. Timothy Webb (London, 1977; repr. 1983), p. xxvi.
29 'Preface', *Lyrical Ballads*, ed. Brett and Jones, pp. 255–6.

2

Novels of the Romantic age

Introduction

The fiction written during the Romantic period is often studied in ways that focus on its historical context but skirt around the issue of its relationship to concepts of Romanticism itself, although many critics regard some concept of Romanticism as central to the interpretation of literature written between 1785 and 1832. Since what we have come to identify as 'Romanticism' is based mainly on readings of the poetry of the period, I intend to discuss not only whether some significant novels of this period can be considered 'Romantic' in a similar way to much of its poetry, but also whether these significant novels enlarge the received notion of what the canon of the Romantic age comprises.

One has to ask whether the 'novels of the Romantic age' can be said to form a coherent group. Recent criticism has tended to group novels of the era thematically, focusing, for instance, on regional novels, such as those by Maria Edgeworth and Sydney Owenson, which are set in Ireland, and by Walter Scott in Scotland; on fiction by women writers, including Austen, Frances Burney, Edgeworth, Mary Shelley and others; or on novelists who engage with some of the political upheavals of the 1790s, such as William Godwin, Elizabeth Hamilton, Mary Hays, Thomas Holcroft and Mary Wollstonecraft. The majority of novels written during this era share some thematic preoccupations, such as sensibility, nationalism, the Gothic, and the sublime in nature to an extent that is unique to the period. A significant number of interesting novels that are not classified as 'Gothic novels' or 'novels of sensibility' nonetheless engage with these preoccupations satirically: Austen's *Northanger Abbey* (1818) and Thomas Love Peacock's *Nightmare Abbey* (1818) both make a central feature of Gothic conventions and language, while Matthew Lewis's uber-Gothic novel *The Monk* (1796) also pokes fun at many conventional Gothic tropes and plot devices. Yet more novels are frequently classified under one sub-genre but gesture towards others: Godwin's *Caleb Williams* is seen as the great Jacobin novel of the 1790s, but it is also a Gothic novel, while Hogg's *Confessions of a Justified Sinner*, set in Scotland, could be described as regional Gothic. Tropes such as the sublime landscape and ancient castle are practically ubiquitous in regional novels as well as in Gothic ones.

In his comprehensive study *English Fiction of the Romantic Period*, Gary Kelly attempts to characterize the Romantic novel in his description of Jane Austen as the 'representative Romantic novelist':

> she deals superbly with the central thematic and formal issues of the novel of the period – the gentrification of the professional classes and the professionalization of the gentry, the place of women in a professionalized culture that denies them any significant role in public or professional life, the establishment of a 'national' culture of distinction and discrimination in the face of fashion and commercialised culture, the re-siting of the authentic self in an inward moral and intellectual being so cultivated as to be able to negotiate successfully the varieties of social experience and cultural discriminations, the establishment of a standard speech based on writing, and resolution of the relationship of authoritative narration and detailed representation of subjective experience.[1]

However, while this description fits many novels of the Romantic age, at least to some extent, the characteristics he lists contrast sharply with what he later refers to as 'the central characteristics and achievements of Romantic poetry . . . intense, transcendent and reflexive subjectivity, supernatural naturalism and discursive self-consciousness'.[2] In a subsequent essay discussing 'Romantic Fiction', Kelly concludes by comparing these two versions of Romanticism, that of poetry and that of fiction, to imply that the predominant aims of the literature of the period were those of its novelists, whom he considers to have achieved as much or more than its poets in exploring domestic affections, local life, and national culture. These aims are not, however, the central concerns in a Gothic novel such as *Vathek* any more than in a poem such as 'Kubla Khan'; whereas 'the domestic affections and local quotidian life',[3] for instance, are as much if differently explored in Wordsworth's poems as they are in Austen's novels.

The majority of the novels of the Romantic age tend to support Kelly's view that their predominant ideology is a bourgeois one, since the almost inevitable resolution of the plot with one or more marriages would seem to valorize middle-class 'quotidian' life and the 'domestic affections', while the 'realism' of many novels also tends to deflate romantic idealism through collision with the commonplace. This deflation occurs in Radcliffe's novels through the marriage plot and her characteristic device of the 'supernatural explained', where she accounts for supernatural events in rational terms, and in Austen's, through her 'punishment' of sensibility in heroines such as Marianne in *Sense and Sensibility* (1811).

A related Romantic project was to valorize the poet and to resist the marginalization of the artist in an increasingly industrialized, mercantile, and bourgeois-dominated British society. This is expressed in autobiographical and semi-autobiographical poems by male poets including Wordsworth and Byron, and epitomized in the construction of the poet as Promethean creator. Many of the most influential and widely read fiction-writers of the period, including Austen, Burney, Edgeworth, Radcliffe, Scott, and Mary Shelley, implicitly or overtly support the changes in British society, although with qualifications, stressing the importance of family life and rational judgement, and implicitly or overtly condemn the perceived 'Romantic' personality cultivated and cult-ified by many Romantic poets.

In *English Fiction of the Romantic Period*, Kelly reveals the limitations of his aforementioned generalizations, since his list of sub-genres of Romantic fiction is an assemblage of contraries: Jacobin novels, anti-Jacobin novels, Gothic, Gothic Romance, novels of sensibility, national tales, moral tales, tales of fashionable life, tales of the heart, tales of real life, historical romances, tales for youth, tales of wonder, Scotch novels, 'silver fork' novels, 'Newgate' novels, and the Romantic quasi-novel. Several of these kinds of novel have little, if anything, in common with Romantic poetry: 'Anti-Jacobin novels', and 'tales of real life', in particular, were thematically and formally in opposition to the Romantic cult of the imagination and sensibility. Yet Gothic novels, for example those by Ann Radcliffe, have much that is in common with Romantic poetry, in terms of both language and themes – for instance the transcendentalizing of nature, and the significance accorded to an emotional response to such landscapes.

Another difficulty in relating the Romantic period novel to a Romantic agenda set by poetry is that during the period, especially in the 1780s and 1790s, the novel was not seen as high art in the way that poetry was, a perception that has lingered on in recent literary criticism. Coleridge, a regular reviewer of fiction for the *Critical Review*, satirized both fiction-readers and fiction-reading, wittily articulating a prevalent view of the novel as an adverse, if transient, mental and moral influence, and moreover a pointless waste of the reader's time:

> For as to the devotees of the circulating libraries, I dare not compliment their passtime, or rather killtime, with the name of reading. Call it rather a sort of beggarly day-dreaming, during which the mind of the dreamer furnishes for itself nothing but laziness and a little mawkish sensibility; . . . this genus comprizes as its species, gaming, swinging, or swaying on a chair or gate; spitting over a bridge; smoking; snuff-taking . . .[4]

While Coleridge's attitude is fairly light-hearted, many other more conservative critics contemporary to him expressed serious moral criticism of the genre as a whole.

Early in the twentieth century, when J.M.S. Tompkins wrote her groundbreaking survey of *The Popular Novel in England 1770–1800*, she made no claims for the quality of the works she included, and rather proclaimed their lack of merit; Ian Watt, in the last chapter of his seminal book on eighteenth-century fiction *The Rise of the Novel*, dismisses the 'mediocre' fiction of the Romantic period, of which only Austen's novels are said to have been of central importance to the development of the genre in the nineteenth century. Many readers will still consider Austen's restrained realism as a mark of 'great fiction', and may view the reverse, the prolixity, emotionalism and unrestrained qualities of novels by writers such as Burney, as a sign of their lack of artistry.

Austen's own defence of the Romantic-era novel, in *Northanger Abbey*, has a surprisingly polemical tone, and is perhaps the most frequently quoted contemporary vindication of novels as a genre. Its unusual status in Austen's novels, as an overt authorial comment on the form in which she is writing, testifies to the strength of compulsion that she, as a novelist, felt herself to be under to make such a justification of her work: 'there seems to be almost a general wish of decrying the capacity, and undervaluing the labour of the novelist, and of slighting the performances which have only genius, wit, and taste to recommend them.'[5] Austen refutes the denigration of novels as intellectually and artistically inferior by simply producing as evidence the artistry of Burney and Edgeworth, the two most respected novelists of the day. This expectation of the reader's concurrence with her assessment of the two novelists suggests the existence of a growing counter-current in opinion towards the belief that the novel did indeed have artistic value.

Of the novels of the Romantic period that have best survived the test of time, and still attract a large readership, it seems to be the more supposedly un-Romantic novelists who predominate – Austen has worn better than the Gothic novelists, although the latter were as popular in their day. In most studies charting the history of the novel, Gothic fiction, novels of sensibility, historical romance, and other kinds of non-realistic fiction have a secondary place. Yet these latter genres seem to manifest a clearer relationship to Romantic poetry, in terms of both content and style, than the more socially realistic novels. Sentimental and Gothic novelists such as Ann Radcliffe and Charlotte Smith wrote lyrical prose, interspersed with poetic quotations from English 'classics' such as Shakespeare and with their own poetry, and endorsed a Romantic belief in the significance of subjective experience, while 'realistic' novelists, such as Maria Edgeworth and Austen, often dealt with more commonplace subjects, in more prosaic terms.

Realism was, according to Margaret Anne Doody in *The True Story of the Novel*, 'new in the eighteenth century and dominant in the nineteenth'.[6] She refers to it as 'prescriptive realism', suggesting that this constrained novelists to write only about what seems plausible or probable in everyday life. Yet sub-genres of fiction that resisted such realism abounded in the Romantic period: the Oriental tale, the Gothic novel, the 'historical romance', and science fiction. These works were, however, censured by contemporary critics both for their lack of realism and for their detrimental moral influence on the reader. A lack of realism, in the perception of some cultural arbiters, who included many literary reviewers and educational reformers as well as some novelists, could exacerbate an immoral influence on the readers of a particular work; and a novel's artistry was at that time assessed on the basis of its moral tendency as well as its formal and stylistic qualities. The journal *The British Critic* (which was funded by a Conservative government) condemned Matthew Lewis's *The Monk* (1796)[7] in terms that linked its immorality and its unrealism: 'Lust, murder, incest, and every atrocity that can disgrace human nature, brought together, without the apology of probability, or even possibility, for their introduction. . . .'[8] Coleridge's negative assessment of Ann Radcliffe's novels in *The Critical Review* indicates that realism or plausibility in fiction had become an automatic expectation, although in his own poems he clearly does not aim to confine himself to what can be observed in real life:

> It was not difficult to foresee that the *modern romance*, even supported by the skill of the most ingenious of its votaries, would soon experience the fate of every attempt to please by what is unnatural, and by a departure from that observance of real life, which has placed the works of Fielding, Smollett, and some other writers, among the permanent sources of amusement.[9]

It seems significant that Coleridge chose from among eighteenth-century novelists two of those whose works least resemble his own Romantic poetry, in order to imply that non-realism and the novel are best not mixed.

Although the term Romantic was not used during the period itself to describe either a cultural movement or the authors now commonly thought of as Romantic, the term 'romance' was frequently used by writers and critics (for example by Coleridge in his review, above) and had a specific, although often debated, meaning when used to describe a work of fiction or a fictional genre. Clara Reeve's *The Progress of Romance* (1785) is a survey, in the form of a Platonic dialogue, of prose fiction written before 1780, which attempts to define the difference between the novel and the romance: 'The Romance is an heroic fable, which treats of fabulous persons and things. – The Novel is a picture of real life and manners, and of the times in which it is written.'[10] Some confusion arises, however, when Reeve divides specific fictional works of the eighteenth century into one or other category – for instance, *A Tale of a Tub*, *Gulliver's Travels*, *Don Quixote*, *Tristram Shandy*, and *The Castle of Otranto* are all considered to be novels, despite having some qualities of romance or mock-romance, whereas Dr Johnson's rather comparable *Rasselas* is not.[11] The term 'romance' or, as Coleridge has it, 'modern romance', was frequently used by critics, and by novelists in sub-titling their work, to describe novels that we might now see as particularly 'unrealistic' – especially Gothic novels, such as Radcliffe's *The Romance of the Forest*, *A Sicilian Romance*, and *The Mysteries of Udolpho, a Romance*, and historical novels, such as

Scott's *Ivanhoe* (1819), sub-titled 'a Romance'. On the other hand, 'realistic' novelists and novelists of 'manners', would frequently sub-title their works 'a Novel', which appears on the title page of all of Austen's novels that were published during her lifetime. Any assumption, however, that 'romance' and 'realistic novel' were always oppositional is misleading, since major 'hybrid' novels such as Scott's combined and integrated both romance and realism.

Gillian Beer, in her monograph *The Romance*, charts the changing nature and status of romance from medieval to recent times. She says of the use of romance conventions during the Romantic age: 'The Romantic attitude to the romance and its associated forms is distinguished by conscious revivalism – revivalism in both senses of the word, since it is present both as pedantic antiquarianism and as a restoring to spiritual life.'[12] This 'conscious revivalism' describes cultural trends such as antiquarianism as well as retrospectively defined movements such as Orientalism. In poetry, this antiquarianism and exoticism was variously characterized by collections of old ballads and oral poetry, such as Percy's *Reliques* (1765), by works of pseudo-antiquity such as MacPherson's Ossian poems (1760–63), and by works that drew on the popular ballad such as Wordsworth's *Lyrical Ballads* (1798). Antiquarianism and exoticism appeared in novels of the period largely in terms of their setting: in remote historical novels set in the medieval past, such as Scott's *Ivanhoe* (1820) and Godwin's *St Leon* (1799), in Gothic novels set in medieval Italy, such as the *Mysteries of Udolpho* (1794), or in novels set in the East, such as William Beckford's *Vathek* (1785). Many novelists, including Beckford, Edgeworth, Owenson, and Scott, appended scholarly notes or glossaries to their works, which create a distance between the voice of the 'editor-narrator', with whom the reader can identify as the voice of reasoned objectivity, and the otherness of past customs or exotic locations. Supposedly informative notes could also provide a superficially orthodox point of view, which might then be challenged by a sympathetic portrayal of the alternative culture, as in Edgeworth's *Castle Rackrent*. Alternatively, such factual notes could become an instrument of propaganda, as they are in Owenson's *The Wild Irish Girl*. Remote settings, such as Roman Catholic Europe or the Islamic East, were also an often used and readily decipherable code through which to criticize English social institutions or comment controversially on contemporary events such as the French Revolution, without risking imprisonment by explicitly criticizing church or king in defiance of the anti-treason test acts, which were in effect from 1795 to 1828. Ann Radcliffe, in a rare use of a footnote in *The Romance of the Forest*, draws the reader's attention to the French Revolution in order to remind the reader that the France in which she sets the novel is pre-revolutionary, but this also serves to bring contemporary political turmoil to the forefront of the reader's mind, inviting a possible interpretation of the novel in the light of such events.

Radcliffe and Romantic Gothic

Ann Radcliffe's Gothic novels have much in common with some Romantic poetry, such as Wordsworth's, especially in terms of the significance given to nature, the language of the picturesque and the sublime used to describe it, and the quasi-religious association attached to the beautiful and the terrifying in nature. Radcliffe was a source of inspiration to several Romantic poets, including Keats, who referred to her as 'Mother Radcliffe' in a letter to George Keats (14 February 1819). In another letter to Reynolds (14 March 1818), he promises that 'I am going among scenery whence I intend to tip you the Damosel Radcliffe – I'll cavern you, and grotto you, and waterfall you, and wood you, and water you, and immense rock you, and tremendous sound you, and solitude you.' The second quoted letter suggests Radcliffe's status as a signifier for a whole set of generic conventions and motifs. Her fiction also influenced many novelists, including Jane Austen, who in *Northanger Abbey* satirizes Radcliffe's hyperbolic language while also weaving elements of Radcliffe's plots into her own.

In Radcliffe's novels, a Romantic appreciation for nature and a volatile emotional sensibility serve as a kind of moral index among her characters: heroines such as Adeline (*The Romance of the Forest*, 1791) and Emily St Aubert (*The Mysteries of Udolpho*, 1794), and idealized, benevolent paternal figures (M. St. Aubert and La Luc), share an almost debilitating emotional susceptibility to nature, an appreciation which extends to its more threatening or terrifying manifestations, such as thunderstorms, as well as its beauties. Radcliffe's villains, evil aristocratic figures like Montoni and the Marquis de Montalt, are impervious to natural beauty; and the responses to nature from her lower-class characters, servants or peasants, are limited to a caricatured patriotism, expressed in conventional and often erroneous terms (for instance, Adeline's servant Peter mistakes mountains for 'hills').

In Radcliffe's second novel, *A Sicilian Romance* (1790), a sublime landscape produces an enjoyable melancholy in Mme de Menon, which reciprocally enhances her perception of the landscape to an almost hallucinatory degree:

> Fancy caught the thrilling sensation, and at her touch the towering steeps became shaded with unreal glooms; the caverns more darkly frowned – the projecting cliffs assumed a more terrific aspect, and the wild overhanging shrubs waved to the gale in deeper murmurs. The scene inspired Madame with reverential awe. . . .[13]

In this passage, as elsewhere in Radcliffe's novels, nature is implicitly represented as an earthly manifestation of the divine. Like Radcliffe, poets who make a similar use of nature, such as Wordsworth or Keats, advocate an anti-rationalist, intuitive emotional response to nature in order to grasp deeper truths about the world.

In Radcliffe's novels, moreover, compassionate empathy with other human beings, as well as an appreciation for nature, is an aesthetic experience as well as a virtue, in a way that is comparable to Wordsworth's poem 'The Wanderer', which aestheticizes an emotional response to the hardship or sadness suffered by others. In Wordsworth's poetry, this heightened responsiveness to nature and to compassion is the preserve of certain privileged individuals, such as the Wanderer or the poet-narrator. Significantly, Radcliffe's sensitive heroines are also themselves poets, whose impromptu verses, interpolated into the novels, seem curiously unreflective of the heroines' predicaments, usually focusing instead on the landscape or on mythical situations – like Wordsworth's Wanderer and the poem's narrator, their poetic sensibility seems to preclude pragmatic action.

The Romantic qualities of Radcliffe's novels are inevitably suppressed at their conclusions, when Gothic and supernatural elements are dispelled, the villains justly punished, and the heroines sequestered in happy bourgeois marriages with tidy inherited fortunes to secure their futures. Radcliffe was, moreover, notorious among her contemporaries as a rationalizer of the supernatural in her novels, to a degree that some reviewers such as Coleridge found yet more implausible than the supernatural events themselves (it is to this that he refers as 'crying wolf' in the review quoted previously, and which Matthew Lewis parodied in *The Monk*). In *The Mysteries of Udolpho* the device of the 'supernatural explained' is used frequently at the novel's conclusion to de-mystify occurrences that include the apparently rotting corpse (a wax figure) behind the veil, and the disappearance of a servant (who was kidnapped by smugglers) from a supposedly haunted room. However, in Radcliffe's novels the presence of the supernatural is never altogether expelled, since it remains inscribed in the potential offered by nature for human contact with the divine.

Radcliffe's luminous descriptions of landscape were influenced by the paintings of the Italian artist Salvator Rosa (1615–73), whose works later came to epitomize the Romantic conception of the 'picturesque' as wild, rugged and asymmetrical, and Radcliffe refers the reader un-ironically to Salvator to emphasize particularly picturesque scenes in several of her novels. Scott also does this, but ironically, in *Waverley*, when his hero meets the robber chief, Donald Bean Lean: 'Waverley prepared himself to meet a stern, gigantic, ferocious figure, such as Salvator himself would have chosen to be the central object of a group of banditti.' Waverley's romantic expectations, however, are abruptly deflated as, in fact, 'Donald Bean Lean was the very reverse . . . thin in person and low in stature'.[14] Owenson too brings in Salvator as testifying to a certain type of beauty ascribed to the Irish landscape: 'if the glowing fancy of Claude Loraine would have dwelt enraptured on the paradisial charms of English landscape, the superior genius of Salvator Rosa would have reposed its eagle wing amidst those scenes of mysterious sublimity with which the wildly magnificent landscape of Ireland abounds.'[15]

Radcliffe also explicitly associates the highest forms of aesthetic pleasure with terror and horror, following Edmund Burke's concept of 'the sublime', as he influentially defined it in his *Philosophical Enquiry into the Origin of Our Ideas of the Sublime and Beautiful* (1756) – 'fitted in any sort to excite the ideas of pain, and danger, that is to say, whatever is in any sort terrible, or is conversant with terrible objects, or operates in a manner analogous to terror, is a source of the *sublime*'.[16] In Radcliffe's *The Romance of the Forest* (1791), for instance, the heroine Adeline wishes to experience the 'dreadful sublimity' of a thunderstorm in the mountains, albeit from a place of safety.[17] The contemplation of a picturesque or sublime spectacle is often associated in Radcliffe's novels both with melancholy reverie and with a pleasure akin to religious ecstasy, in a way that is typical of many other popular and influential works of this era, including Goethe's *The Sorrows of Young Werther* (1774, first translated into English in 1779 as *The Sorrows of Werter*) and Wordsworth's *Prelude* (composed 1798?–1850, first published 1850).[18] In Goethe's fiction, as in Radcliffe's, susceptibility to nature and to melancholy are presented as virtues: in *The Sorrows of Young Werther*, Werther's acute enjoyment of walking in the mountains at the start of the novel is one of his most endearing characteristics, while his growing nihilism later on corresponds to his increasing inability to respond to nature.[19]

Political novels of the 1790s: Wollstonecraft and Godwin

Many novels, as well as poems, of the Romantic period, especially those written during the 1790s, participated in the conflict between conservative and radical politics in Britain that escalated following the French Revolution in 1789. The two intellectual standpoints were in many ways epitomized by the sentimental conservatism of Edmund Burke's *Reflections on the Revolution in France* (1790), on the one hand, and the rationalism and political radicalism (or 'Jacobinism') of Thomas Paine's *Rights of Man* and Godwin's *Enquiry Concerning Political Justice* on the other. Even novels without an overt political agenda participate in this debate – for instance, although Radcliffe makes use of Burke's earlier ideas on the sublime, she questions and subverts the chivalric code and the location of authority within the aristocracy that Burke defends in his *Reflections*. The latter work contained a warm advocacy of a society that is based not on a rationally devised constitution guaranteeing equal rights, but rather on uncritical respect for monarchical power and an unspoken chivalric code. Burke re-appropriates the term 'prejudice' and gives it a positive gloss, and conversely denigrates 'reason' and 'enlightenment'.[20]

One of the first published ripostes to Burke's polemic was Mary Wollstonecraft's *A Vindication of the Rights of Men* (1790), in which she directly attacked Burke's privileging of sensibility and sentiment over reason. In *A Vindication of the Rights of Woman* (1792) she criticized this at greater length, particularly emphasizing the detrimental effects for women of his advocacy of chivalry and sentiment, an issue against which she had already protested in her first fictional work, *Mary* (1788). In the first chapter of this novel, she parodies the kind of sentimental novels that encourage sensibility in their female readers:

> If my readers would excuse the sportiveness of fancy and give me credit for genius, I would go on and tell them such tales as would force the sweet tears of sensibility to flow in copious showers down beautiful cheeks, to the discomposure of rouge etc. etc.

A special kind of sensibility is, however, championed as a virtue in her eponymous heroine of *Mary*:

> Sensibility is the most exquisite feeling of which the human soul is susceptible: when it pervades us, we feel happy; and could it last unmixed, we might form some conjecture of the bliss of those paradisiacal days, when the obedient passions were under the dominion of reason, and the impulse of the heart did not need correction.[21]

Wollstonecraft here links sensibility with reason and well-disciplined emotions, as opposed to 'passions', so that her seeming ambivalence towards sensibility is nonetheless self-consistent, and, in *Mary* as well as in her non-fiction, she makes a distinction between feelings that are 'artless' and 'unaffected' as opposed to those that are artificially cultivated. In Wollstonecraft's unfinished second novel, *The Wrongs of Woman, or, Maria*[22] (published posthumously in 1798), the heroine's sensibility is portrayed as both a virtue and a liability in its excess, which is fostered in middle-class women by the limitations of their education. In this novel Wollstonecraft re-appropriates a familiar Gothic motif, which opens with her heroine confined in a madhouse by a scheming villain, but reverses generic expectations with the revelation that the villain is Maria's husband, and that this horror takes place in middle-class England. Even more subversively, Wollstonecraft defends the right of a woman thus circumstanced to look outside of her marriage for love. In both of her novels she condemns a society in which, as she saw it, intelligent, sensitive women could be freely abused by men and were prevented from seeking fulfilment through other channels.

William Godwin's philosophical treatise *An Enquiry Concerning Political Justice*[23] (1793), was one of the most significant polemics, alongside Thomas Paine's *Rights of Man* (1792), to be written following the French Revolution and in reaction against Burke's *Reflections*. The brand of rationalist idealism advocated in *Political Justice* influenced Wordsworth and Coleridge as well as overt radicals such as Wollstonecraft in the 1790s, and also inspired a later generation of writers, including Mary and Percy

Shelley, the daughter and son-in-law of Godwin and Wollstonecraft. In his first novel *Things as they Are, or the Adventures of Caleb Williams* (1794), Godwin sought to express his critique of society, outlined in *Political Justice*, through the powerful medium of fiction, through which he hoped to reach a wider readership than he had with his political treatise, since novels were rapidly gaining a mass readership and could be rented cheaply from circulating libraries. In his 1794 preface to the novel, Godwin stated its potentially inflammatory purpose:

> It is now known to philosophers, that the spirit and character of the government intrudes itself into every rank of society. But this is a truth highly worthy to be communicated to persons whom books of philosophy and science are never likely to reach. Accordingly it was proposed, in the invention of the following work, to comprehend ... a general review of the modes of domestic and unrecorded despotism by which man becomes the destroyer of man.[24]

Almost 40 years later, in his preface to the 1832 edition, Godwin focused instead on the psychological genesis of the novel, and de-emphasized the political message set out in the 1794 preface. By 1832, Godwin perhaps realized that his novel was dominated by its suspenseful plot, which overshadows the political aim set out in the 1794 preface, and makes the novel seem too sensational to be read as a realistic portrayal of 'domestic despotism'.

In order to serve as an exposé of 'things as they are', or at least to explore the ramifications of an extreme abuse of existing social institutions and power structures, Godwin's characters and situations need to seem 'socially typical, the consequence of systemic injustice'.[25] But Godwin closes off the possibility of perceiving either the narrator Caleb or the aristocratic anti-hero Falkland as representatives of their respective social classes, since the atypical characteristics and abilities of both men are emphasized throughout the novel. Both men are obsessive, Caleb with satisfying his 'curiosity', Falkland with his 'reputation', and both, ultimately, with each other. Falkland is a talented poet and conversationalist, the perfect cultivated patrician, while Caleb has seemingly inexhaustible talents, acting over the course of the novel as secretary, librarian, journalist, teacher of geography and mathematics, carpenter and watchmaker, and disguising himself variously as a tramp, an Irishman and a Jew. The ending of the novel seems strangely ambivalent, if the novel is to be interpreted as a social critique; Falkland's tyrannous abuse of power does not prevail, but this is because Caleb confronts him and he confesses to his previous crimes – in other words, his unjust persecution of Caleb comes to an end because of personal individual acts, rather than because of the workings of social justice.

Godwin's portrayal of Falkland's obsession with honour and reputation as the originating cause of the evils of despotism in the novel can nevertheless be read as a critique of Burke's idea that English society is best as it is, based on a foundation of supposedly traditional chivalry and 'prejudice'. Caleb criticizes Falkland's hypocritical adherence to a notion of chivalry that has motivated him to kill and lie, against his other principles, in order to preserve his 'honour' – an honour that consists more in reputation, or the preservation of his 'good name', than in genuine virtue. Yet Caleb, too, is concerned to protect his own 'good name' and reputation, although he never admits this to be common ground between himself and Falkland. Caleb's self-analysis seems inconsistent in another revealing way, since, although he insists on the 'innocence' of the curiosity that leads him to 'spy on' his master Falkland, he seems to extract a sadistic pleasure from the power he wields over him. And, while Caleb announces himself at the start of the novel as the victim of persecution, for the first volume he appears to be the persecutor and Falkland the victim, although these roles are reversed for most of the latter two volumes. Godwin at several points describes the pleasure Caleb takes in the sensation of fear combined with illicit power which he experiences while spying on Falkland, in a way that corresponds to the Burkean sublime, as a tingling sensation which fills him with extraordinary energy.[26]

In *Caleb Williams*, Godwin reprises a number of conventional Gothic motifs and settings: dark secrets, despotic tyrants, imprisonment, and pursuit in gloomy ancestral estates, dark dungeons and wild landscapes – and, like many Gothic novels, *Caleb Williams* explores 'the nature of power, the source of its authority in the oppressive past'[27]. However, the way in which these Gothic tropes are deployed is often atypical of Gothic novels, since they are *not* located in a Roman Catholic or continental past, but in contemporary England, and this reversal of Gothic convention can make for trenchant social criticism. The description of Caleb's 'dungeon' is based upon Godwin's observation[28] of prisons he had actually visited, since several of his friends had been arrested while he was writing the novel, and many others were imprisoned in cells resembling Caleb's dungeon:

> Our dungeons were cells, 7½ feet by 6½, below the surface of the ground, damp, without window, light or air, except from a few holes worked for that purpose in the door. In some of these miserable receptacles three persons were put to sleep together.[29]

This reverses a number of Gothic conventions: first, Godwin is very precise in describing the cell, including its dimensions to the nearest six inches, a specificity which resists the Gothic tendency to describe in terms such as 'indescribable'; second, the language is the reverse of Gothic hyperbole, and most of the salient details are given by negatives ('without window, light or air'); and third, whereas Gothic novels usually locate their dungeons in the safely remote world of medieval continental Europe, Godwin is describing the uncomfortable reality of such horrors in modern England, leading to the disconcerting likening of English prisons to the recently demolished Bastille. At times, Godwin achieves an Austen-esque type of understatement quite unlike the excessive emotional language typical of Gothic fiction: when Caleb has just escaped his prison, and is forced to spend a day standing concealed in a shallow cavern to evade detection by his erstwhile guards, the perilous situation and his state of hunger and exhaustion are described as productive of 'no very agreeable sensations'.[30] However, the hyperbolic language of Caleb's paranoia – for instance, he eventually starts to believe that Falkland is omniscient – became Godwin's most lasting contribution to Gothic fiction, influencing writers such as his daughter Mary Shelley and the American Gothic novelist Charles Brockden Brown.

Nationalism and the regional novel: Edgeworth, Owenson, and Scott

Maria Edgeworth's *Castle Rackrent* (1800),[31] Sydney Owenson's *The Wild Irish Girl: A National Tale* (1806), and many of Scott's novels (1814 onwards) are all usually linked under the banner of the 'regional novel', as all three share an interest in representing and valorizing recent or passing cultures that were perceived to be 'other' than English within the newly united Britain. (The Act of Union between England and Scotland was passed in 1707, and that between Britain and Ireland in 1800.) All three novelists differ from one another in the degree to which they realistically specify the society and individualize the inhabitants of the regions they describe. Owenson's novel is overtly pro-Irish, and romanticizes the landscape and the people, whereas Edgeworth satirically exposes both a decaying Irish feudal system in *Castle Rackrent* and also the abuses of the Irish by their English landlords and their corrupt bailiffs in *The Absentee*. Scott treads a kind of middle ground in his Scottish novels, where the past is alternatively a site of nostalgia or social criticism. However, the three novelists ultimately seem to advocate a conciliatory approach to the divisions and differences between England and the 'regions' of Scotland and Ireland: Owenson concludes her novel with a symbolic Anglo-Irish union, in the marriage between the dispossessed Irish princess Glorvina and the narrator, who is the English heir to her family's former lands. Scott similarly ends *Waverley* with a marriage between the English hero Edward Waverley and Rose Bradwardine, the daughter of the old-style Scottish laird. Edgeworth, in her 'Irish' novels, tends to idealize by contrast a course of action similar to that taken by her own Anglo-Irish landowning family, who lived on and managed their property, and were accepted and even liked by their Irish tenants.

In both *The Wild Irish Girl* and *Waverley*, Ireland and Scotland are portrayed as seen for the first time by young, aristocratic Englishmen, who fall in love with beautiful, musical, patriotic native heroines, as well as with the country itself. In both novels, a central feature of the novel's landscape is the Gothic convention the ancient castle, in surroundings described in highly wrought language, and in terms of the picturesque and the sublime – and these otherworldly settings contribute to the 'otherness' of the scene for both English hero and English readers. Owenson heightens the hero's first glimpse of the heroine, the Irish princess Glorvina, by linking it with his awe at the sublimity of the landscape: to the hero, 'all still seemed the vision of awakened imagination – surrounded by a scenery, grand even to the boldest majesty of nature, and wild even to desolation'. His newly awakened sentimental appreciation for landscape is contrasted with his former life of cynical leisure in England, which he learns, through Glorvina and Ireland, to perceive as consisting of 'hackneyed modes', 'vicious pursuits' and 'unimportant avocations'.[32]

Scott describes Waverley, coming across Flora as she gazes on a waterfall, in a way that similarly links the hero's appreciation of the natural sublime with his appreciation of Flora's beauty, and thus associates his love with the element of danger or pain present in the vertiginous landscape:

> At a short turning, the path, which had for some furlongs lost sight of the brook, suddenly placed Waverley in front of a romantic waterfall. . . . After a broken cataract of about twenty feet, the stream was received in a large natural basin. . . . Eddying round this reservoir, the brook found its way as if over a broken part of the ledge, and formed a second fall, which seemed to seek the very abyss . . .

However, whereas *The Wild Irish Girl* is, as a whole, enthusiastically and even naively romantic, about both Ireland and love, in *Waverley* Scott deconstructs the hero's patriotic and romantic idealism. The hero of *The Wild Irish Girl*, Horatio, begins the novel as a cynical louche jaded by society, and experiences an emotional reawakening through his encounter with both the heroine and the landscape. In *Waverley*, on the other hand, Edward Waverley is full of romantic illusions at the outset of the novel, but through his encounter with Flora McIvor and her brother, and his involvement in their political and military campaign, he loses some of this idealism, and by the end of the novel he is sequestered in happy bourgeois marriage to the less glamorous second heroine Rose Bradwardine. His idealistic aspirations and romantic illusions are treated ironically throughout the novel. Following Waverley's encounter with Flora at the waterfall, Scott describes, in terms of approbation, Flora's pragmatic and rather unromantic reaction to Waverley's evident admiration:

> Flora, like every beautiful woman, was conscious of her own power, and pleased with its effects, which she could easily discern from the respectful, yet confused address of the young soldier. But as she possessed excellent sense, she gave the romance of the scene, and other accidental circumstances, full weight in appreciating the feelings with which Waverley seemed obviously to be impressed.[33]

Scott's later novel *The Heart of Midlothian* (1818), a hybrid of historical realism and romantic fable, is yet more deconstructive of the Romantic personality. Whereas Waverley's romantic leanings signify merely his immaturity, in *The Heart of Midlothian*, the anti-hero George Staunton's quasi-Byronic 'Romantic temperament' is signalled by his volatility, melancholia, and self-dramatizing language and gestures, and is a cause of disruption and danger to other characters. The heroine, Jeanie Deans, distrusts Staunton, and her character could be described as the opposite of his – placid, honest, self-disciplined, and religious.

Authenticity and anti-Romanticism: Burney and Austen

Austen, like Scott, frequently ironizes and undercuts Romantic sensibilities and character traits in her fiction, and in novels such as *Sense and Sensibility*, *Mansfield Park*, and *Persuasion* she vindicates characters who practise self-control and adhere to social codes. However, although the 'excessive' (and partly self-cultivated) emotionalism of Marianne Dashwood is suspect, heroines such as Fanny and Anne, and even Marianne's counterpoint Elinor, are in their own way equally sensitive. In Austen's fiction, a lot of value is accorded to authentic subjective feeling, while artificiality, sentimentalism, or pursuit of emotional desire to the exclusion of concern for others are represented as being both risible and harmful.

The representation of the 'authentic' inner self and the emphasis on its value are central concerns in much fiction and poetry of the Romantic era, and in many novels the 'action' and plot are determined by the portrayal of the inner life and subjectivity of the central character, usually a heroine, as women were seen as being especially sensitive, and were, moreover, restricted to a largely 'private' life by societal constraints. Thus the field of action for many heroines of this era lies in their power to make correct choices in a moral or emotional sphere. Frances Burney's novelistic career spans a large part of the period under discussion: her first novel, *Evelina*, was published in 1788, and her last, *The Wanderer*, in 1814. Like Austen (on whom she was a significant influence), she portrays the inner or 'moral' life of her heroines as the gauge of their merit, in resistance to superficial or meretricious standards of female worth imposed by their social peers, such as beauty, wealth, or 'accomplishments'. The heroine's 'true' worth is, in these novels, a way of ultimately triumphing over the judgements and restrictions imposed on them by their immediate society, in order to win the love (and sometimes also the money) of the hero. This can be seen as a manifestation of one major strand of Romantic idealism, the privileging of the 'true' inner self over the 'social' persona that interacts in society. This plot structure, however, had been an important strand in a novelistic tradition since Richardson's *Pamela* (1740), in which the intrinsic merit and idealism of a servant girl, who resists several violent attempts to corrupt her 'virtue', eventually triumphs over worldly pressure and wins marriage to her would-be rapist, as well as access to his wealth. Burney's first novel, *Evelina*, which charts the progress of its naive but intelligent and beautiful heroine from her uncertain 'Entrance into the World' (the novel's sub-title) to marriage, wealth, and legitimacy, is further associated with this tradition by its epistolary form, which facilitates the direct expression of the heroine's private thoughts.[34] Burney's second novel, *Cecilia* (1782), follows a roughly similar plot trajectory, except that the heroine's trials are greater, and, instead of gaining a fortune by marriage, she begins the novel an heiress but loses her fortune by the end of the novel. In this novel Burney leaves the epistolary form, but nonetheless maintains the reader's intimacy with the heroine's inner life through what has come to be termed 'free indirect discourse', that is, the reporting of a character's thoughts in the language that we associate with their character rather than in the narrator's voice.

As Kelly points out, the use of 'free indirect discourse' by novelists from Burney onwards invited readers to identify strongly with the hero or heroine, as well as, briefly, with other characters.[35] This method of revealing a character's mental processes usually gives the reader an even greater sense of psychological authenticity, since thoughts are reported 'directly' and are not filtered through a character's self-conscious story-telling persona, as would be the case with a first-person narrative.

Austen is known to have been an admirer of Burney's novels: Austen's name appears on the list of subscribers to *Camilla* (1796), and she cites both *Cecilia* (1782) and *Camilla* in *Northanger Abbey* as great works of fiction. Burney's final novel, *The Wanderer* (1814),[36] was published in the same year as Austen's *Mansfield Park*. These later novels by Austen and Burney are less comic than their earlier works, and their respective later heroines are more Romantically idealistic and appreciative of nature. As Margaret Ann Doody points out in *Frances Burney: The Life in the Works*, the title of Burney's *The Wanderer* (1814) refers to 'the truly Romantic figure',[37] alongside Wordsworth's 'Wanderer', Coleridge's 'Ancient Mariner', and Maturin's *Melmoth the Wanderer* (1820).[38] Doody analyses Burney's description of Juliet wandering on Salisbury Plain, where she meditates on her life, and contrasts the 'sophisticated civilization represented by Wilton', the town where Juliet has been staying, and the 'grand, strange and primitive', represented by Stonehenge, in a way that trivializes the former in comparison with the latter.[39] Juliet's loneliness is emphasized in this situation, which adequately reflects the alienation she experiences in daily life, because she is happier here than she is in most human company. However, the novel's co-heroine manqué, Elinor, seems almost a parody of the Romantic pursuit of self-realization, personal happiness, and radical political ideals. Although she is not self-satisfied or uncharitable as are most of the novel's other characters, the kindness she shows Juliet is generated more by egotism than altruism.

Burney, however, is pragmatically realistic in her concentration on hours, pay and conditions for working women, and she extends the social criticism begun in *Cecilia* (1782) – in which the heroine befriends a builder's wife, Mrs Hill – by making Juliet of *The Wanderer* earn her own living out of necessity, first by teaching music and then as a seamstress. Both types of employment gave Burney the opportunity to represent the many ways in which the rich are complacent, insensitive and cruel to the poor and dependent, as well as revealing the relentless drudgery of normal working conditions for working women.

Austen's two most obviously 'serious' novels, *Mansfield Park* (1814) and *Persuasion* (1818), describe sensitive, introspective heroines, the characterization of whom could be seen as somewhat akin to constructions of selfhood in Romantic poetry. Fanny Price in *Mansfield Park* displays, at times, a Wordsworthian appreciation of nature and solitary contemplation, and meditates aloud on the wonders of nature and memory to an unappreciative Mary Crawford.[40] In many other ways, however, Austen appears not to endorse such poetically 'Romantic' states of mind. In *Mansfield Park*, the concept of 'propriety' is given a strong positive emphasis, and both this word and its antonym, 'impropriety', are used frequently and significantly – an emphasis that suggests the importance of self-control and conformity in one's outward behaviour to societal norms. This form of discipline is antithetical to the Romantic 'cult of the self' which privileges individual desire. The novel thus presents a conflict for the heroine as well as other characters between the benefits of expressing or acting on one's feelings and opinions and the benefits of controlling them, a conflict that is also played out in Austen's earlier novel *Sense and Sensibility* (1811). Austen ultimately resolves this conflict by placing Fanny in a position where it is acceptable for her to express herself – as Edmund's wife and equal and also as the moral superior to the figure of male authority who remains at Mansfield, Sir Thomas. However, she has been able to achieve this position not only simply because her superiority has at last been recognized but also because of her self-control during most of the novel – indeed, her self-control and self-abnegation are necessary to her superiority.

The relevance to Romantic poetry of Austen's portrayal of the conflict between self-expression and self-control is made explicit in *Persuasion*, during a scene in which the heroine Anne Elliott recommends that Captain Benwick, who has recently been bereaved of his fiancée, read instructive essays rather than Romantic poetry in order not to exacerbate his grief:

> he repeated, with such tremulous feeling, the various lines which imaged a broken heart, or a mind destroyed by wretchedness, and looked so entirely as if he meant to be understood, that she ventured to hope he did not always read only poetry; and to say, that she thought it

> was the misfortune of poetry, to be seldom safely enjoyed by those who enjoyed it completely; and that the strong feelings which alone could estimate it truly, were the very feelings which ought to taste it but sparingly. . . . she ventured to recommend . . . such works of our best moralists, such collections of the finest letters, such memoirs of characters of worth and suffering, as occurred to her at the moment as calculated to rouse and fortify the mind by the highest precepts, and the strongest examples of moral and religious endurances.[41]

Ironically, later in the novel Benwick comes to epitomize male inconstancy, and is cited as an example of this in a later conversation between Anne and Captain Harville (whose sister had been Benwick's fiancée) after Benwick rapidly recovers his broken heart and gets engaged to the shallow Louisa Musgrove.[42] Austen's negative characterization of Benwick's emotional volatility reflects her attitude to his reading-matter, Romantic poetry, which, it is implied, encourages him to prolong a grief that is more pleasurable than sincere.

Austen's earlier fiction is also in many ways a satirical antidote to the preoccupations of Romantic literature. Beginning in her juvenilia in the 1790s, Austen mercilessly parodies novelistic portrayals of sensibility, and then goes on in *Northanger Abbey* to target the un-realism and sensationalism of Gothic fiction, although, as many recent critics have pointed out, Catherine's intuitive perception of General Tilney as a Gothic villain is to some extent justified by the cruelty of his subsequent behaviour towards her. Marianne in *Sense and Sensibility* (1811) is Austen's most Romantic heroine, with a propensity for violent emotion and a desire for emotional expression and fulfilment at all costs, yet she is taught that such behaviour can be self-destructive and also have negative consequences for those around her.[43] However, Austen's satire of Marianne is directed toward the manner in which Marianne seeks emotional fulfilment, and does not denigrate this as an aim in itself. Her characterization of Elinor represents an alternative and more pragmatic possibility for realizing this goal, rather than a championing of 'sense' as a kind of cold reason that precludes intense feeling.

Frankenstein and the Romantic dialectic

Mary Shelley's *Frankenstein* (1818) also engages with the central conflict present in Austen's novels, between the relative value of restraining or pursuing individual desire. In spite of its fantastic story and poetic prose, in *Frankenstein* Shelley seems to advocate a vision of rational domestic harmony similar to that which triumphs at the end of Austen's novels, and constructs this vision as oppositional to the Romantic ambitions that lead to the creation of the monster.

Like many Romantic novels and poems, *Frankenstein* contains intense, lyrical descriptions of sublime landscapes and sensations, such as that of Frankenstein's walk to the summit of Montanvert:

> It is a scene terrifically desolate. In a thousand spots the traces of the winter avalanche may be perceived, where trees lie broken and strewed on the ground; some entirely destroyed, others bent, leaning upon the jutting rocks of the mountain, or transversely upon other trees. . . . The sea, or rather the vast river of ice, wound among its dependent mountains, whose aerial summits hung over its recesses. Their icy and glittering peaks shone in the sunlight over the clouds. My heart, which was before sorrowful, now swelled with something like joy.[44]

However, this description, and others like it, jars with the natural sublimity represented in many other Romantic works: this is a vision of destruction and barrenness, yet paradoxically it fills Frankenstein with 'something like joy', reflecting his estrangement from more natural sources of pleasure. Later, when Frankenstein is on the Rhine with Henry Clerval, he is unable to enjoy the lush scenery that delights his companion. The omnipresence of ice here is a re-echoing of the desolate arctic scenes at the start and end of the novel, with which the monster is strongly associated.

Mary Shelley also, in this scene, suggests the transience of an emotion inspired by the merely visual, since Frankenstein is immediately cast back into despair by an encounter with his monster. The monster usually reappears in overtly sublime landscapes; indeed he says that he can live happily among the glaciers, although humans cannot. This link between the natural sublime and the monster implies a connection between the celebration of nature and sublimity by the Romantic poets and the inhumanity of the monster.

Frankenstein's hubristic act of creation can be read as a critique of the egotism of poetic creation. While obsessively engaged in his work of building the monster and giving it life, Frankenstein cuts himself off from his family and from all other kinds of human affection. In the retrospective frame narrative of the opening chapters, Frankenstein reflects with hindsight that:

> A human being in perfection ought always to preserve a calm and peaceful mind, and never to allow passion or a transitory desire to disturb his tranquility. I do not think the pursuit of knowledge is an exception to this rule. If the study to which you apply yourself has a tendency to weaken your affections, and to destroy your taste for those simple pleasures in which no alloy can possibly mix, then that study is certainly unlawful, that is to say, not befitting the human mind.[45]

'Unlawful' and 'not befitting the human mind' are very strong terms, effectively imposing a taboo upon knowledge or desire beyond the confines of 'simple pleasures' and domestic affections.

Mary Shelley sub-titled the novel 'The Modern Prometheus', inviting a reading of her novel as a critique of her husband's Romantic self-image. According to Anne K. Mellor, Prometheus was 'an often invoked self-image among the Romantic poets' – in 'Prometheus Unbound' by Percy Bysshe Shelley, as well as in poems by Blake, Coleridge, and Byron. In one version of the myth, Prometheus shaped the first man, and later the first woman, out of clay. Mellor also points out that in choosing the name 'Victor' Mary Shelley was referring readers who were familiar with her husband's work to Percy Shelley himself – Victor was an early pseudonym of his, and in his poetry Shelley frequently uses the words 'victor' and 'victory'. Mellor goes on to draw attention to numerous other similarities between Frankenstein and the actual Percy Shelley.[46]

Like Victor Frankenstein, the Romantic poets invoked in their writing the potential for immortality through the use of their intellect and imagination, although for Frankenstein the product of his mind is to be an entire race and not just art. Far from achieving for Victor the immortality he craves, the creature destroys his peace of mind and eventually his family. This destruction results, more or less directly, from Victor's abandonment of his creation at the moment of 'birth'; the creature claims to have been born 'benevolent and good' and that he was only made a 'fiend' by lack of affection.[47] In demonstrating how this corruption came about, Mary Shelley echoes Rousseau's idea that humans are innately good but can be corrupted by society and bad education, and thus suggests that reason and imagination, without appropriate guidance, are insufficient to create happiness or moral good.

While Mary Shelley condemns Frankenstein's egotistical acts of solitary creation, she conversely advocates bourgeois family life and 'the domestic affections' as the means of achieving happiness and futurity, through the conventional and legitimate method of conjugal procreation. The character of Clerval, Frankenstein's friend and alter ego, is an idealization of the cultivated middle-class man, and he is also remarkably self-sacrificing: for instance, he nurses Frankenstein through a long illness even though this deprives him of benefiting from his stay at the university. In contrast with Clerval, Frankenstein pursues his thirst for knowledge and greatness at the expense of his family and friends, forgetting them for months at a time while pursuing his overriding obsession into 'charnel houses' and graves for body parts. Before his monster has been created, Frankenstein himself has come to seem monstrous.

The dialectic Mary Shelley sets up between bourgeois family values and Romantic idealism is, as I have said, central to many novels of the Romantic era; and in most fiction the advocacy of domesticity over free pursuit of desire seems to mark a key difference between the agendas of novelists and poets. As I suggested at the start of this chapter, Gary Kelly's re-defined characterization of the 'Romantic' novel, which he sees as emphasizing the worth of everyday, middle-class family life, is oppositional to the kind of

Romantic poetry that seeks to put into words the transcendence of the self over everyday matters.

The Gothic elements that are prevalent in much of the fiction of the Romantic period, and the outright fantasticality of a number of Gothic novels, seem something of an aberration from the 'realism' that is generally said to characterize much mid-eighteenth-century and Victorian fiction, and Gothic characteristics do seem to denote a kinship with similar features in the poetry of the period. On the other hand, many novels that contain elements of Gothic fantasy nevertheless conclude with happy marriages that seem to valorize bourgeois society and domesticity. The prevalence of the 'courtship plot', in some form, in fiction of the period suggests that, in some cases at least, it might be meaningless in terms of the novel's overall ideology; but in most of the cases I have discussed the courtship plot is central to the novel as a whole, providing the heroine with scope to exercise significant moral judgement. The exceptional Romantic-era novels that do not end in this way, such as Beckford's *Vathek*, Godwin's *Caleb Williams*, Lewis's *The Monk*, Shelley's *Frankenstein*, Hogg's *Private Memoirs and Confessions of a Justified Sinner*, and Maturin's *Melmoth the Wanderer*, are usually dominated by a male hero or anti-hero who overreaches himself and tends to collapse into self-destruction or eternal damnation, which in a sense also valorizes marriage and domesticity by way of contrast. Wollstonecraft posed two radical alternatives to this pattern. Her first heroine, in *Mary*, is left at the end of the novel trapped in an unconsummated marriage to an absent and inadequate husband. Wollstonecraft's second novel, *Maria*, was left unfinished at her death, but her draft endings show that she had contemplated concluding with either the heroine's suicide or the establishment of an all-female family consisting of Maria, her daughter, and Jemima, the working-class woman who befriends Maria while she is confined in a madhouse.

The uniqueness of the Romantic period should not be overstated, however, since some of the major novelists at both the beginning and end of the Victorian period were to some extent neo-Romantic: for instance Anne, Charlotte, and Emily Brontë, and Joseph Conrad; and much of the Victorian poetry by Tennyson and Browning continued to echo the diction as well as the imagery and values of major poets of the Romantic age. The literary scene in the Romantic age, as in the succeeding Victorian period, was complex and at times contradictory.

Notes

1 Gary Kelly, *English Fiction of the Romantic Period 1789–1830* (London, 1989), p. 19.

2 *Ibid.* p. 197.

3 Gary Kelly, 'Romantic Fiction', in *The Cambridge Companion to British Romanticism*, ed. Stuart Curran (Cambridge, 1993), p. 215.

4 Samuel Taylor Coleridge, *Biographia Literaria* (Princeton, 1983) p. 48.
5 Jane Austen, *Northanger Abbey* (Harmondsworth, 1995), pp. 33–4.
6 Margaret Anne Doody, *The True Story of the Novel* (New Brunswick, 1996), p. 294.
7 Matthew Lewis, *The Monk* (Oxford, 1998).
8 *The British Critic*, 7 (1796), 677. Quoted by Emma McEvoy in her introduction to *The Monk* (Oxford, 1998), i.
9 Coleridge's review of Ann Radcliffe's *The Italian*, in *The Critical Review*, June 1798, pp. 166–9.
10 Clara Reeve, *The Progress of Romance* (New York, 1970), p. 111.
11 *Ibid.* pp. 53–4.
12 Gillian Beer, *The Romance* (London, 1970), p. 59.
13 Ann Radcliffe, *A Sicilian Romance* (Oxford, 1998), p. 104.
14 Walter Scott, *Waverley* (Harmondsworth, 1986), p. 80.
15 Sydney Owenson, Lady Morgan, *The Wild Irish Girl* (New York and Poole, 1995), p. 53.
16 Edmund Burke, *A Philosophical Enquiry into the Origin of Our Ideas of the Sublime and Beautiful* (Oxford, 1990), p. 36.
17 Ann Radcliffe, *The Romance of the Forest* (Oxford, 1998), p. 265.
18 William Wordsworth, *The Prelude* (New York, 1979).
19 Johann Wolfgang von Goethe, *The Sorrows of Young Werther* (Harmondsworth, 1989), p. 65.
20 Edmund Burke, *Reflections on the Revolution in France* (Harmondsworth, 1986), p. 183.
21 Mary Wollstonecraft, *Mary and Maria,* Mary Shelley, *Matilda*, ed. Janet Todd (Harmondsworth, 1992), p. 6.
22 Wollstonecraft, *Mary*, p. 43.
23 William Godwin, *An Enquiry Concerning Political Justice* (Harmondsworth, 1985).
24 William Godwin, *Caleb Williams* (Harmondsworth, 1987), p. 3.
25 Gary Kelly, 'Romantic Fiction', p. 204.
26 *Caleb Williams*, p. 247.
27 Fiona Robertson, 'Novels', in *An Oxford Companion to the Romantic Age: British Culture 1776–1832*, ed. Iain McCalman (Oxford, 1999), p. 291.
28 The description of Caleb's 'dungeon' is no Gothic fantasy, but was based on Godwin's personal observation of conditions in British jails: William St Clair, *The Godwins and the Shelleys* (Baltimore, 1989), pp. 114 and 118.
29 *Caleb Williams*, pp. 187–8.
30 *Ibid.* p. 216.
31 Maria Edgeworth, *Castle Rackrent and Ennui*, ed. Marilyn Butler (Harmondsworth, 1992).
32 *The Wild Irish Girl*, pp. 156–7.
33 *Waverley*, pp. 105–6.
34 Frances Burney, *Evelina: Or the History of a Young Lady's Entrance into the World* (Harmondsworth, 1994).
35 Gary Kelly, 'Romantic Fiction', p. 201.
36 Frances Burney, *The Wanderer; or, Female Difficulties* (Oxford, 1991).
37 Margaret Ann Doody: *Frances Burney: The Life in the Works* (New Brunswick, 1988), p. 328.
38 Charles Maturin, *Melmoth the Wanderer* (Harmondsworth, 2000).
39 *Frances Burney: The Life in the Works*, pp. 362–3.
40 Jane Austen, *Mansfield Park* (Harmondsworth, 1996), p. 222.
41 Jane Austen, *Persuasion* (Harmondsworth, 1985), pp. 121–2.
42 *Ibid.* pp. 235–8.

43 Jane Austen, *Sense and Sensibility* (Harmondsworth, 1995).
44 Mary Shelley, *Frankenstein* (New York, 1996), pp. 64–5.
45 *Ibid.* p. 32.
46 Anne K. Mellor, *Mary Shelley* (London, 1988), pp. 70–80.
47 *Frankenstein*, p. 81.

3

Ballads and lyric poetry in Scotland

From the time of the Act of Union between England and Scotland in 1707, literary entrepreneurs, editors, poets, and scholars in Scotland sought to record or to remake their earlier and contemporary tradition of the composition of lyric songs and ballads, which had been one of the noteworthy achievements of the English language known either as 'Scots English' or simply 'Scots'. The literary historian Kurt Wittig describes this eighteenth-century Scots poetry as embodying 'the tunes, verse forms, and rhythms of popular song and dance. . . . These poets were not writing in an ivory tower, but recited or sang their verses, as it were, on the sounding board of the community, and a special stimulus came from the clubs of Edinburgh'.[1] The origins of much Scots oral balladry is a matter of argument, however, though it has been ascertained that many of the older and newer ballads and songs originated either in northeast Scotland around Aberdeenshire, Banff, Moray, and Kincardineshire or to the south in 'the Borders' where Scotland had been in frequent warfare with England. By the 1790s, a considerable amount of this Scots oral poetry had been collected into a written literary tradition by means of widely read publications such as James Watson's *Choice Collection* (1706–11), Allan Ramsay's *Ever Green* (1724), David Herd's *Ancient and Modern Scots Songs* (1776), and other anthologies.The publication of anthologies of oral ballads and songs was often, though not always, linked intrinsically to the notion of preserving Scots English, at least for literary and social purposes, in the face of the standard English that came more and more to be used for official, educational, and business purposes after the Act of Union.

The collecting of oral ballads nevertheless held problems for anthologists. Should they modify or alter the phrasing and content according to their own or their publishers' tastes, taboos, and editorial judgements? Should they record these ballads entirely in Scots English or with an admixture of standard English? If entirely in Scots English, which written form of Scots English should be used, when each different region of Scotland had built up its own variant usages of vocabulary and grammar?

Some later collector-editors of songs and ballads, such as George Thomson in the early nineteenth century, had recourse to John Jamieson's *Etymological Dictionary of the Scottish Language* (1808). But, prior to Jamieson's linguistic work, anthologists and poets relied on their own personal judgement of usage, or tried to imitate a specific folk-singer's usage, or drew on usages in works by other Scots poets. This rediscovery and reworking of eighteenth-century and earlier Scottish ballads and lyric songs had a profound influence on what came to be known later as 'Romanticism'.

After the 1707 Act of Union, a number of intellectual 'clubs' arose in Edinburgh, such as Allan Ramsay's Easy Club of 1712. Roderick Watson, the social and literary historian, describes the members of the Easy Club as 'a group of mild Jacobites dedicated to "mutual improvement in conversation" and to reading the *Spectator* aloud at each meeting'.[2] The members of the Easy Club might contribute to or read the Scots English-language *Ruddiman's Magazine*, and were generally intent on reviving Scottish traditions of language and literature. At the same time, another group, who called themselves the *literati*, founded the Select Society and wrote for or read the standard English, but evidently misnamed, *Scots Magazine*. This latter group in Edinburgh congregated around non-fiction prose writers such as David Hume (1711–76), the leading philosophical writer of the day, and were intent on purging their language of Scotticisms, which they understandably considered to be ill-suited to their needs as European philosophers and historians. These 'clubs' were argumentative and their members a contrary mixture when considering questions of Scottish culture, especially that of language; but they provided the focus of a literate reading public and a publishing industry through which creative writers as diverse as Robert Burns and Walter Scott could write freely in the language of individual choice.

The two cultural groups in both Edinburgh and Glasgow – the Scots language devotees and the academic *literati* – although ostensibly opposing forces, were nevertheless both concerned with conserving their Scottish heritage, particularly in relation to 'literary antiquities'. Nowhere can this interest be seen more clearly than in the disproportionate rumpus over James Macpherson's mid-eighteenth-century publication of what purported to be a literal translation of a Celtic cycle of mythology from a Gaelic-language area of the Scottish Highlands.

In his forerunner to the Romantic age, what did James Macpherson put together in the way of prose poems that made him admired on the one hand and despised on the other? In 1759, some of the Edinburgh *literati* such as John Home and Hugh Blair persuaded Macpherson to translate from the Gaelic language some oral ballads that he had purported to write down when he visited the Highlands. Macpherson's style and content can be seen from a sample of his freely translated prose poems in his anonymous *Fragments of Ancient Poetry*:

> I sit by the mossy fountain; on the top of the hill of winds. One tree is rustling above me. Dark waves roll over the heath. The lake is troubled below. . . . Sad are my thoughts as I sit alone. Didst thou but appear, O my love, a wanderer on the heath! Thy hair floating on the wind behind thee . . .[3]

These 'fragments' mesmerize in their evocation of sublime scenery, wandering hero, ghostly heroine, blasted heath – and many more of the props of Gothic and alienating imagery, which captivated an audience across northern Europe, and were to influence the production of later Romantic literature. But soon several among the Scottish academic establishment began to turn on Macpherson and treat his prose poetry as fabrications. He had added to and at times altered some of his Gaelic-language oral sources, and, moreover, in doing so, he had not used Scots English but had invented his own pastiche of standard poetic English.

Even so, many major poets and some of the novelists of the later Romantic age in both Scotland and England continued to regard the pre-Romantic Macpherson and his Gaelic-inspired prose poems as an inspiration, if not also some kind of paradigm. Burns claimed Ossian as one of his 'glorious models after which I endeavour to form my conduct';[4] and, in 1810, Joanna Baillie declared, 'I am still a great admirer of Ossian'.[5] Sir Walter Scott concluded that Macpherson was 'a bard, capable not only of making an enthusiastic impression on every mind susceptible of poetical beauty, but of giving a new tone to poetry throughout all Europe.'[6] The 'model' that Burns, Baillie, and Scott are referring to is not only that of encouraging Scottish poets and novelists to look to their own Scottish past oral culture for sources of inspiration; even the major Romantic poets in England, most notably William Blake, Lord Byron, and Samuel Taylor Coleridge, found in Macpherson a way of transmuting into poetry the mystical in life and the sublime in nature. The influence of Macpherson, however, was not always a beneficial one, particularly in some of the work of Walter Scott and Joanna Baillie.

The beginning of the revival of Scots English balladry can be seen in the popularity of Allan Ramsay's *Tea-Table Miscellany* (1724) and Herd's much later *Ancient and Modern Scottish Songs* (1776; 1791). Both Ramsay and Herd, however, edited the language of these ballads in order to remove some of the bawdiness as well as some of the Scotticisms that they thought might displease the educated reader. A related influence on Scottish writers just prior to and during the Romantic period was the collector Thomas Percy's *Reliques of Ancient English Poetry* (1765), in which Percy followed the essayist Joseph Addison in considering oral ballads to have a 'pleasing simplicity',[7] although he too amended and added to the texts of oral works. He thus incurred the disapproval of those who wanted authentic texts as well as texts matched with tunes.

Robert Burns also joined these collectors when he accepted the invitation of James Johnson (*c.* 1750–1811), an important printer and engraver in

Scotland, to discover lyrics with their accompanying tunes for his series, *The Scots Musical Museum*, which eventually ran to six volumes (1787–1803). Burns responded enthusiastically, because Johnson, unlike many previous publishers, wished to reprint the authentic 'favourites of Nature's Judges – the Common People'.[8] Subsequently, in 1792, Burns agreed to contribute to George Thomson's project, *A Select Collection of Scottish Airs*, of which only the first volume had been published in 1793 before Burns's death in 1796. Burns was less enthusiastic about collecting ballads for Thomson, since he suspected that Thomson would erode Burns's interpretation of the authenticity of the songs because of a desire to please genteel readers. The critic and literary historian, Robert Crawford, argues that, in contributing to these two anthologies, Burns acted as 'a cultural broker between the oral folk-culture and the cultivated reading public of Edinburgh'.[9] Eighteenth-century Scottish interest in the oral ballads of the 'common people', however, was prompted more by a desire to keep intact the use of the lowland Scots English language than by an interest in the lives of ordinary people. Whatever the motives of his readers or his publishers, Burns's stated desire was to transmit ballads that ordinary people could relish. Moreover, in his own lyrics he adapted old tunes for the expression of egalitarian sentiments such as in these succinct and pithy lines from his 'Song: For a' that and a' that' (1794):

> Is there, for honest Poverty,
> That hings his head, and a' that;
> The coward-slave, we pass him by,
> We dare be poor, for a' that.
> For a' that, and a' that,
> Our toils obscure, and a' that,
> The rank is but the guinea's stamp,
> The man's the gowd for a' that.[10]

Burns himself realized that this song, which he sent to George Thomson in January 1795, broke away from traditional themes for songs:

> A great critic, Aikin on songs, says that love and wine are the exclusive themes for song-writing – The following is on neither subject, and consequently is no Song; but will be allowed, I think, to be two or three pretty good *prose* thoughts, inverted into rhyme.[11]

Burns is here using the appellation '*prose* thoughts' ironically in order to emphasize that songs and ballads might be written on any subject.

Crawford shows also how Scottish poets such as Burns and Scott drew stimulus from the collecting of earlier oral ballads:

> Ramsay, Burns, and Scott were as much major collectors as major creative artists. Writing in a culture under pressure, each sought to bind that culture together, to preserve it and celebrate it through

> anthology, which was closely bound up with creative endeavour. Sometimes, as in the case of the Ossianic works, collection and creation became so confused as to be virtually inextricable, but the mixed urge to preserve and, at the same time, to build or develop a tradition is shared by Macpherson and Scott, along with other major Scottish eclectic writers, most notably Burns.[12]

Crawford here seems to imply that, however much the antiquarian scholars might criticize, these creative writers were bound at times to transform oral poems with whatever creative alterations their own individual imaginations and tastes might impose.

The difficulties of ascertaining, for example, what Burns actually wrote down when he collected oral poems can be seen in regard to one of the most highly regarded lyric poems, 'A Red, Red Rose'. On the one hand, Kenneth Simpson asserts that Burns improved the earlier versions of this lyric collected from the folk tradition:

> Burns's finest love lyrics are unrivalled in direct emotional appeal. Though there were chapbook models for each stanza of 'A Red, Red Rose', Burns made the material his own, enriching the most trite of similes by the intensifying effect of the repetition of 'red'.[13]

But James Kinsley states that:

> We may be doing an injustice to oral tradition in regarding 'A Red, Red Rose' even as a reconstruction by Burns. . . . There is nothing in the letter to [Alexander] Cunningham [from Robert Burns] to suggest that Burns made any changes in the song; he had not even adjusted it to fit an air . . .'[14]

On the latter evidence, the striking expression of the hyperbolic metaphors in 'A Red, Red Rose' seem probably to have emanated from the folksong tradition with only the assistance of Burns as an amanuensis.

In other oral songs and ballads, however, such as 'My Nanie O', 'A Weary Pund o' Tow', and 'Fy Let Us A' to the Bridal', Burns evidently made both minor and major changes, sometimes completely rewriting words in order to convey a different political, social, or sexual meaning. In 'A Weary Pund o' Tow', for example, Burns rewrote an earlier ballad, and, according to his editor, James Kinsley, 'transformed this into a neat and witty domestic comedy'. Burns used the form of 'Fy Let Us A' to the Bridal' as a model for a political broadside which he wrote in order to satirize the opposition candidate who stood against one of his patrons, Patrick Heron – the Whig candidate for the Stewardry of Kirkcudbright in 1795.[15]

In relation to his early song, 'My Nanie O' (April, 1784), for example, Burns commented:

> I have often thought that no man can be a proper critic of Love composition, except he himself, in one, or more instances, have been a

> warm votary of this passion. – As I have been all along, a miserable dupe to Love, and have been led into a thousand weaknesses and follies by it, for that reason I put the more confidence in my critical skill in distinguishing foppery and conceit, from real passion and nature. – Whether the following song will stand the test, I will not pretend to say, because it is my own; only I can say it was, at the time, real.[16]

His editor, James Kinsley, then demonstrates how others, including the poet's brother, Gilbert Burns, tried to confirm the song was Burns's 'own', by attempting to identify the woman whom Burns had in mind when he wrote 'My Nanie O':

> Gilbert Burns told [George] Thomson (1819) that she was probably Agnes Fleming, daughter of a Tarbolton farmer, to whom Burns paid a little of his 'roving attention': 'her charms were indeed mediocre, but what she had were sexual, which was characteristic of the greater part of the poet's mistresses; for he was no platonic lover, however he might otherwise pretend, or suppose of himself.'

Burns offered 'My Nanie O' to George Thomson on 26–27 October 1792 for his *Select Scottish Airs*, which Thomson printed, after proposing alterations that Burns accepted. Burns, however, might have been working from other verses in *Orpheus Caledonius*, 1725, No. 38, or from Ramsay's *Ever Green* or from David Herd's *Ancient and Modern Scottish Songs* (1776), which was a reprinting from Ramsay's *Ever Green*.[17]

Burns's idealized view of romantic love in 'My Nanie O' can be contrasted with Joanna Baillie's rewriting of this earlier oral ballad, which appeared in her own collection *Fugitive Verses* (1840). Her source for her version is not known, although she might have used an oral source that she heard in the late 1770s. George Thomson, for whom Baillie had already composed a considerable number of Scots, Welsh, and Irish poems for the airs he stipulated, asked her if he could reprint her poem 'My Nanny O', along with two other of her Scots poems, in his next edition of his six-volume *Collection of the Songs of Burns, Sir Walter Scott, Bart, and other Eminent Lyric Poets* (1841). At first Baillie agreed to Thomson's request:

> As to my three amended Scottish songs, 'Willie was a Wanton Wag' ['The Merry Bachelor'], 'Fee him, father, fee him', and 'Wi' lang-legged Tam the bruise I tried' ['My Nanny O'], you are heartily welcome to put them into your next publication of Scotch music. I shall be pleased to see them there; and you have no leave to ask any Bookseller, for they are entirely my own property.[18]

But Baillie soon changed her mind when she discovered that Thompson wanted to set her words to different music from the traditional 'My Nanny O':

> I . . . thank you for the pains you are willing to take in favour of Lang-legged Tam ['My Nanny O'], but I should not like to have him joined to any other music than the old air of My Nanny O. It is one of those Scotch airs that may be made plaintive or joyous as you choose to sing or play them: my song was intended to be in the last character, and Burns or Percy [Percy's *Reliques*] having written words for it, suited to the former, is a matter of no importance in itself; though I readily agree that there would be a confusion and waywardness in its appearing in its joyous mood in your last volume when it has keen melancholy and sentiment in the first. We shall, therefore, if you please think no more about it.[19]

To Thomson, Baillie puts herself on a level with Burns as a songwriter, and she identifies the main distinction between their two very different versions of 'My Nanny O'. She observes that her words convey satiric humour about masculine dallying with love, whereas Burns's stanzas have a mournful quality in relation to his protagonist's concept of love.

In Baillie's 'My Nanny O', for example, the male speaker cannot be deterred from his obsessive attraction by even the disapproving matriarchs of his beloved Nanny's family:

> Like swallow wheeling round her tower,
>   Like rock bird round her cranny o,
> Sinsyne I hover near her bower
>   And list and look for Nanny o.
>
>   . . .
>
> Her angry mither scalds sa loud,
>   And darkly glooms her granny o;
> But think they he can e'er be cowed,
>   Wha loves and lives for Nanny o?[20]

On the other hand, Burns in his version conveys the stereotype of the devoted man who pins all his aspirations on conventional notions of 'love'. His speaker can resign himself to the work of driving a plough for the owner or tenant of a small estate or farm, so long as he is sustained by his love for 'my Nanie O':

> Our auld Guidman delights to view
>   His sheep and kye thrive bonie O;
> But I'm as blithe that hauds his pleugh,
>   An' has nae care but Nanie O.
>
> Come weel come woe, I care na by,
>   I'll tak what Heav'n will sen' me, O;
> Nae ither care in life have I,
>   But live, an' love my Nanie O.[21]

Baillie's version has a satiric humour that deflates masculine protestations of 'love', whereas in Burns's lyric lies an implication that declarations of undying 'love' might be taken seriously.

Baillie's 'The Merry Bachelor' represents a tale of the stereotypical bachelor who flirts with all women, married and single:

> And aye he led the foremost dance,
>   Wi' winsome maidens buskit braw,
> And gave to each a merry glance
>   That stole, a while, her heart awa'.
>
> The bride forgot her simple groom,
>   And every lass her trysted Joe;
> Yet nae man's brow on Will could gloom,
>   They liked his rousing blitheness so.[22]

Will, the popular bachelor, has been forced to emigrate, however, and this ballad ends on a forlorn note of loss. 'Wanton Willie', to which Baillie alludes as the source of her tune, is a bawdy ballad that Burns might have once collected, but never rewrote.[23]

Baillie wrote and sang Scots ballads before Burns published his poems, and he in fact admired the humour in Baillie's 'Fee him, father, fee him'.[24] The speaker in this ballad implores her father to hire a young man to whom she is attracted. Her father demurs because the young man has not even a shirt to his back. But the speaker is insistent, telling her father that she will supply the shirt, and her man will not only drive the plough and thresh the corn, but he will also enliven their home because 'lang I trow/We've dull and dowie been'. In this ballad, Baillie recognizes the strength of woman's desire, as well as her protagonist's determination to have her own way.

Some poet-collectors were less apt than Burns or Baillie in transmitting or transmuting the oral tradition of poetry in Scots English. Sir Walter Scott (1771–1832), for example, in *Minstrelsy of the Scottish Border* (3 vols, 1802–03), edited and altered ballads in ways he believed would suit his eighteenth-century audience, so that his collection is not only inaccurate, but also at times anodyne or pretentious. Subsequently, Scott composed ballads of his own, such as *The Lay of the Last Minstrel* (1805), which were also immediately popular and sold well, but are not very highly regarded now.

Scottish interest in the revival and reworking of Scottish ballads had coincided throughout the eighteenth century with attempts to write new poems in other forms in Scots English. The pre-Romantic Allan Ramsay (1685–1758) epitomizes the new kind of literary entrepreneur who arose after the Act of Union. After publishing his famous collection of Scots songs, he wrote several poems in the 'standard habbie' mock elegiac form about low life in Edinburgh, as did Robert Ferguson (1750–74), who used the 'habbie' for humorous poems such as 'Daft Days' and 'Auld Reekie'. The 'standard habbie' was a stanza form that dated from the sixteenth century, and which Robert Sempill (?1595–?1669) had revived in his mock elegy 'The Life and Death of the Piper of Kilbarchan, or The Epitaph of Habbie Simson'. This stanza form later became known as the 'Burns stanza' because Robert Burns used this form to such good effect.

The pre-Romantics Ramsay and Ferguson wrote 'standard habbies' that stand out because of their realism and ironic use of vernacular Scots, as this stanza from Ramsay's 'Answer to the Third Epistle' (1721) indicates:

> I think, my friend, as fowk can get
> A doll of rost beef pypin het,
> And wi' red wine their wyson wet,
>   And cleathing clean.
> And nae be sick, or drown'd in debt,
>   They're no too mean.

These lines epitomize the 'standard habbie' form in that the first six lines, which relate the ordinary man's minimal desires for a good life, are then undercut by an allusion to the actual hardships of the lower classes.

In fact, the Scottish broadcaster and literary historian Maurice Lindsay considers that Allan Ramsay's few 'habbies' have 'a taut and racy urban originality' which make these poems not only a precursor but also an equal to Burns's later achievement with this traditional poetic form.[25] Burns, however, recognized that this stanza form suited the use of irony and satire; for example, in 'To A Louse, On Seeing one on a Lady's Bonnet at Church' (1786), he mocks the social airs and graces of a young Scotswoman who unwittingly harbours lice. His final stanza implies that, if only she could see the louse making free with her hair and bonnet, she would drop all pretension, particularly at prayer:

> O wad some Pow'r the giftie gie us
> *To see oursels as others see us!*
> It wad frae monie a blunder free us
>   An foolish notion:
> What airs in dress an gait wad lea'e us,
>   And ev'n Devotion!

The narrator uses the final two lines of the 'habbie' to underline his entire send-up of the richly dressed female with her exaggerated closing of her eyes and clasping of hands in prayer, as well as to point a moral to the reader.

Burns must have seemed to William Wordsworth an example of the 'common man' writing in his own voice, although Wordsworth did not attempt to use a demotic Northumbrian dialect in his 'lyrical ballads' about ordinary people. Wordsworth read Robert Burns's *Poems, Chiefly in the Scottish Dialect* (1786) with his sister, Dorothy, during his summer vacation at Penrith, before going to Cambridge University in October 1787. One of Wordsworth's modern biographers, Mary Moorman, describes the influence of Burns's poetry on Wordsworth:

> It is almost impossible to over-estimate the effect of Burns's poems on Wordsworth.... The character, both in subject-matter and in versification, of the poetry of his own mature years is often drawn from Burns, while Burns's proud claim, 'My Muse, tho' hamely in attire,/May touch the heart', became his own faith and doctrine.[26]

Burns tried to impress a susceptible audience if not also to ensure good sales figures for his first book of his own poems, *Poems, Chiefly in the Scottish Dialect* (Kilmarnock, 1786), by writing a Preface that played on the sympathies of the reading public who were often aware of notions of Rousseau's 'noble savage' and the desirability of experiencing 'genuine' passion through the process of reading and identifying with an author's authentic feelings. He describes himself as 'an obscure, nameless Bard', a description that encouraged his readers, including Samuel Taylor Coleridge, to take him as a 'Doric rustic' or 'unlettered shepherd'. In fact, Burns was the son of a Scots 'cottar' – a farm worker who was leased a cottage with its own plot of land – and he worked on the land with his father at first. But his father also ensured that his son, Robert, was educated through what were known as 'adventure schools' for which a group of parents paid a tutor, and the breadth of Burns's literary education was increased by his going on summer courses and by his independent study of Scots anthologies as well as Shakespeare, Milton, Dryden, Addison, Thomson, Gray, Shenstone, and others. The 'ploughman poet' knew his Scots and English literary tradition, as well as Latin, trigonometry, and French.[27]

Scottish women songwriters and collectors who were contemporaries of Burns but who did not attempt to represent themselves in ways that caught the attention of the reading public have almost been forgotten. Yet, as Kirsteen McCue points out, 'About thirty of the Scottish songwriters published during the period were women', and several lyrics by Isobel Pagan (1741–1821), Jean Glover (1758–1801) and Carolina Nairne (1766–1845) have possibly been wrongly attributed to Robert Burns. Jean Glover, for example, is said to have been the author of 'Ca' the Yowes to the Knowes', which, McCue asserts, 'Burns claimed that he noted down initially from a clergyman called Clunzie'. McCue adds, 'Many collections published in this [twentieth] century quote this song in its first form ("As I gaed down the waterside,/There I met a shepherd lad") as Pagan's lyric.' Robert Burns's editor, James Kinsley, comments:

> The original song ['Ca' the ewes to the knowes'] has been attributed to an Ayrshire woman, Isobel Pagan (1741–1801); who kept a drinking howff near Muirkirk; but it is unlikely that Burns, had he accepted this, would have missed a chance to celebrate a local notability in his manuscript notes.[28]

These various comments, however, are less than conclusive about the authorship of this oral song.

Nairne thought that she had a duty to 'purify' oral ballads in Scots English of corrupt phrasing or awkward style, as well as any content of a kind that did not cohere with the social mores of the day. In 'The Laird of Cockpen', for example, she gives the poem an evocative power via an emphatic characterization of a genteel but impoverished woman refusing to accept the wealthy, well-dressed 'laird o' Cockpen' in marriage because she does not love him. Nairne's version – apart from a somewhat similar first line – is completely different from the version that James Kinsley publishes in *The Poems and Songs of Robert Burns*, in which a 'laird' seduces a collier's daughter. Burns's version has the stereotypical storyline of the oral ballad, whereas Nairne, in her literary adaptation, alters this narrative so as to introduce a comic irony from a woman's perspective: the presumptuous 'laird' receives his comeuppance and yet he still believes that he is God's gift to women: '"She's daft to refuse the laird o' Cockpen"'.[29] Two further stanzas, which are attributed to either George Thomson or Susan Ferrier, have sometimes been published in order to undo the heroine's untoward refusal in marriage of Cockpen, but these corrupt stanzas only serve to denude Nairne's ballad of dramatic irony.

Joanna Baillie, in another underrated ballad of the Romantic period, also narrates a tale of a Scottish 'laird' on the prowl, but, in her poem 'It was on a morn, when we were thrang', the 'laird' unsuccessfully seeks a pretty young mistress in order to revivify his fading prowess as a lover:

> Then awa flung the Laird, and loud muttered he,
> 'A' the daughters of Eve, between Orkney and Tweed o'
> Black or fair, young or auld, dame or damsel or widow,
> May gang in their pride to the de'il for me!'[30]

Like Nairne, Baillie represents her anti-hero ironically condemning himself in his own voice.

As well as her songs in Scots English, Baillie also wrote two extended lyrics, 'A Winter Day' and 'A Summer Day', which exemplify her skill in writing pastoral poetry of the late eighteenth-century Scottish landscape. These two long poems should be read in tandem since there are both contrasts and linkages between the themes and imagery of each. Through the use of a covert narrator, the differences between the seasons are highlighted, and, at the same time, a social commentary is adumbrated in relation to some aspects of rural life.

In both poems, family life and the countryside are evoked in detail and celebrated with greater realism and less mawkishness than in Burns's 'The Cotter's Saturday Night' (1785–86). Moreover, unlike Burns, Baillie uses the more natural rhythms of blank verse rather than the Spenserian stanza, which had become associated – through Shenstone and Beattie – with supposedly rustic themes. The difficulties of the domestic and economic circumstances of the yeomanry are described in detail by Baillie, unlike some of the distancing from the subject-matter that is apparent in some of the blank verse poems of another of her compatriots, James Thomson. In his poem 'Winter' (1726), for example, Thomson describes 'the cottage-swain' who:

> Hangs o'er th' enlivening blaze and, taleful, there
> Recounts his simple frolic: much he talks
> And much he laughs, nor recks the storm that blows
> Without, and rattles on his humble roof.[31]

Thomson's 'swain' seems more generalized and less distinctive than Baillie's 'hind' whom she characterizes in detail in 'A Winter Day'.

These two poems are therefore both aligned with, as well as subversive of, the tradition of the pastoral, in that they not only carry echoes of Thomson's *The Seasons* (1726–39) but also are an ironic response to Alexander Pope's *Four Pastorals* (1709); for example, she eschews neo-classical musing on winter and summer, and uses less elevated language than Pope or Thomson.

In an incomplete and unpublished memoir, Baillie describes the genesis of 'A Winter Day':

> One dark morning of a dull winter day, standing on the hearth in Windmill Street [London] and looking at the mean dirty houses on the opposite side of the street, the contrast of my situation from the winter scenes of my own country came powerfully to my mind. . . . With little further deliberation I forthwith set myself to write 'the Winter day' in blank verse.[32]

By drawing on her detailed observation of the lives of the country people whom she knew as a child and adolescent in her father's parishes at Bothwell and Hamilton, and later on at her mother's family estate in the Scottish Lowlands, she represents the joys and sorrows of men and women in Scottish rural surroundings. Baillie's poems cannot be taken as patronage of those in a class lower then herself; for, as she herself noted later, she had taken part in their lives:

> Traits in human nature whether in books or in real life have always had most power in arresting my attention and keeping place in my recollection. This has often made me a watcher of children at play or under any excitement, and/or frequenter in early life of the habitations of labouring and country people which happily for me I had many opportunities of doing.[33]

Baillie here definitively identifies the sources of these pastoral poems in her life in rural Scotland in the latter half of the eighteenth century.

In 'A Winter Day', the narrator concentrates on the smallholding yeoman farmer and his family, showing how he is slow to get up in the cold darkness, wryly wishing that he 'were a lord,/That he might lie a-bed'. The family's breakfast is the porridge that was usual in cottage meals of that time; the children play on snow and ice; a black cock is shot wantonly by a fowler; and a mendicant soldier is given a bed for the night. In 'A Summer Day', the narrator centres on a labourer, who, in the first light of morning, 'quits his easy bed' and 'with good will begins his daily work' of digging with spade and hoe. Children play in the early sunshine, and a housewife separates curd and whey in making cheese. When, at noon, 'all the freshness of the morn is fled', scythes are used to cut the hay. Everyone joins in – 'old and young, the weak and strong' – to stack the new-cut hay in a haystack. Children bring lunch for a meal in the field; a siesta follows, and then more haying. At sundown everyone returns to the village, where young men and women flirt, and children play. A pedlar arrives and the villagers are attracted to his flashy wares. The poem concludes with an image of sleep for everyone except for a frustrated lover who lurks in a copse hoping to waylay 'his darling maid'.[34]

The main difference between Baillie's two season poems lies in their tone and mood. In 'A Winter Day', a sense of foreboding and desolation is created through the use of adjectives in phrases such as 'bleak and dreary' and 'the rugged face of scowling winter'. In 'A Summer Day', a mood of joyful labour and fulfilment is created in phrases such as 'the cheerful voice of industry' and 'thus do they jest, and laugh away their toil'. In 'A Winter Day', the imagery is dominated by violence, such as the shooting of the cock, and the old soldier's tales. In 'A Summer Day', the imagery is connected with ripeness and sexuality; for example, the housewife is assisted in making cheese by 'her brown dimpled maid, with tucked-up sleeve,/And swelling arm' and the haymaking is accompanied by laughter and flirtation.

Inherent in Baillie's celebrations of the pastoral is a critique of the artificiality of town life with its incessant quest for pleasure in contrast with the 'natural' existence of the rural yeomanry with their balance between physical labour and calm relaxation. In 'A Winter Day', after listening to 'tales of war and blood', the villagers retire not 'torn with vexing cares,/Nor dancing with the unequal beat of pleasure'. The main enemy that the yeoman fears is an accepted fact of nature – storms, which 'break in dreadful bellowings o'er his head'. Those who are unluckily excluded from a family circle are represented as pitiable. The mendicant soldier, for instance, who is taken in for the night by the yeoman farmer, is not easily rehabilitated into civilian society:

> They gaze upon him,
> And almost weep to see the man so poor,
> So bent and feeble, helpless and forlorn,
> That oft has stood undaunted in the battle
> Whilst thundering cannons shook the quaking earth,
> And showering bullets hissed around his head.[35]

This representation of battle contrasts dramatically with the rural haven in which the farming community lives, and alludes indirectly to the period between 1775 and 1783 during which Britain was at war with France and Spain as well as with the American colonists.

Baillie's 'A Winter Day' and 'A Summer Day' are a new departure in British poetry of 1790 in that she depicts, in standard English enriched with a few lexical and structural features from modern (post-1700) Scots English, the lives of the Scottish 'hind' and his family. She reveals, through imagery developed by means of close observation, details of how these rural Scots men and women obtain their livelihoods as well as how they enjoy their recreation. In her 1840 reprinting of these two poems, however, she deleted a few Scotticisms, such as the word 'grumly', which she replaced with 'dismal', and 'knotted shoes', for which she substituted 'studded shoes'.[36] In her first publication of these two poems, however, Baillie uses standard English with an admixture of scattered Scotticisms so as to create original poems which are as evocative and vivid as her songs in Scots English are. Baillie and Burns exemplify that interchange between late eighteenth- and early nineteenth-century Scots and English cultures, which led to a deepening of both Scots and English poetry. Both poets reveal in their work their strong Scottish roots. In Baillie's case – as is demonstrated by her remarkable Scots songs that she wrote in the 1840s – these roots remained just as strong even after living for 50 years in London.

Notes

1 Kurt Wittig, *The Scottish Tradition in Literature* (London, 1958), p. 156.
2 Roderick Watson, *The Literature of Scotland* (Basingstoke, 1984), p. 172.
3 *The New Oxford Book of Eighteenth-Century Verse*, ed. Roger Lonsdale (Oxford, 1984), p. 487.
4 Letter from Robert Burns to Murdoch, 15 January 1783, in *The Letters of Robert Burns*, ed. G. Ross Roy (2 vols, Oxford, 2nd edn, 1985).
5 *The Collected Letters of Joanna Baillie,* ed. Judith Slagle, Vol. 2 (2 vols, Madison, USA), p. 1117.
6 *Edinburgh Review*, 6 July 1805, p. 462.
7 Alan Bold, *The Ballad* (London, 1979), pp. 11–12.
8 James Johnson, 'Preface', *The Scots Musical Museum*, 2, 1788, p. iii.
9 Robert Crawford, *Devolving English Literature* (Oxford, 1992), p. 107.
10 *The Poems and Songs of Robert Burns*, ed. James Kingsley, Vol. II (3 vols, London, 1968) p. 762.
11 Letter to George Thomson, *The Poems and Songs of Robert Burns*, Vol. III, p. 1467.
12 Crawford, *Devolving English Literature*, pp. 113–14.
13 Kenneth Simpson, ed., 'Introduction', *Burns Now* (Edinburgh, 1994), p. xii.
14 *The Poems and Songs of Robert Burns*, Vol. III, p. 1455.
15 See *The Poems and Songs of Robert Burns*, Vol. II, pp. 622–3 and 777–80; Vol. III, pp. 1395, 1474, and 1476–9.
16 'First Commonplace Book' (April, 1784), quoted in *The Poems and Songs of Robert Burns*, Vol. III, p. 1006.
17 *The Poems and Songs of Robert Burns*, Vol. III, pp. 1007–8.

18 Letter to George Thomson, 1 May 1841, BL Add. MS. 35265, f. 286, repr. in *The Collected Letters of Joanna Baillie*, Vol. 1, p. 147.
19 Letter to George Thomson, 10 May 1841, BL Add. MS. 35265, fos. 290–1, repr. in *The Collected Letters of Joanna Baillie*, Vol. 1, p. 148.
20 *The Selected Poems of Joanna Baillie*, ed. Jennifer Breen (Manchester, 1999), p. 123.
21 *The Poems and Songs of Robert Burns*, Vol. I, p. 9.
22 *The Selected Poems of Joanna Baillie*, pp. 123–4.
23 *The Poems and Songs of Robert Burns*, Vol. II, p. 930.
24 See Margaret Carhart, *The Life and Work of Joanna Baillie* (London and New Haven, 1923), p. 182.
25 See Maurice Lindsay, *History of Scottish Literature* (London, 1977), pp. 172–4.
26 Mary Moorman, *William Wordsworth: The Early Years, 1770–1803* (Oxford, 1957), p. 74.
27 Nicholas Roe, 'Authenticating Robert Burns', in *Robert Burns and Cultural Authority*, ed. Robert Crawford (Edinburgh, 1997), p. 163.
28 Kirsteen McCue, 'Burns, Women and Song', in *Robert Burns and Cultural Authority*, ed. Robert Crawford (Edinburgh, 1997), pp. 41 and 49. See also Kirsteen McCue, 'Women and Song, 1750–1850' in *A History of Scottish Women's Writing*', ed. Douglas Gifford and Dorothy McMillan (Edinburgh, 1977), p. 60; and *The Poems and Songs of Robert Burns*, Vol. III, p. 1252.
29 *Women Romantic Poets, 1785–1832: An Anthology*, ed. Jennifer Breen (London, 1992, 2nd edn, 1994), p. 144.
30 *The Selected Poems of Joanna Baillie*, p. 85.
31 *The New Oxford Book of Eighteenth-Century Verse*, p. 182, ll. 128–32.
32 Wellcome Institute for the History of Medicine, London, MS 5613/68/1–6.
33 *Recollections: Written at the Request of Miss Berry*, 1831, Hunter Baillie Collection, Vol. 2, no. 56, Royal College of Surgeons Library, London.
34 *The Selected Poems of Joanna Baillie*, pp. 36–45.
35 *The Selected Poems of Joanna Baillie*, p. 35.
36 *Women Romantic Poets, 1785–1832: An Anthology*, pp. 51 and 48.

4

Literary ballads and lyrical poetry in England

Variations of the ballad form began to be used in English poetry in the literary journals and magazines of the 1790s, thus undermining the almost universal use of the heroic couplet, a verse form that up till then had been predominant in eighteenth-century poetry. Robert Mayo, in his seminal article 'The Contemporaneity of the "Lyrical Ballads"' describes the difficulties of defining the 'ballad' as a form:

> In the magazines . . . any *narrative poem* in stanzas, or any *lyric* which hoped to appeal to a large circle of readers, or any combination of both, was likely to be termed a ballad. Half of the so-called 'ballads' which appeared in the *Gentleman's Magazine*, the *Lady's Magazine*, and the *Edinburgh Magazine* in the last years of the eighteenth century have no resemblance to the traditional balladry of the non-literary classes, nor do they even tell a story.

Mayo indicates here that the definition of 'ballad' needs to be extended if the kinds of poems that were denominated as 'ballads' in the 1790s are to receive consideration. In relation to Wordsworth's and Coleridge's invention of the hybrid collocation 'lyrical ballads', Mayo comments that their title 'does not represent a significant innovation in 1798, nor as a term is it particularly appropriate to the contents' of *Lyrical Ballads*.

Moreover, as Mayo points out, the *Lyrical Ballads* did not embody a completely new style of writing poetry:

> The new poets were everywhere striving for artless expressions of sensibility. . . . Conversational informality and freedom from artificiality or affectation were hallmarks of 'simplicity' – so that the bald style of the ballads and, to some extent, the theory of diction advanced in the Advertisement would be likely to be taken as more or less aggressive attempts to achieve 'simplicity' . . . these poems were merely the fulfilment of a tendency which a great number of contemporary poets, without the benefit of Wordsworth and Coleridge's aesthetic theories,

> were already showing. To most readers this feature of the volume would seem less a revolution, therefore, than an excess of a new orthodoxy.[1]

William Wordsworth and S.T. Coleridge, who, along with Joanna Baillie and Robert Southey and other poets of the Romantic period, tried out demotic forms combined with an unaffected poetic diction, were merely part of an ideological change that permeated the English literary scene in the 1790s and even earlier. Moreover, eighteenth-century interest – particularly that of dissenters – in childhood education led to an increase in the publication of poetry specifically for children. This poetry, such as that by William Blake and Mary Lamb, tended to be written in quatrains and in language that could be understood more readily by the child reader.

This generally 'new' kind of informal poetic diction emerged partly as a response to earlier eighteenth-century works of literature such as the collector Thomas Percy's *Reliques of Ancient English Poetry: Consisting of Old Heroic Ballads, Songs, and Other Pieces of Our Earlier Poets; together with Some Few of Later Date* (1765) and partly in reaction to Hugh Blair's *A Critical Dissertation on the Poems of Ossian* (1763), and his later *Lectures on Rhetoric and Belles Lettres* (1783). Coleridge introduced the second volume of the latter work to Wordsworth in 1798, the year in which they were engaged in writing *Lyrical Ballads*.[2] Blair advocated, *inter alia*, a return in literary art to replication of the more primitive stage of the oral ballad when the 'bard' could represent his feelings without the refinements of poetic decorum or ornate diction.

Wordsworth and to some extent Coleridge adapted the oral ballad famously in *Lyrical Ballads* (1798), but Joanna Baillie had already written, on the theme of infancy and childhood, what might be considered versions of what Wordsworth later termed the 'lyrical ballad' – which, if you read the poems that Wordsworth printed under that title, seems to imply any semi-ballad or lyric poem. Baillie's two semi-ballads in sixains about relationships between adults and children, which were published as early as 1790, reflect that newly developed eighteenth-century interest in the psychological and moral development of children. In 'A Mother to Her Waking Infant', Baillie, through the use of a disingenuous narrator, describes in minute detail the behaviour of a young baby. A devoted mother muses over her baby's lack of physical coordination and inability to form words or even to express by gesture a range of appropriate feelings:

> From thy poor tongue no accents come,
> Which can but curb thy toothless gum;
> Small understanding boasts thy face,
> Thy shapeless limbs nor step nor grace:
> A few short words thy feats may tell,
> And yet I love thee well.[3]

In this lyric poem, which is composed of sestets of rhyming tetrameters that conclude with a trimeter, Baillie shows the play of feeling in a mother in relation to her observation of her helpless baby. In another lyric with a similar form, 'A Child to His Sick Grandfather', the first-person speaker is a devoted young grandson addressing his elderly grandfather who is on the threshold of death. The naiveté of the child's monologue induces the reader to contemplate the mystery and randomness of the moment of death.

In her 1790 *Poems*, Baillie seems to have been putting into practice her later theories about the writing of poetry and drama, which she published as 'Introductory Discourse' to her 1798 *Plays on the Passions*, a volume that Coleridge and Wordsworth read when it first appeared.[4] Baillie wrote, in reference to poetry:

> let one simple trait of the human heart, one expression of passion genuine and true to nature, be introduced, and it will stand all alone in the boldness of reality, whilst the false and unnatural around it, fades away upon every side, like the rising exhalations of the morning. . . . The highest pleasures we receive from poetry, as well as from the real objects that surround us in the world, are derived from the sympathetic interest we all take in beings like ourselves.[5]

Wordsworth, in his influential 'Preface' of 1800, was merely endorsing a change in poetry that had already taken place. His originality lay in introducing the notion that poetry about common life should also reflect the psychology of the individual, that is, what he termed 'the primary laws of our nature'. Wordsworth, however, had to contend with the attempts of Mary Robinson (1758–1800), a more facile versifier than either Wordsworth or Coleridge, to appropriate his title. Robinson published many of her own poems under different pseudonyms when she was editor of the poetry columns of the *Morning Post*, and, as an admirer of *Lyrical Ballads*, reprinted in the *Morning Post* (2 April 1800) Wordsworth's 'The Mad Mother' with her editorial:

> We have been so much captivated with the following beautiful piece, which appears in a small volume *Lyrical Ballads*, that we are tempted to transgress the rule we have laid down for ourselves. Indeed, the whole collection, with the exception of the first piece, which appears manifestly to have been written by a different hand, is a tribute to genuine nature.

Two months later, Robinson was planning to have her *Lyrical Tales* published, and she began to promote this projected volume in the context of Wordsworth's 1798 *Lyrical Ballads*: 'The volume will consist of Tales, serious and gay, on a variety of subjects in the manner of Wordsworth's Lyrical Ballads.'[6] Robinson's self-promotion in relation to Wordsworth demonstrates both her commercial acumen as well as her desperation to finance herself and her daughter, Maria. Wordsworth, however, discovered that his publishers, Longman and Rees, had published Mary Robinson's volume of poetry, *Lyrical Tales*, a month before the second edition of *Lyrical Ballads* was to appear, and he immediately tried to alter the title of the second edition of his own similarly titled work. Curran describes how Wordsworth, 'apprised that she had boldly usurped his title . . . that autumn attempted without success to have it changed simply to *Poems in Two Volumes*'.[7] Curran also points out that Robinson's poetry at that time was a highly marketable commodity, and the publisher thought that he would thereby increase the sales of both books of poetry.

Judith Pascoe, who recently edited a selection of Robinson's poetry, compares 'All Alone', in *Lyrical Tales*, to Wordsworth's 'We Are Seven'. She notes, 'Certainly, in Robinson's rewriting of "We Are Seven", her replacement of the fey child, who plays and sups by her sibling's graves, with a boy whose catalogue of deprivation – of father, mother, baby goat, family dog, cottage – makes the little girl Wordsworth describes seem perhaps a little too charming'.[8] Curran also compares these two poems to the detriment of Wordsworth's: 'the orphan of "All Alone", like Wordsworth's young girl of "We Are Seven", is soberly rational. In immediate contrast with Robinson's portrayal, however, Wordsworth's elaboration of the saving continuities of memory perhaps seems facile.'[9]

But Wordsworth's 'We Are Seven' is more than an 'elaboration of the saving continuities of memory': the poet uses the representation of naiveté in a young child so as to bring home the difficulty young children have in appreciating the actuality of death and loss. His ballad is based on his meeting a young girl who refused to accept that her brother and sister were dead, but continued to see them as spiritually alive in their nearby graves. Wordsworth's conclusion to this poem is ambiguous, and the reader is left to think that in some ways the small girl is correct because her brother and sister are imaginatively still alive in her mind:

> 'But they are dead; those two are dead!
> Their spirits are in heaven!'
> 'Twas throwing words away; for still
> The little Maid would have her will,
> And said, 'Nay, we are seven!'

The reader is thereby forced to reassess his or her attitude to death in order to accommodate the young girl's idea that her brother and sister can still be responded to emotionally even if they are physically dead. In their 'Notes' to *Lyrical Ballads*, R.L. Brett and A.R. Jones describe the context of the composition of 'We Are Seven'. They relate how Wordsworth met an eight-year-old girl, and, in recollection of this meeting, tried 'to illustrate the perplexity and obscurity which in childhood attend our notion of death, or rather our utter inability to admit that notion'. Wordsworth himself commented on his own attitude in childhood to death:

> Nothing was more difficult for me in childhood than to admit the notion of death as a state applicable to my own being. . . . I was often unable to think of external things as having external existence, and I communed with all that I saw as something not apart from, but inherent in, my own immaterial nature. Many times while going to school have I grasped at a wall or tree to recall myself from this abyss of idealism to the reality. At that time I was afraid of such processes.[10]

Wordsworth suggests here that for some people, if not everyone, communication between the human spirit and the spirit of nature is as significant as any other kind of human interaction. In other words, Wordsworth seems to think that physical death does not lead to the death of the spirit.

Robinson's 'All Alone' uses a similar theme to that of Wordsworth in 'We Are Seven' but she reverses the narrator's approach to the supernatural. Whereas Wordsworth's protagonist believes that her brother and sister live in spirit after their deaths, the small boy in Robinson's poem affirms that, because all his family and friends are physically dead, he is entirely alone in the world. He rejects any idea of the immanence of nature or of any spiritual life after death. Moreover, Wordsworth's ballad is less melodramatic than is Robinson's in that the interlocutor in 'We Are Seven' implies that to be remembered by the living is one way that people can be kept alive in spirit. Another way for the spirit to live on is through works of literature and other art, which might continue to resonate in succeeding centuries.

Although Mary Robinson's 'All Alone' is an inventive parody of 'We Are Seven', her use of poetic diction tends toward the archaic with words such as 'yon' and 'yonder'. Robinson also resorts to an excessive use – even for the eighteenth century – of capitalization and italics:

> 'My Father never will return,
> He rests beneath the sea-green wave;
> I have no kindred left, to mourn
> When I am hid in yonder grave!
> *Not one*! to dress with flow'rs the stone; –
> *Then – surely*, I AM LEFT ALONE!'[11]

'All Alone' invites the reader to indulge a lachrymose sentimentality, whereas 'We Are Seven', in plain language, merely asks us to question whether, in relation to death, all might not be as it seems.

Probably it is more useful to look at both Wordsworth's and Robinson's lyric poems in the context of the other poetry that was being published at the same time. As Robert Mayo concludes:

> The more one reads the popular poetry of the last quarter of the eighteenth century, the more one is likely to feel that the really surprising feature of these poems in the *Lyrical Ballads* (as well as of many of the others) – apart from sheer literary excellence – is their intense

> fulfilment of an already stale convention, and not their discovery of an interest in rivers, valleys, groves, lakes, and mountains, flowers and budding trees, the changing seasons, sunsets, the freshness of the morning. This fact is a commonplace. Yet it is astonishing how often responsible Wordsworthians go astray in this respect, and tend to view Wordsworth and Coleridge as reacting with a kind of totality against contemporary fashions in verse. The question is not whether the *Ballads* were altogether conventional, which no one would attempt to affirm, but whether they were completely out of touch with popular taste.

Mayo then dismisses some of the other writers of lyric poetry of that period, who were in touch with 'popular taste': Helen Maria Williams, Anna Seward, W.L. Bowles, Charlotte Smith, and Mary Robinson are to him 'a deservedly forgotten generation'.[12] Yet both the authors of *Lyrical Ballads* responded or reacted to some of these authors' writings, particularly those of Mary Robinson, who had an influential position, from 1799 until her death in 1800, as poetry editor of *The Morning Post*.

Antiquarian recovery of the poetry of previous centuries, however, was often beset with quarrels about authenticity. Kathryn Sutherland, in her account of the late eighteenth-century dispute over the importance of the 'minstrel' as composer or mere performer of sung ballads, summarizes Thomas Percy's role as a collector of ballads and lyric poems: 'Percy gave the figure of the minstrel a bold, imaginative coherence, as he did to the ballads he so freely emended, providing a national poet and a national song.'[13] Percy and Joseph Ritson (1752–1803), collector of balladry and bibliographer of early English poetry, argued over the role of the minstrels, but their main dispute was concerned with whether Percy's or Ritson's recovered ballads were authentic rather than with who originally composed and sang them. Percy freely amended his chosen 'ancient works' especially if these ballads and lyric poems were incomplete, whereas Ritson made no editorial changes whatsoever. Percy defended his emendations in *Reliques of Ancient Poetry* by asserting that his changes led to 'improvement' in 'old copies'.[14] Despite the fact that Ritson's anthologies were more authentic, Percy's various editions became more popular with the readers, and, as Nick Groom notes, William Wordsworth, in his 'Essay, Supplementary to the Preface' of the *Lyrical Ballads* (1815), 'celebrated' Percy's *Reliques* 'as belonging to "the region of true simplicity and genuine pathos"'.[15] Although other anthologies of lyric poems had been published in Scotland and England, Percy's was by far the most successful in sales and influence.

Stuart Curran describes how access to 'Percy's and Warton's antiquarian researches' led to the reprinting of poetry of earlier centuries in various anthologies from the 1780s onwards:

> A landscape flooded with couplets was drained to reveal a remarkable topography of forms and, with them, opportunities for formal experi-

> ment, testing, arrangement, revisionism. . . . For the first time there was an actual *history* not of literature *per se*, but of poetry in English. The generation beginning in the 1780s and truly emerging into artistic leadership in the 1790s was the first ever to know that history.[16]

The 'generation beginning in the 1780s' included Joanna Baillie along with William Wordsworth and S.T. Coleridge, even though Joanna Baillie at times reverted to the earlier eighteenth-century use of couplets in her various satires such as 'A Disappointment' (1798). A preoccupation that Wordsworth and Coleridge shared with Baillie was an interest in the working of the human mind coupled with attempts to render in poetry their ideas about the expression and meaning of human feeling and emotion. William Wordsworth's and S.T. Coleridge's *Lyrical Ballads* are now seen as merely one part of a drive towards building up a tradition of English poetry in which the importance of the authentic poet, who could emerge from any class, is stressed.

Kenneth R. Johnston, in *The Hidden Wordsworth: Poet, Lover, Rebel, Spy,* summarizes the cultural milieu in which Wordsworth's and Coleridge's *Lyrical Ballads* emerged:

> The desire to go back to simple places with simple manners and sincere language was often extended historically into a broad program for recovering older, more genuine ways of living and speaking. Sometimes this focused on the era just before the national trauma of the civil war, the reign of Elizabeth I, but more often it tried to go "all the way" back, not only to the antique Greek and Roman patterns of England's Neoclassical myth, but to ancient or fictitious traditions of Welsh, Scottish, and generally Celtic bards and minstrels, as in [Thomas] Percy's *Reliques of Ancient English Poetry* (1765) and [James] Beattie's *The Minstrel* (1770).

Johnston demonstrates how both Wordsworth himself and his sister, Dorothy Wordsworth, thought that Beattie's fictional poet-hero, Edwin, resembled Wordsworth: 'The earliest commentator to recognize Beattie's influence on Wordsworth was his sister, Dorothy. . . . [In letters of 1787 to Jane Pollard] she presents "my dear William" as a version of Beattie's model'.[17]

Wordsworth himself, in 'Essay, Supplementary to the Preface', commented on the effect of Thomas Percy's *Reliques of Ancient Poetry*:

> This work [*Reliques of Ancient English Poetry*] did not steal silently into the world, as is evident from the number of legendary tales, that appeared not long after its publication; and had been modelled, as the authors persuaded themselves, after the old Ballad.

Wordsworth later cited Percy's anthology as an important influence on his own poetry.[18]

But Wordsworth was more interested in representing how the mind worked, rather than telling a traditional narrative in the ballad form. He claimed in his Preface of 1800 that in *Lyrical Ballads* he was attempting:

> to illustrate the manner in which our feelings and ideas are associated in a state of excitement. But speaking in less general language, it is to follow the fluxes and refluxes of the mind when agitated by the great and simple affections of our nature. This object I have endeavoured ... to attain by various means; by tracing the maternal passion through many of its more subtle windings, as in the poems of the IDIOT BOY and the MAD MOTHER.[19]

Wordsworth's poems in *Lyrical Ballads*, however, do not illustrate much about how the mind operates, except insofar as to reflect upon how seeming irrationality can be explained by examining mental and emotional conflict within the individual psyche. In a few ballads, Wordsworth deconstructs the obsessive behaviour of various characters: the woman in 'The Female Vagrant' who subsists alone without seeking help from her in-laws; the mother of the dead baby in the poem 'The Thorn' who wanders distractedly in the vicinity of the place where her illegitimate infant is buried, perhaps the victim of her infanticide; and Harry Gill, in 'Goody Blake and Harry Gill', who suffers psychosomatic fits of shivering. In 'The Mad Mother', the poem that Robinson reprinted in the *Morning Post*, a narrator introduces the monologue of a deranged mother whose love for her infant temporarily assuages her mental anguish. Thus Wordsworth astutely responds to the interests of his readers: at that time attitudes to insanity oscillated between severity and compassion. The author, Mary Lamb, for example, after killing her mother in a manic outburst, was released by a court into the care of her brother, Charles, instead of being committed to Bedlam.[20]

Wordsworth not only attempted to meet the desire of his contemporary readers for more understanding of human nature, but he also, as Coleridge recognized, presented his insights into human feeling in language that was devoid of artificial embellishment:

> I shall hardly forget the sudden effect produced on my mind, by his [Wordsworth's] recitation of a manuscript poem, which still remains unpublished, but of which the stanza, and tone of style, were the same as those of the 'Female Vagrant' as originally printed in the first volume of the 'Lyrical Ballads'. There was here, no mark of strained thought, or forced diction, no crowd or turbulence of imagery. ... the occasional obscurities, which had arisen from an imperfect controul [*sic*] over the resources of his native language, had almost entirely disappeared.[21]

In these lines, Coleridge identifies Wordsworth's use of the diction of ordinary men and women that avoided poetic language that was strained and inappropriate to the natural processes of imaginative thought. Coleridge's notion that the lyric poem in unforced imagery and plain language emerges from a kind of organic process in the mind of the poet was taken up subsequently by John Keats who counted the following as one of his 'Axioms' for the composition of poetry: 'if Poetry comes not as naturally as the Leaves to a tree it had better not come at all'.[22]

Keats's ballad, 'La Belle Dame Sans Merci' (April, 1819), however, which might be thought to have evolved organically in the mind of the poet, reveals a variety of influences such as Thomas Percy's *Reliques of Ancient Poetry*, Alain Chartier's fifteenth-century French ballad 'La Belle Dame Sans Merci', Robert Burns's Scottish ballads and lyric poems, and Wordsworth's and Coleridge's *Lyrical Ballads* (1798).[23] Keats, in 'La Belle Dame Sans Merci', reverses the central theme of Coleridge's ballad 'Love', which was first published in the *Morning Post,* 21 December 1799, as 'Introduction to the Tale of the Dark Ladie', and reprinted in a different version in the second edition of *Lyrical Ballads* (1800). Coleridge employs the device of a 'tale within a tale' so that his young female auditor becomes entranced with the narrator because of the sentimental effect of his tale. In the ballad, the narrator describes a medieval knight who saves a damsel in distress because he is 'crazed' and in the grip of a 'cruel scorn':

> . . . unknowing what he did,
> He leaped amid a murderous Band,
> And saved from outrage worse than death
> The Lady of the Land.

The narrator proceeds to describe how the grateful 'Lady' in her turn nurses the Knight in his madness:

> And that she nursed him in a cave;
> And how his madness went away
> When on the yellow forest-leaves
> A dying man he lay . . .

But the reader is not privy to his 'dying words' because the narrator's story is interrupted by his auditor's declaration of her love for him:

> She wept with pity and delight,
> She blushed with love, and virgin-shame;
> And, like the murmur of a dream,
> I heard her breathe my name.[24]

This sentimental ballad plays on the feelings of the reader in a way that reinforces one of the common stereotypes of that period: young women are easily swayed in their feelings by what they read or hear read to them. But in 'La Belle Dame Sans Merci' the 'Lady in the Mead' seduces the knight and then abandons him. Keats thus avoids the sentimentality of much of the 'magazine poetry' of his day.

A major problem with Keats's 'La Belle Dame Sans Merci' arises from the fact that Keats wrote two versions, both of which have been published side by side recently. Critics do not agree about which is the better version, or which is the version that Keats himself preferred. In his influential anthology, *The New Oxford Book of Romantic Period Verse* (1994), Jerome McGann reprints the first published version of 'La Belle Dame Sans Merci' from Leigh Hunt's the *Indicator* instead of the manuscript version from Keats's letter (14 February–3 May 1819 to his brother and sister-in-law, George and Georgiana Keats), which is the version now preferred by most editors. John Barnard states that the version in the *Indicator* 'is a revision of the first draft which Keats wrote in his journal letter to George and Georgiana Keats', but that this revised version 'introduces several changes, which most editors have agreed are for the worse'.[25] McGann's *Indicator* version, for example, opens with the line, 'Ah, what can ail thee, wretched wight . . .' instead of 'O what can ail thee knight-at-arms . . .' from Keats's manuscript version.[26] According to the COD, 'wight' means 'person (especially *luckless*, wretched, etc.)', but 'wight' is an archaism that does not have the resonance of 'knight-at-arms', whatever meaning it held for the poet himself when he wrote this alternative opening line.

Usual publishing practice is to print the first version that the author saw through the press, which is the *Indicator* version. But because some critics, such as Sidney Colvin, have suggested that the version in *The Indicator* was marred by the introduction of editorial infelicities from the hand of the editor, Leigh Hunt, most critics, apart from Jerome McGann, who makes a cogent argument for the literary quality of the *Indicator* version, prefer the unrevised journal-letter version. 'La Belle Dame Sans Merci' epitomizes the effects of transforming the oral ballad into a literary work. One of the main effects is to allow for indeterminacies of meaning through the use of allusion and symbolism, effects that the 'minstrel' or ballad-singer did not seek when communicating a narrative to a live audience.

John Barnard suggests that 'La Belle Dame Sans Merci' 'is an oblique expression of some aspects of Keats's feelings for Fanny Brawne'. He adds: 'Recent critics differ widely over the meaning of the poem, and whether La Belle Dame is wilfully cruel to the knight, or whether it is the knight's inability to maintain the vision that causes his return to the "cold hill side".'[27] But such readings appear to be too literal, especially when this ballad is read in the context of the *Lyrical Ballads*, which is dominated by poems with indeterminate endings, and which preceded Keats's ballad.

New ways of reading 'La Belle Dame Sans Merci' have been revealed more recently by feminist and psychoanalytic critics. In 'Harassing the Muse', for example, Karen Swann places this ballad in the context of theories about language in relation to psychoanalysis, and suggests that the 'lady' of this ballad is a projection – in late twentieth-century terminology of 'the Other' – and is therefore bound to be mysterious and unattainable:

> As I've just described it, this 'world' resembles not the 'real world' of just a short time ago, when critics found something tragically incompatible between the poet/knight's love for a life of imagination, and real, mortal existence, but the new criticism's equivalent, the symbolic order – the order of language, in which subject knights must bow to a deathly law, and where, according to Jacques Lacan, 'the Woman does not exist' except as a fantasmatic construct, which, insofar as it occupies the place of the unattainable Other, figures the imaginary unity of identity 'itself'.[28]

Swann is here re-interpreting Graves' reading of the 'lady' of 'the meads' as the poetic Muse that disappoints the male poet who strives to discover her through language. Women readers, according to Swann, recognize that the 'faery's child' is merely a figment of the imagination that the poet works toward, but the disappearance of the female subject is inevitable. But Swann's analysis here is only a reworking of the old rhetorical question 'Is there a woman in this text?' The significant point is that Keats's ballad gives us – in a popularist form – a narrative that causes the reader to question the nature of language and the symbolic ordering of human existence through language. If we had no language, existence would be meaningless. If we had no literary language, the numinous – in its very nature part of the symbolic order of things – would prove to be unattainable. Keats's triumph in this ballad is to give the reader a story on more than one level so that readers are encouraged to explore events through the interpretation of symbols, such as 'a faery child', 'kisses four', 'horrid warning gaped wide', which remain enigmatic.

Of the generation of English poets who succeeded Wordsworth, P.B. Shelley showed an interest in using the ballad form to reach a wide readership. In fact, Shelley can be shown to have considered publishing a collection of his own songs and ballads to be entitled *Popular Songs*. Richard Holmes and, subsequently, M.H. Scrivener, list the poems that might have appeared in this work: 'The Mask of Anarchy', 'Lines Written during the Castlereagh Administration', 'Song to the Men of England', 'Similes for Two Political Characters', 'What Men Gain Fairly', 'A New National Anthem', 'Sonnet: England 1819', 'Ballad of the Starving Mother', and perhaps 'Ode to Liberty' and 'Ode to the West Wind'. Such a projected work has obvious affinities with Wordsworth's and Coleridge's *Lyrical Ballads*, especially if we consider Wordsworth's own attempts to draw the attention of the politician Charles James Fox to his poems such as 'The Brothers' and 'Michael'. Wordsworth and Coleridge sent a copy of *Lyrical Ballads* to Fox, and in their accompanying letter (of which Wordsworth was the sole signatory) they pointed out the political significance of this volume.[29]

But Shelley uses the ballad form in 'The Mask of Anarchy' (September, 1819) in order to create a demotic allegorical satire of a recent political event, a political rout that later became known as 'the Peterloo Massacre'. In *Shelley: the Pursuit*, Richard Holmes describes how Holman Hunt had called a meeting at St Peter's Field near Manchester on 16 August 1819 in order to discuss how the reform of the House of Commons could be effected. Although the Home Secretary had arranged extensive military support, the local Yeomanry were used first to arrest Hunt as soon as he arrived. When they arrested Hunt, at the same time, because of the dense crowd, they inadvertently knocked down a woman and child, killing the child. The crowd encircled the Yeomanry in order to ridicule them, and the 15th Hussars were ordered to rescue them. In the general fracas, which did not last long, 11 were killed, and at least 421 people were injured; more than a third of these sustained sword injuries.[30]

Shelley responded dramatically in a letter to Thomas Love Peacock: 'The tyrants here [at St Peter's Field] as in the French Revolution, have first shed blood. ... I still think there will be no coming to close quarters until financial affairs decidedly bring the oppressors and the oppressed together.'[31] Perhaps his composition of *The Mask of Anarchy* is an attempt to provoke a more sustained – even if passively resistant – response from the 'oppressed' to their 'oppressors'. Shelley himself had come into embattled contact with the Lord High Chancellor over the custody of his children, and *The Mask of Anarchy* opens with Shelley's indictment of his *bêtes noires* who include Castlereagh, who as Foreign Secretary was associated with militarism in Ireland as well as in the Napoleonic wars with France, and the Lord Chancellor. Satire in this ballad is achieved through the use both of mocking hyperbole and of the personification of abstractions such as 'Fraud':

> Next came Fraud, and he had on,
> Like Eldon, an ermined gown;
> His big tears, for he wept well,
> Turned to mill-stones as they fell,
>
> And the little children who
> Round his feet played to and fro,
> Thinking every tear a gem,
> Had their brains knocked out by them.

In 1817, Eldon had refused Shelley, because of his supposed immorality and atheism, custody of his two children by his first wife, Harriett Westbrook, who had committed suicide in 1816.[32] But Shelley here is referring generally to the Lord Chancellor's renowned 'crocodile tears' on the Bench, particularly in relation to the custody of children, whom he is reputed to have usually removed from parental care.

In *Mask of Anarchy* elsewhere, however, an attack is mounted on the State's misrule by means of abstractions rather than through specifying individual men. The State's rulers are represented in the telling abstraction

Anarchy, and, instead of order, bring chaos. Moreover, Anarchy wears a crown, which is supposed to symbolize God and Law, but which in this case symbolizes the wearer trampling 'to a mire of blood/The adoring multitude'. A 'mighty troop', all supposedly in the service of order, but actually in the pay of Anarchy, 'Waving each a bloody sword,/For the service of their Lord', puts fear into the hearts of everyone. Hope, however, is not finally extinguished, but rises again in misty splendour, and mother Earth herself is portrayed as calling on the populace to seize their freedom:

'Rise like Lions after slumber
In unvanquishable number,
Shake your chains to Earth like dew
Which in sleep had fallen on you –
Ye are many – they are few.

This allegory proceeds to explode the notion that the lower classes should remain subservient by suggesting that lack of freedom brings about starvation and that attaining freedom leads to a full life for all:

No – in countries that are free
Such starvation cannot be
As in England now we see.[33]

And Freedom as an abstract is displayed through 'Science, Poetry and Thought' leading to Freedom's virtues of 'Spirit, Patience, Gentleness'.

In the closing stanzas, Shelley represents a pacifist view of revolution in which the narrator advocates passive resistance to tyranny in order to overcome, through sheer weight of numbers, the suppression of their freedom: 'Ye are many – they are few.' Shelley's view of a revolution that can be achieved by simple resistance to unlawful tyranny concludes this allegorical ballad, which was never published in Shelley's lifetime. Thus Leigh Hunt, who was offered this work for his liberal journal *The Examiner*, lost, through his pusillanimity, the chance to take a stand against the anti-reformers of his day. Shelley's ballad, moreover, has never received the critical attention that has been devoted to Wordsworth's and Coleridge's *Lyrical Ballads* as well as to Keats's 'La Belle Dame Sans Merci', despite, or because of, the fact that Shelley had the temerity to satirize, in his *Peter Bell the Third*, Wordsworth's poem *Peter Bell*. Wordsworth's reputation as a poet was not much enhanced by the publication of this long narrative ballad, *Peter Bell* (composed 1798; published 1819), which he prefaced with an address to Robert Southey, the then poet laureate. In his Preface, Wordsworth discounts ideas of the supernatural, and instead asserts that the 'imagination' can arise 'in the humblest departments of daily life', without having to be stimulated by supposedly supranormal events – or such events that are imagined to be above the ordinary.

Peter Bell begins with a Prologue that serves as a means for the narrator to dismiss wild fantasy as a part of poetic invention in favour of 'life's daily prospect'. The imaginary boat in which the narrator sails through the skies to be given a bird's-eye view of earth probably owes something to the invention of the hot-air balloon by the Montgolfier brothers in 1782, an experiment to which Anna Barbauld alluded in her poem 'Washing Day' (1797). Joanna Baillie's 'Preface' to her collection *Fugitive Verses* (1840) carries an echo of Wordsworth's dismissal of the fantastic:

> Modern poetry, within these last thirty years, has become so imaginative, impassioned, and sentimental, that more homely subjects, in simple diction, are held in comparatively small estimation. . . . He who has been scouring through the air in a balloon, or ploughing the boundless ocean in the bark of some dauntless discoverer, or careering over the field on a warhorse, may be very well pleased after all to seat himself on a bench by his neighbour's door, and look at the meadows around him, or country people passing along the common from their daily work. [34]

Baillie in these sentences aligns herself with the preoccupations of Wordsworth's 'Preface' to *Peter Bell*: 'the faculty [of imagination] may be called forth as imperiously, and for kindred results of pleasure, by incidents within the compass of poetic probability, in the humblest departments of daily life'.

In Wordsworth's somewhat bathetic tale, Peter Bell is represented as a hawker, who, despite his travels in rural society, shows no feeling or imagination. In other words, he is not given to the 'silent raptures' of the poetic person in the face of nature. But his character alters when he experiences a vision of his dead wife that brings about in him feelings of remorse that are intensified by the 'saving grace' of the words of a Methodist preacher. Thus Wordsworth's narrative, despite his efforts at using an improved poetic diction, remains sentimental in its religiosity in the idea that, if a man can be helped to experience remorse for wrongs that he has done, then he will be 'saved' for a good life.

In fact, Wordsworth claimed, in the 'Preface' to *Peter Bell* that he addressed to the then poet laureate Robert Southey, that he had attempted to perfect this poem over a period of 21 years in order 'to fit it for filling *permanently* a station, however humble, in the Literature of our Country'.[35] Such a pretension was an invitation to Shelley's ridicule in his 'Dedication' to his parody, *Peter Bell the Third*, the title of which alludes to both Wordsworth's poem and *Peter Bell* by John Hamilton Reynolds. The latter had appeared in *The Examiner* in April 1819 prior to Wordsworth's poem of the same name, because Reynolds had some inkling of Wordsworth's aims and tried to mock them before Wordsworth could publish the poem.

In *Peter Bell the Third*, the main protagonist is consigned to Hell by the Devil, which, like the 'Hell' in Wordsworth's poem, turns out to be London:

There is great talk of revolution –
And a great chance of depotism –
German soldiers – camps – confusion
Tumults – lotteries – rage – delusion –
Gin – suicide – and methodism.

Shelley's satiric style here is comparable to that of the earlier Mary Robinson. In equating 'Hell' with 'methodism' – the form of Christianity that ostensibly 'saved' Wordsworth's character Peter Bell – Shelley ironically links a supposedly transforming source of 'grace' with all the ills of society of the day. This reworking of 'methodism' thus mocks Wordsworth's representation of Bell's contrition for his life of sin. Both the sentimental sources of Bell's contrition in Wordsworth's poem – the vision Bell has of his dead wife, and the fervent sermons of a Methodist preacher – are not convincing in the face of Wordsworth's earlier construction of Bell as an inveterate rogue and seem ripe for Shelley's satiric approach to Wordsworth's narrative.

Elsewhere Shelley attacks Wordsworth's messianic conviction about himself as a poet:

And some few, like we know who,
Damned – but God alone knows why –
To believe their minds are given
To make this ugly Hell a Heaven,
In which faith they live and die.

Shelley turns Wordsworth's conception of himself as a poet – 'a man speaking to men' – into an absurd obsession that he is condemned to live by throughout his life.

Shelley's characterization of Peter Bell appears to satirize Wordsworth's personality; for example, Peter Bell is converted from evil transgressor to 'moral eunuch' who 'touched the hem of nature's shift,/Felt faint – and never dared uplift/The closest, all-concealing tunic'.[36] These lines imply that Wordsworth as a poet held a naive view of nature as a beneficent source of inspiration, and that he was afraid to discover nature's inherent power in relation to humankind. By Part VII of *Peter Bell the Third*, the characterization of Peter Bell and Shelley's construction of Wordsworth the poet seem inextricably linked, so that the final section appears to describe Shelley's negative view of Wordsworth's poetry.

Despite the overly sentimental quality of his ballad *Peter Bell*, which seemed to invite satiric attacks, Wordsworth established himself as central to the poetry of the Romantic age by virtue of his revivifying – along with other poets who included S.T. Coleridge – of the oral ballad form, but also because he created lyric poems in a personal voice in which he expressed philosophic truths about life and art. His narrative and meditative poems in blank verse – 'Michael', 'The Brothers', 'Lines written a few miles above

Tintern Abbey' and 'Lines left upon a Seat in a Yew-tree which stands near the Lake of Esthwaite' for example – illuminate that period in English history just prior to and around the time of the many Acts of Enclosure which resulted in small leasehold farms and tracts of common land being amalgamated into much larger units run by the big landowners. Yeomen leaseholders and their farm workers were forced to leave their rural lives and seek work in factories in the towns.

In 'Michael', the main protagonist, a shepherd, is forced to send his only son, Luke, to the 'dissolute city' in order that he can earn enough to pay off his father's debt that he incurred on behalf of his brother's son. Luke becomes corrupted in his urban environment, and he 'gave himself to evil courses', and has to seek a new life abroad. After Michael and his wife died, the land that his son would have inherited was sold. In telling this tale, which the poet avers he heard as a boy, he demonstrates his interest in the lives and 'passions' that were not his own. In doing this, he is passing on not only history, but his method of telling it poetically:

> Therefore, although it be a history
> Homely and rude, I will relate the same
> For the delight of a few natural hearts
> And with yet fonder feeling, for the sake
> Of youthful Poets, who among these Hills
> Will be my second self when I am gone.[37]

Wordsworth, through his characterization of Michael, adumbrates here his philosophical beliefs: that what matters in life is natural human feeling, without artifice; and that only those who appreciate the need to maintain the tradition of an existence which is in harmony with the natural world will also respond to this poem. Yet the mere telling of the tale is not his main object. He hopes that younger poets will learn to seek their subjects in nature as well as to express their poetic thoughts in a natural diction.

Percy Bysshe Shelley to some extent followed both Wordsworth and S.T. Coleridge in his representations of elements of spirituality in nature. In his blank verse poem 'Mont Blanc', for example, he plays with imagery of a divine presence, which might be said to animate the natural world. Desmond King-Hele draws attention to the similarity between Shelley's epigraph to 'Mont Blanc' – 'Lines Written in the Vale of Chamouni' – and Coleridge's earlier poem 'Hymn before Sunrise in the Vale of Chamouni'.[38] Whereas Shelley's poem is dated by the day he visited Chamonix in the French Alps, Coleridge's poem is based on a German hymn and not his experience of Chamonix, which he never visited.[39]

The themes of 'Mont Blanc', moreover, are closely related to Wordsworth's responses to nature, particularly those in 'Lines written above Tintern Abbey', in which he extols the 'presence' that he senses in the natural world:

a sense sublime
Of something far more deeply interfused,
Whose dwelling is the light of setting suns,
And the round ocean, and the living air,
And the blue sky, and in the mind of man,
A motion and a spirit, that impels
All thinking things, all object of all thought,
And rolls through all things. [40]

Wordsworth's imagining of a divine spirit, which imbues the natural environment, is the antithesis of an objective, materialist attitude to nature. Shelley also, even though he became knowledgeable about scientific discoveries and technological inventions, in his meditative and philosophic poem 'Mont Blanc' remains quintessentially 'Romantic' in his celebration of 'the secret strength of things/Which governs thought' and which he postulates 'inhabits' Mont Blanc. Shelley adds his own authentic note to these Wordsworthian musings: that any perception of Mont Blanc might be a projection of the thoughts of the observer and not an inherent quality of the mountain. His final lines – which are reminiscent of his later rhetorical question at the close of 'Ode to the West Wind' – imply that it is merely the human imagination that projects impressions to fill the 'vacancy' of the mountain's 'silence and solitude'.[41]

The restoration of the lyric mode of the oral ballad and its transformation into a literary form by, among others, Wordsworth and Coleridge, followed by Keats and Shelley, directed English poetry into a more fruitful path than that of contrived poetic diction and the constricting literary form of heroic couplets. Moreover, the use of the blank verse form in a conversational mode by Coleridge and Wordsworth at the turn of the century, followed later by Shelley in the early years of the nineteenth century, further enhanced the lyric potential of English poetry. In addition, the revival of the sonnet form from the 1780s onwards by various poets such as Charlotte Smith, Mary Robinson, William Wordsworth, John Keats, and P.B. Shelley, can be shown to have fostered that note of individual introspection that marked the poetry of the Romantic age, at the same time as the reinstitution of this neglected form encouraged in poetry a disciplined expression of feeling.

Notes

1 Robert Mayo, 'The Contemporaneity of the *Lyrical Ballads*', *Publication of the Modern Language Association*, Vol. 69 (New York, 1954), 494–5.
2 See Duncan Wu, *Wordsworth's Reading 1770–1799* (Cambridge, 1993), 16, 181–2, 184, and 85–6; see also G.L. Little, 'A Note on Wordsworth and Blair', *Notes & Queries*, New Series 7 (Oxford, 1960), 254–5.
3 *The Selected Poems of Joanna Baillie*, ed. Jennifer Breen (Manchester, 1999), p. 74.

4 See Duncan Wu, *Wordsworth's Reading 1770–1799*, p. 8.
5 Joanna Baillie, 'Introductory Discourse', *Plays on the Passions*, 1798, repr. in *Women Romantics 1785–1832: Writing in Prose*, ed. Jennifer Breen (London, 1996), pp. 100–1.
6 Robinson's letter to an unknown publisher, 17 June 1800, quoted in Judith Pascoe, 'Introduction', *Mary Robinson: Selected Poems* (Ontario, 1999), p. 54.
7 Stuart Curran, 'Mary Robinson's *Lyrical Tales* in Context', in *Re-visioning Romanticism: British Women Writers, 1776–1837*, ed. Carol Shiner Wilson and Joel Haefner (Philadelphia, 1994), pp. 17–18.
8 Pascoe, *Mary Robinson: Selected Poems*, pp. 54–5.
9 Wilson and Haefner, *Re-visioning Romanticism*, p. 32.
10 William Wordsworth and S.T. Coleridge, *Lyrical Ballads*, ed. R.I. Brett and A.R. Jones (London, 1968, 2nd edn, 1991), pp. 68 and 286.
11 Pascoe, *Mary Robinson: Selected Poems*, p. 187.
12 Mayo, 'The Contemporaneity of the *Lyrical Ballads*', pp. 486–522.
13 Kathryn Sutherland, 'The Native Poet: The Influence of Percy's Minstrel from Beattie to Wordsworth', *Review of English Studies*, 33 (132) (Oxford, November, 1982), 418–19.
14 'Preface', *Reliques of Ancient English Poetry*, 1765, repr. 1864 (Edinburgh, James Nicol; London, James Nesbit House), p. xxix.
15 Nick Groom, *The Making of Percy's Reliques* (Oxford, 1999), pp. 8–9, and p. 3.
16 *The Cambridge Companion to Romanticism*, ed. Stuart Curran (Cambridge, 1993), p. 225.
17 Kenneth R. Johnston, *The Hidden Wordsworth: Poet, Lover, Rebel, Spy* (New York and London, 1998), pp. 78 and 85.
18 Wordsworth, *Poetical Works*, ed. Thomas Hutchinson (London, 1904; new edn, rev. Ernest de Selincourt, 1936), p. 748.
19 Repr. in *Lyrical Ballads*, ed. Brett and Jones, p. 247.
20 See Jane Aaron, '*On Needlework:* Protest and Contradiction in Mary Lamb's Essay', in *Romanticism and Feminism*, ed. Anne K. Mellor (Bloomington, Indianapolis, 1988), pp. 177–8.
21 S.T. Coleridge, *Biographia Literaria*, ed. Nigel Leask (London and Vermont, 1997), p. 53.
22 *Letters of John Keats*, edited Robert Gittings (London, 1979, repr. 1982), p. 70.
23 See John Keats, *The Complete Poems*, ed. John Barnard (Harmondsworth, 1973; 2nd edn, 1977), p. 637.
24 Samuel Taylor Coleridge, *Poems*, ed. John Beer (London and Vermont, 1993), pp. 335–8.
25 John Keats, *The Complete Poems*, ed. John Barnard, p. 637.
26 Jerome J. McGann, ed., *The New Oxford Book of Romantic Period Verse* (Oxford, 1993), pp. 526–7.
27 See *John Keats, The Complete Poems*, ed. John Barnard, pp. 636–7.
28 Karen Swann, 'Harassing the Muse', in *Romanticism and Feminism*, ed. Anne K. Mellor, p. 90.
29 *The Early Letters of William and Dorothy Wordsworth (1787–1805)*, ed. Ernest de Selincourt (Oxford, 1935), pp. 312–15.
30 Richard Holmes, *Shelley: the Pursuit* (London, 1974), pp. 529–31.
31 Quoted in Holmes, *Shelley: the Pursuit*, p. 531.
32 *Ibid.*, pp. 356–7.
33 'Mask of Anarchy', *Selected Poems*, ed. Timothy Webb (London, 1977; repr. 1983), pp. 69 and 71.
34 *The Selected Poems of Joanna Baillie*, pp. 195–6.
35 Wordsworth, *Poetical Works*, p. 188.
36 P.B. Shelley, *Selected Poems*, pp. 79, 81 and 84.

37 Wordsworth, *Poetical Works*, p.104.
38 Desmond King-Hele, *Shelley: His Thought and Work*, 3rd edn (London, 1984), pp. 70–71.
39 Thomas de Quincey, *Reminiscences of the English Lake Poets*, ed. John E. Jordan (London, 1961), p. 24.
40 Wordsworth, *Lyrical Ballads*, ed. R.L. Brett and A.R. Jones, ll.96–103, p. 116.
41 P.B. Shelley, *Selected Poems*, pp. 3–6.

5

The revival of the sonnet

The sonnet in English became important during the Romantic period after seldom being used during the early part of the eighteenth century when poets and their readers seemed to prefer the heroic couplet as a suitable medium for narration and description as well as for satire. The sonnet had originated in southern Italy around 1250, and, according to the critic Paul Oppenheimer, 'the birth of the sonnet heralds a departure from the tradition of lyrics as performed poems and introduces a new, introspective, quieter mode, a mode that is to dominate the history of Western poetry for at least the next seven centuries'.[1] He also stresses the way in which the sonnet pursues a logical argument within one persona constructed in the poem, with the octet setting out a problem, which is resolved in the sestet. Moreover, this quarrel within the constructed persona can be engaged with by a single reader rather than be performed to a large audience. The Italian sonnet is usually now known as the Petrarchan sonnet, after Francis Petrarch (1304–74) who followed three earlier generations of Italian sonneteers including Dante Alighieri (1265–1321). Dante's series of love sonnets, *Vita Nuova*, is remarkable for the way in which Dante constructs – within the same poetic persona – both an observing narrator and a subject who is being observed. The usual stanzaic form of the Petrarchan or 'legitimate' sonnet became an octet of two quatrains with the rhymes ABBA ABBA, succeeded by a sestet of two tercets with the rhymes CDE CDE.

The English sonnet, as R.G. Spiller notes, began in approximately 1525 with Sir Thomas Wyatt (?1503–42) who modified the Italian sonnet and 'reinvented' the rhyming couplet as a summation at the end of each sonnet, with a rhyme scheme ABBA ABBA CDCD EE. Another sonneteer, the Earl of Surrey (?1517–47), also used the rhyming couplet in closure, although his preceding three quatrains significantly altered the rhyme to ABAB CDCD EFEF GG; this pattern of three blocks of thought followed by a summation was later used by Shakespeare (1564–1616), and subsequently became known as the Shakespearean or 'illegitimate' sonnet.[2]

The English innovation in the sonnet form is postulated as having arisen from the differences in the Italian and English languages: 'English poets, finding their language harder to rhyme in than Italian poets, clung to a sonnet in seven rhymes as something of itself more congenial than a sonnet in four or five rhymes.'[3] Possibilities of similar rhymes were greater in Italian, and therefore the intricate pattern of two similar quatrains of ABAB in the octet and two similar tercets of CDC CDC in the sestet was easier to achieve in Italian than in English. The most significant difference, however, between the Petrarchan and Shakespearean sonnet – in whatever way the rhymes of each poem's quatrains are arranged – is that in the Italian form the poet sets up his argument or point of view in the octet, and then comments on this proposition in his sestet. In the Shakespearean sonnet form, the poet has three quatrains in which to formulate his proposition and then must close his argument in an epigrammatic summary of a couplet. Thus in the Petrarchan sonnet the *volta* or turn occurred at the end of the octave, whereas in the Shakespearean sonnet the turn was delayed until the end of the third quatrain. This alteration in the Shakespearean or 'illegitimate' sonnet meant that a longer argument could be made, which was then succeeded by a witty or enlightening summation at the close.

According to Spiller, during the seventeenth century – after the appearance of Shakespeare's sonnet sequence – 'the sonnet declined in popularity as the sonnet sequence passed out of favour'. It was then that John Milton (1608–74) adapted – in both Italian and English – the Petrarchan sonnet form:

> Milton is exceptional in his direct adoption of an Italian pattern, an Italianate rhetoric and a persona neither conventionally Petrarchan nor penitentially religious: the civic humanist, servant and adviser, and also poet and moralist, is his projected /I/ throughout. Because this is a persona designed to sound like a guide, philosopher and friend, and because Milton himself stood in something like that relation to later poets, the sonnets are easily read as intimate poems, and their mode of discourse became congenial to Romantic poets in Britain.[4]

Although neo-Classical early eighteenth-century poets had rejected the sonnet form, readers and writers in the Romantic period found a new interest in the sonnets of Milton and Shakespeare and others. Romantic sonneteers experimented with the form, mixing Shakespearean characteristics with those adapted by Milton from the Petrarchan sonnet.

John Fuller has identified when the sonnet – after its unaccountable eighteenth-century decline – began to be used by English poets again: 'The significant moment of revival occurs in the 1780s with the work of [Thomas] Warton (1728–90), [William] Bowles (1762–1850), and Charlotte Smith.'[5] Another critic, Stuart Curran, suggests, however, that Thomas Gray's elegiac 'Sonnet on the Death of Mr Richard West' (1775) marks the beginning of the revival of the sonnet form that came to dominate the Romantic age.[6] Subsequently, some of Warton's sonnets appeared in his *Poems* (1777), and William Lisle Bowles' *Fourteen Sonnets Elegiac and Descriptive, Written during a Tour* was published in Bath in 1789. By far the most popular and influential sonneteer of the early Romantic period was Charlotte Smith, whose volume *Elegiac Sonnets* was published in 1784 at her own expense.

In these sonnets, which, except for a few Petrarchan sonnets, were mainly varieties of the Shakespearean form, she caught the mood of the day with her predominant tone of elegiac gloom, which she expressed in her first-person descriptions of nature linked to her actual or imaginary feelings. Although Smith's sonnets are not sequential, they are coherent in mood and theme, representing losses of various kinds – ranging from the loss of the beloved of Goethe's fictional hero, Werther, to the poet's significant losses in her own life. Those sonnets which refer most movingly to her recognition of mutability and the transience of life's pleasures are perhaps reflective of her own now well-known failures – her disappointing marriage that left her to support eight children and a spendthrift absent husband, and her frustrated attempts to gain the inheritance left to her in 1776 by her father-in-law.

Smith's echoes of Milton occur in some of her more accomplished and less theatrical contemplations of mutability. In 'To Spring', for example, her final couplet, 'Thy sounds of harmony, thy balmy air,/Have power to cure all sadness, but despair' acknowledges her source in Milton's comparable expression of sentiments in Book IV, *Paradise Lost*, ll. 154–6: 'To the heart inspires/Vernal delight and joy, able to drive/All sadness but despair.' Smith's allusions to her forerunner, Milton, are also particularly apt in 'On the departure of the nightingale' in which she recalls his more famous 'First Sonnet' and evokes her feelings via a metaphor from nature.[7]

Throughout *Elegiac Sonnets*, Smith encapsulates the Romantic notion that inherent in life are disappointment and loss, which can lead to despair, and she constructs in *Elegiac Sonnets* the typically Romantic persona of the despairing poet. As Stuart Curran, in 'Romantic Poetry: The I Altered', has suggested, when he comments on Smith's 'Written at the Churchyard at Middleton in Sussex' (1789), which describes the ocean invading a seaside cemetery:

> But if extreme, the sonnet is of a piece with the collection that surrounds it, the whole portraying a disembodied sensibility at the mercy of an alien universe and without discernible exit from its condition. The entire sonnet revival of the Romantic period was impelled into existence by this vision, and, even where (as with Wordsworth) the tonalities are reversed, the underlying dynamic of an isolated sensibility informs all the sonnets written in Smith's wake.[8]

Smith herself was defensive about interpretations which saw her as projecting not her own lived experience, but rather a theatrical persona of the embattled woman poet; and she wrote in her 'Preface to the Sixth Edition' (May 14, 1792):

> It was unaffected sorrows that drew them [her sonnets] forth: I wrote mournfully because I was unhappy – And I have unfortunately no reason yet, though nine years have elapsed, to *change my tone*. The time is indeed arrived, when I have been promised by 'the Honourable Men' who, *nine years ago*, undertook to see that my family obtained the provision their grandfather designed for them, – that 'all should be well, all should be settled.' But still I am condemned to feel the 'hope delayed that maketh the heart sick.' Still to receive – not a repetition of promises indeed – but of *scorn and insult* when I apply to those gentlemen, who, though they acknowledge that all impediments to a division of the estate they have undertaken to manage, are done away – will neither tell me *when* they will proceed to divide it, or *whether they will ever do so at all....*'[9]

Anna Seward (1742–1809), the poet, describes Smith's sonnets as 'a perpetual dun on pity',[10] but Smith's personal sonnets, such as 'Written at Bignor Park in Sussex, in August, 1799', although hyperbolic, are also reflective and sharp in her view of society in relation to her civic status as a woman: '... too late/The poor Slave shakes the unworthy bonds away/Which crush'd her!' The legal system in the eighteenth-century society in which Smith lived did not permit her to inherit money, which her father-in-law left to her for herself and her children, and to which she had a just claim: this 'fate' she now understands late in life, but the 'rosy hours' of her youthful pleasure at Bignor Park can never be returned to her. The persona Smith constructs here is that of the mature social critic who comprehends how she has been cheated, but who can do nothing about her social and legal position as a woman.[11]

The sonnet was a particularly useful form for Charlotte Smith and other poets such as Anna Seward to employ to represent an inner life, since its strict iambic metre with a formal layout and pattern of rhymes encouraged concision of thought and feeling in imaginative selectivity rather than confessional outpourings. Moreover, in following Milton or Shakespeare, poets could invoke a tradition of sonneteering to which they felt they belonged. In an age in which reason jostled with sensibility and other outré Romantic tendencies, the sonnet seemed peculiarly apt to meet the demands of rationality at the same time as allowing individual expression of a personal and emotional kind.

Mary Robinson (1758–1800), unlike Charlotte Smith in her *Elegiac Sonnets*, adopted Milton's Petrarchan sonnet form for her sonnet sequence *Sappho and Phaon* (1796):

> I have ventured to compose the following collection, not presuming to offer them as imitations of Petrarch, but as specimens of that species of sonnet writing, so seldom attempted in the English language; though adopted by that sublime bard, whose Muse produced the grand epic of Paradise Lost, and the humbler effusion,

> which I produce as an example of the measure to which I allude, and which is termed by the most classical writers, the *legitimate sonnet*.[12]

The central theme of *Sappho and Phaon* is a poetic exploration of the nature of obsessive sexual love. Possibly in order to establish herself as a serious poet, Robinson chose the legendary Sappho's love for the youth Phaon as the subject of her sequence. In 1779–80, Robinson had been the mistress of the Prince of Wales for one year, and she might have anticipated readers' presumptions that her sonnets were a semi-autobiographical sequence. Moreover, she might have also wanted to distance herself, through the use of mythology, from readers assuming that her intimate knowledge of sexual love arose from her various other liaisons.

Her sonnet sequence is introduced by her reflection on the power of 'Poesy' to enlighten humankind and 'calm the miseries of man' – especially those who are obsessed with 'hopeless love' – by showing how spiritual joys will console in the face of loss of love. Her second sonnet represents Sappho in the resplendent 'Temple' of 'Chastity':

> The steps of spotless marble, scatter'd o'er
> With deathless roses arm'd with many a thorn,
> Lead to the altar. On the frozen floor,
> Studded with tear-drops petrified by scorn,
> Pale vestals kneel the Goddess to adore,
> While Love, his arrows broke, retires forlorn.

Sappho might seek a passionless existence, but in Robinson's narrative Reason is soon overcome by Desire, as Sappho becomes entranced with Phaon. In this sestet, Robinson's description of the temple of the vestal virgins is compelling in its use of figurative language to represent the death of sexual desire – 'frozen floor', 'teardrops petrified by scorn', and, finally, the arrow of Eros broken.

Robinson then proceeds by portraying, from the point of view of Sappho, the compulsive nature of erotic love that cannot be modified by the voice of Reason:

> Love steals unheeded o'er the tranquil mind,
> As summer breezes fan the sleeping main,
> Slow through each fibre creeps the subtle pain,
> 'Till closely round the yielding bosom twin'd.
> Vain is the hope the magic to unbind,
> The potent mischief riots in the brain,
> Grasps ev'ry thought, and burns in ev'ry vein,
> 'Till in the heart the tyrant lives enshrin'd.[13]

In this octet, Robinson has constructed convincingly the voice of Sappho deprecating the 'magic' tyranny of feelings of sexual love. Throughout

Sappho and Phaon, she anticipates many of the romanticizing archetypes that other poets of the Romantic age, such as Samuel Taylor Coleridge and John Keats, employed.

In 'Mary Robinson and the Myth of Sappho', Jerome McGann argues that Robinson describes poetically how young women are driven through their lack of education to seek the delusive attractions of erotic love:

> In certain (obvious) ways, *Sappho and Phaon* might be taken as a perfect illustration of Wollstonecraft's complaint: its central subject is love, it scrutinizes 'sensual feelings', it works up an elaborate philosophical rationale for itself, it tells the story of a suicide. And behind it all stands the notorious figure of 'Perdita' Robinson, whose personal life was a scandal.[14]

But *Sappho and Phaon* is based on mythology, however much Robinson might draw on her own experience of sexual passion. In *Sappho and Phaon*, she explores aspects of erotic obsession in relation to the powerlessness of Reason to modify such obsession. Robinson's sonnet sequence reverses the masculine rationale of earlier sonnet sequences about love, such as that of the poet Petrarch and his addresses to Laura. Robinson represents Sappho as the progenitor as well as the recipient of Love, and shows her embracing the folly of an excessive sexual passion, which leads to her suicide when Phaon rejects her.

Smith's and Robinson's sonnets predate those of two of their contemporaries, Charles Lamb (1775–1834) and William Wordsworth (1770–1850), who wrote sonnets after reaching their maturity as poets. Wordsworth's most recent biographer, Kenneth Johnston, states that Wordsworth 'owed large debts to the tradition of Sensibility especially . . . Charlotte Smith and Helen Maria Williams'.[15] Smith and Wordsworth were acquainted, and Smith had given Wordsworth some introductions to her friends in France. In 1783, Wordsworth began writing sonnets according to the Shakespearean model, but these were formulaic and trite.

Wordsworth's later Petrarchan sonnet, 'Composed Upon Westminster Bridge' (1803), however, is more successful in capturing an evanescent moment. The octet consists of a description of Westminster Bridge seen at sunrise, and the sestet is a brief meditation on the effects of this exceptional sight, which for the poet has a deeply calming effect. The poet personifies the houses, which are lit by the sunrise in their seeming sleep, and London itself, which for him is stilled, like he is, in the calm of the morning. By comparing his calm to the repose of a great city he intensifies his exceptional, isolated feelings. 'Composed Upon Westminster Bridge' can be seen as a direct inheritor of Smith's *Elegiac Sonnets* which epitomize the poetry of the isolated sensibility. But both poets are writers of their age, catching a public interest in sensibility, and expressing individual feelings in language that is well chosen and schooled to the demands of the sonnet form, whether it is Shakespearean or Petrarchan.

In some respects, John Keats (1796–1821), who tried out poetic experiments with both the Petrarchan and English sonnet forms, is more of a direct heir to the sonneteering style of Mary Robinson than to that of Leigh Hunt, with whom, in relation to the sonnet, his early sonnets are usually associated. His early sonnets are often variations of the Petrarchan or 'legitimate' model; for example, one of his early poems, 'Woman! when I behold thee flippant, vain' (March–December, 1815), resembles an ode but is actually a trio of Petrarchan sonnets, with variant endings. In these sonnets, he addresses 'woman' as an abstract entity, and expresses several conventions of his day about attributes of womanhood such as meekness, kindness and tenderness, 'creamy breast', and other 'lures'. The poet then centres on what he thinks attractive in 'women': 'when I mark/Such charms with mild intelligences shine,/My ear is open like a greedy shark,/To catch the tunings of a voice divine.' His masculine ear resembles that of a hungry 'shark' whereas 'she is like a milk-white lamb that bleats/For man's protection.'[16] This contrast between the woman-eating shark who is out for himself and the innocent 'lamb' who charms her man is the kind of false gendered attitude that Wollstonecraft criticized in *A Vindication of the Rights of Woman* (1792):

> How many women thus waste life away the prey of discontent, who might have practised as physicians, regulated a farm, managed a shop, and stood erect, supported by their own industry, instead of hanging their heads surcharged with the dew of sensibility, that consumes the beauty to which it first gave lustre: nay, I doubt whether pity and love are so near akin as poets feign, for I have seldom seen much compassion excited by the helplessness of females, unless they were fair; then, perhaps, pity was the soft handmaid of love, or the harbinger of lust.[17]

In Keats's final sestet, nevertheless, the poet allows himself to be engulfed mentally by his deceptive vision of woman.

In his two sonnets to fame (30 April 1815), Keats tries out two differing varieties of the sonnet on the same subject. In his first sonnet, 'Fame', which is Shakespearean, the poet pictures this abstraction as a type of wanton female who will only bestow herself on those who can do without her. In his second, which is a variant of a Petrarchan sonnet with an unusual rhyming sestet (EFEGGE), fame is portrayed as a kind of self-prostitution that should be resisted as a 'miscreed'.[18] The use of this made-up word suggests that Keats had a problem with his rhymes, but nevertheless this word implies that a belief in fame is a kind of wrongdoing to one's own person.

His sonnet written a year later, 'On First Looking into Chapman's Homer' (October 1816), reverts to the strict Petrarchan model. In this highly regarded poem, Keats celebrates the pleasures of the imagination, revealing how mental exploration is as evocative, pleasurable, and spiritually rewarding as is the exploratory labour of mapping new territory or, in the skies, a new planet:

Then felt I like some watcher of the skies
When a new planet swims into his ken...[19]

Keats's imagery in this sonnet reflects the basis of eighteenth-century enlightenment: that anyone might experience the excitement of discovery of new knowledge from astronomy to geography, even though Keats here seems to have got his historical geography slightly wrong. Indirectly, the poet also celebrates the pleasures of the sonnet by means of which he can explore imaginatively the powers of the English language.

Keats carries this metaphoric exploration of the uses of the English language further in his attempts to develop a sonnet more suitable for his style of English. His much later 'On the Sonnet' (1819) expounds in poetic language the difficulties and problems in meeting the formal demands of regular sonnets:

If by dull rhymes our English must be chained,
And, like Andromeda, the Sonnet sweet
Fettered, in spite of pained loveliness,
Let us find out, if we must be constrained,
Sandals more interwoven and complete
To fit the naked foot of Poesy . . .[20]

Here Keats has reversed the usual format of the Petrarchan sonnet by placing his sestet ABC ABD first, as a lead-in to a way of balancing the demands of the sonnet form with an exploration of the fluidity and intricacies of English poetic diction. His irregularly rhyming octet CABC DEDE implies that poets must not only 'weigh the stress' of each syllable but also avoid clichéd diction: 'let us be/Jealous of dead leaves in the bay wreath crown'. This sonnet is an inverted Petrarchan sonnet, and was part of Keats's experimentation at that time with the sonnet form. Keats described his ventures to his brother and sister-in-law, George and Georgiana Keats:

> I have been endeavouring to discover a better sonnet stanza than we have. The legitimate does not suit the language over-well from the pouncing rhymes – the other kind appears too elegiac – and the couplet at the end of it has seldom a pleasing effect – I do not pretend to have succeeded – It will explain itself . . .[21]

Keats's final three sonnets follow the model of Sir Philip Sidney's sequence of sonnets *Astrophel and Stella*, in that he uses the Italian break between the octave and the sestet – signalled by a dash as well as by the sense of the words – followed by the closing couplet of the Shakespearean sonnet form, despite his cavil about the couplet at the end 'seldom [having] a pleasing effect'. Therefore he retains the logic of the Petrarchan model combined with the elegiac note of the Shakespearean. The sonnet 'The day is gone, and all its sweets are gone!' (10 October 1819) is ostensibly concerned with the transient enjoyment of one day in the presence of his beloved, and carries an elegiac note. The octet describes the 'paradise' of being in the presence of his beloved; the sestet recounts the loss of this love at nightfall at a time when lovers might expect to experience 'fragrant-curtained love' which 'begins to weave/The woof of darkness thick, for hid delight.'[22] But the couplet ends on a note of renunciation of love in favour of the contentment of voluntary celibacy that the poet sees not as deprivation but paradoxically as a reward for his semi-religious celebration of love during the day. In a letter of 13 October 1819 to Fanny Brawne, Keats expounds his comparison between love and religion:

> I have been astonished that Men could die Martyrs for religion – I have shudder'd at it – I shudder no more – I could be martyr'd for my Religion – Love is my religion – I could die for that – I could die for you. My Creed is Love and you are its only tenet . . .[23]

In another sonnet that is modelled on Sidney's and composed at about the same time, 'I cry your mercy, pity, love – ay, love!' (? October, 1819), the poet offers himself a choice between love and death: in the octet is set out the obsessive nature of the lover's desire for 'all' of his beloved, and in the sestet the poet implies that if she refuses to give herself completely then he will either die literally, or else metaphorically, from the strength of his compulsion: 'the palate of my mind/Losing its gust, and my ambition blind!'[24] In this kind of romantic overstatement, Keats reflects both the much earlier Shakespearean influence as well as the more immediate one of Charlotte Smith and Mary Robinson of the early Romantic period.

In the third sonnet of these three parallel sonnets, 'Bright star, would I were steadfast as thou art', the poet desires the eternal bliss of being 'pillowed' on his 'fair love's ripening breast', and, if such a desired physical union is impossible, the poet would then prefer death. What is interesting about this sonnet is the way in which Keats imputes a religious significance to nature in which the 'bright star' acts as a devotee to the ocean's action of cleansing 'earth's human shores'. The paradoxically religious setting which the poet projects in nature is contrasted with that of the secular lovers in which the poet-lover wishes to deny the mutability of human love by forever remaining awake in 'sweet unrest' to listen to his beloved's 'tender-taken breath'.[25] The imagery of obsessive religious devotion serves to heighten the sensuous and sensual passion of the lover who could become a martyr for that love.

Percy Bysshe Shelley (1792–1822) also experimented in various ways with the sonnet form, and in his 22 sonnets he only used each of his rhyme schemes once. One of Shelley's sonnets, 'Ozymandias', for example, preserves a moment of invented prehistoric time by way of a tale within a tale: the persona or first-person speaker relates an anecdote that he has been told by 'a traveller from an antique land'.[26] The tale implies that even significant works of art such as the statue of the king

Ozymandias, commissioned by himself, might perish, however much the person commissioning or executing the work might seek immortality through this statue. We can never know the beauty of this crumbling 'colossal wreck' even though its relic is preserved in the work of art that is Shelley's sonnet.

Shelley experimented with the sonnet form, transforming a sequence of five linked sonnets into an ode – 'Ode to the West Wind' – with a *terza rima* rhyme scheme. In his account of Shelley's sonnets, Francois Jost demonstrates, *inter alia*, how Shelley's 'Ode to the West Wind', which ostensibly appears to be in the form of Dantean *terza rima*, can also be regarded as a sequence of five sonnets, all rhyming ABAB CBCD CEFE FF.[27] Shelley reframes and transforms the ode into a vehicle for personal expression, which the author has framed in a note which gives the ode an authentic setting:

> This poem was conceived and chiefly written in a wood that skirts the Arno, near Florence, and on a day when that tempestuous wind, whose temperature is at once mild and animating, was collecting the vapours which pour down the autumnal rains. They began, I foresaw, at sunset with a violent tempest of hail and rain, attended by that magnificent thunder and lightning peculiar to the Cisalpine regions.[28]

But, as critic Jennifer Ann Wagner suggests, 'Shelley employs *terza rima* to escape the constraints of the conventional sonnet form; it lends to these sonnet stanzas an inherently oppositional attitude, as it were, towards themselves.'[29] Shelley's linked rhyme scheme of *terza rima* throughout this sequence allows for a fuller exploration of a lyric moment than a single sonnet permits.

Shelley's use of the sonnet combined with *terza rima* in order to form an ode is an adept experiment. Keats also composed his famed odes in a variety of stanzaic forms, but both these poets kept to the traditional mode of the ode in that these poems addressed a person, such as Shelley's elegiac ode to Keats, 'Adonais', or a personified object, such as Keats's 'Ode on a Grecian Urn', or an abstraction, such as Keats's 'Ode on Melancholy'. Both Shelley and Keats keep to the conventional Greek pastoral tradition of Theocritus in their odes with an exalted and elegiac tone. Keats's pastoral imagery in 'To Autumn', for example, reflects the poet's awareness of his mortality as well as his apprehension of death: 'barred clouds bloom the soft-dying day' and 'in a wailful choir small gnats mourn/Among the river sallows . . .'[30] imply the transience of existence as well as mortality. Many of Keats's odes in particular are expressed in imagery that is related to mutability in life in which suffering and mourning predominate.

Poets and critics during the Romantic period did not give the single sonnet the same weight as a sonnet sequence. Wordsworth, in a letter to Walter Savage Landor, complained about miscellaneous sonnet-writing as time-wasting: 'from want of resolution to take up anything of length, I have filled up many a moment in writing Sonnets, which, if I had never fallen into the practice, might easily have been better employed.'[31] Wagner also suggests that the composition of miscellaneous sonnets in the Romantic period was thought to be of lesser importance than the writing of any kind of longer poetry, which aspires to the weightiness of 'epic' and which 'was still unequivocally man's literary territory'. Mary Robinson's substantial sonnet sequence *Sappho and Phaon* (1796) can then be seen as an attempt by a woman poet to establish herself as equal to male poets. In fact, it might be argued that Robinson in *Sappho and Phaon* came as close as any Romantic poet to creating an 'epic' achievement, despite the fact that in her 'Preface' to *Sappho and Phaon* she praised *Paradise Lost* as 'the grand epic' and referred to both her own and Milton's sonnets as 'the humbler effusion'.

According to Wagner, Wordsworth's ambitious aim of giving his sonnets an 'epic' quality led him to group all his sonnets thematically – from his *Ecclesiastical Sonnets in Series* (1822) to his various miscellaneous sonnets – in sequences:

> Wordsworth's sonnet writing would itself take on a sort of epic proportion, the lyric plot of the individual sonnet developing into the narrative plotting of the *Miscellaneous Sonnets*. Wordsworth's rearrangement of his early sonnets into a long sequence in later years would make of his short poems only a different *kind* of autobiographical long poem. Those 'moments' that he wasted by 'filling' them with sonnets became moments that would open out into a large conception of his own life history.[32]

Wordsworth followed the examples of both Charlotte Smith and Anna Seward, who had collected their own miscellaneous sonnets into sequences in book form.

The individual sonnet and the sonnet sequence were 'rediscovered' in the Romantic period because of various reasons. One paramount reason was that these forms allowed some poets to describe and interpret memories or actual moments of intense feeling in order to reveal aspects of themselves in relation to the Romantic age in which they lived. Additionally, another reason was that the sonnet form, although often employed in trite exercises, required that the feelings and perceptions of the addresser be represented with some concision as well as order. Moreover, when a number are written in a sequential arrangement, the sonnet form becomes highly versatile, allowing a lyrical and descriptive form to become a narrative work of some weight. This use of the sonnet sequence, along with English variants of the classical Pindaric and Horatian odes, illustrate that experimentation with a variety of forms in English verse – from the ballad to the sonnet sequence and the ode – that was a significant element of the poetry of the Romantic age.

Notes

1 Paul Oppenheimer, *The Birth of the Modern Mind: New Facts and a Theory* (New York and Oxford, 1989), p. 187.
2 Michael G. Spiller, *The Development of the Sonnet: An Introduction* (London, 1992), p. 98.
3 John Fuller, *The Sonnet* (London, 1972, repr. 1978), p. 15.
4 Spiller, pp. 196 and 201.
5 Fuller, p. 9.
6 Stuart Curran, *Poetic Form and British Romanticism* (New York and Oxford, 1986), p. 30.
7 *Elegiac Sonnets* in *The Poems of Charlotte Smith*, ed. Stuart Curran (New York, 1993), p. 17. All subsequent references to poems by Smith are to this edition.
8 Stuart Curran, 'The I Altered', in *Romanticism and Feminism*, ed. Anne K. Mellor (Bloomington and Indianapolis, 1988), p. 200.
9 *The Poems of Charlotte Smith*, pp. 5–6 and 78.
10 Quoted in 'Introduction', *The Poems of Charlotte Smith*, p. xxv.
11 *The Poems of Charlotte Smith*, p. 78.
12 Preface to *Sappho and Phaon*, 1796, repr. in Mary Robinson, *Selected Poems*, ed. Judith Pascoe (Ontario, Canada, 2000), p. 144. All subsequent references to poems by Robinson are to this edition.
13 *Sappho and Phaon* in *Selected Poems*, pp. 158 and 165.
14 Jerome McGann, 'Mary Robinson and the Myth of Sappho', *Modern Language Quarterly* (March, 1995), p. 67; repr. in *The Poetics of Sensibility: A Revolution in Literary Style* (New York, 1996).
15 Kenneth Johnston, *The Hidden Wordsworth* (London, 1998), p. 180.
16 John Keats, *The Complete Poems*, ed. John Barnard (Harmondsworth, 1973; 3rd edn, 1988), pp. 49–50.
17 See Mary Wollstonecraft, *A Vindication of the Rights of Woman*, repr. in *Women Romantics, 1785–1832: Writing in Prose*, ed. Jennifer Breen (London, 1996) pp. 17–18.
18 Keats, *The Complete Poems*, p. 343.
19 Keats, *The Complete Poems*, p. 72.
20 Keats, *The Complete Poems*, p. 340.
21 *Letters of John Keats: A Selection*, ed. Robert Gittings (London, 1970; repr. 1982), p. 255.
22 Keats, *The Complete Poems*, p. 449.
23 *Letters of John Keats*, p. 334.
24 Keats, *The Complete Poems*, pp. 451–2.
25 Keats, *The Complete Poems*, p. 452.
26 P.B. Shelley, *Selected Poems*, ed. Timothy Webb (London, 1977; repr. 1983), p. 11.
27 Francois Jost, 'Anatomy of an Ode: Shelley and the Sonnet Tradition', in *Comparative Literature*, 34 (1982), p. 232.
28 P.B. Shelley, *Selected Poems*, p. 76.
29 Jennifer Ann Wagner, *A Moment's Monument: Revisionary Poetics and the Nineteenth-Century English Sonnet* (New Jersey and London, 1996), p. 76.
30 Keats, *The Complete Poems*, pp. 434–5.
31 Letter to Walter Savage Landor, 20 April 1822, *Letters of William and Dorothy Wordsworth*, 1821–1828, Vol. IV, The Later Years, Part 1, ed. Ernest de Selincourt, 1939; 2nd edn, rev. and ed. Alan E. Hill (Oxford, 1978), pp. 122–6.
32 Wagner, *A Moment's Monument*, pp. 38–40.

6

Satire in Romantic literature

In the English literary tradition, satire is conventionally defined as 'composition in verse or prose that ridicules a prevailing vice or folly, or a person or institution that the author holds in contempt' (*Concise Oxford Dictionary*). Arthur Pollard suggests that the satiric author is:

> always acutely conscious of the difference between what things are and what they ought to be. . . . For him to be successful his society should at least pay lip service to the ideals he upholds. . . . He is then able to exploit more fully the differences between appearance and reality and especially to expose hypocrisy.[1]

Satire was an important mode not only in the late 1600s in the poetry of John Dryden (1631–1700) but also in the eighteenth century, especially in the poetry of Alexander Pope (1688–1744). It also continued in the late 1700s and early 1800s to be a significant element in both poetry and prose writing of what subsequently became known as 'Romantic' literature. Different forms of satire, such as mock-heroic and mock-epic, parody, burlesque, and satiric comedy and satiric irony, are all to be found in the Romantic age. It is worth exploring these works in order to understand some of the conflicting attitudes of the period towards some of the dominant social mores and moral and religious beliefs of the times. Satirical authors, in exposing vices or follies, are also identifying major elements in society that they think it necessary to highlight by means of parody, exaggeration, caricature, irony, invective, sarcasm, wit, and other linguistic devices.

Steven Jones, in *Satire and Romanticism*, seems to argue that the 'satiric' mode cannot coincide with 'Romantic modes of writing'.[2] In fact, in some important works of the Romantic period, these two modes are intertwined. Thomas Love Peacock's two novels, *Nightmare Abbey* (1818) and *Crotchet Castle* (1831), which mock many aspects of what has come to be termed 'Romanticism', contain a deconstruction of the 'sublime', as does P.B. Shelley's parody *Peter Bell the Third*. P.B. Shelley, Lord Byron, and William Wordsworth and S.T. Coleridge – who later became central figures in

Romantic studies – had already become central figures in Peacock's satiric representations of some of the follies and vices of his day. Peacock knew Shelley and was an acquaintance of Byron, Coleridge, and others of their circles; he used his personal observations to caricature Shelley's intellectual pretensions in the character of Scythrop in *Nightmare Abbey*, along with Byron (Mr Cypress) and Coleridge (Mr Flosky). The character Scythrop is the author of a philosophical work 'filled with hints of matter deep and dangerous, which he thought would set the whole nation in a ferment'. Scythrop's work, however, is so obscure and esoteric that the unsold copies are returned to him by his publisher 'with a polite request for the balance' of money after a sale of only seven copies. Scythrop, however, turns even this publishing flop into a significant experience for himself: 'Seven is a mystical number, and the omen is good. Let me find the seven purchasers of my seven copies, and they shall be the seven golden candle-sticks with which I will illuminate the world.' Here authors generally, as well as Shelley, are mocked for their lack of common sense in publishing their work.

In addition, Scythrop is a caricature who embodies 'Romantic' melancholy, which he is shown to actively cultivate in a manner that results in bathos. He is revealed, for example, as a comic epitome of the 'Romantic' solitary in that he seeks a remote tower of 'Nightmare Abbey' that is 'ruinous and full of owls'. Moreover, here he reads Goethe's *The Sorrows of Werther*, which was much sentimentalized by actual readers at that time; and he immerses himself in 'gloomy reverie, stalking about the room in his nightcap, which he pulled down over his eyes like a cowl, and folding his striped calico dressing gown about him like the mantle of a conspirator'. This 'congenial solitude of Nightmare Abbey' fosters in Scythrop some of the tendencies that Mr Flosky [Coleridge] has introduced to him: 'the distempered ideas of metaphysical romance and romantic metaphysics had ample time and space to germinate into a fertile crop of chimeras, which rapidly shot up into vigorous and abundant vegetation.'[3] Peacock successfully satirizes various adumbrations of these kinds of romantic ideas throughout *Nightmare Abbey*.

Peacock not only mocks the foibles of friends such as P.B. Shelley and other poets including Byron, Wordsworth, and Coleridge, but he also implies a hollowness at the heart of notions about the 'beautiful' and the 'sublime'. Peacock has Mr Flosky describe his own and Mr Sackbut's (William Wordsworth's) devious poetic machinations:

> It is very certain, and much to be rejoiced at, that our literature is hag-ridden. Tea has shattered our nerves; late dinners make us slaves of indigestion; the French Revolution has made us shrink from the name of philosophy, and has destroyed, in the more refined part of the community (of which number I am one), all enthusiasm for political liberty. That part of the *reading public* which shuns the solid food of reason for the light diet of fiction, requires a perpetual adhibition of

> *sauce piquante* to the palate of its depraved imagination. It lived upon ghosts, goblins, and skeletons (I and my friend Mr Sackbut served up a few of the best), till even the devil himself, though magnified to the size of Mount Athos, became too base, common, and popular, for its surfeited appetite. The ghosts have therefore been laid, and the devil has been cast into outer darkness, and now the delight of our spirits is to dwell on all the vices and blackest passions of our nature, tricked out in a masquerade dress of heroism and disappointed benevolence; the whole secret of which lies in forming combinations that contradict all our experience .[4]

In his fabrication of these lines for Mr Flosky, Peacock ridicules Coleridge's and Wordsworth's *Lyrical Ballads* (1798) in having Mr Flosky imply that their attempts at poetry were merely to meet the need of their reading public for Gothic horror – 'ghosts, goblins, and skeletons'. By 1818, according to Peacock, the two poets were seeking to express 'combinations that contradict all our experience', that is, the opposite of what Wordsworth in particular claimed made good poetry.

Peacock satirically provides Mr Flosky with speeches that make various attributes of the popular poets of his circle seem risible. In the following passage, for example, Peacock uses allusions to *Childe Harold* to convey the flavour of Byron's actual language at his most misanthropic, and then provides a commentary from Mr Flosky upon Byron's so-called philosophy:

> A most delightful speech, Mr Cypress. A most amiable and instructive philosophy. You have only to impress its truth upon the minds of all living men, and life will then, indeed, be the desert and the solitude; and I must do you, myself, and our mutual friends, the justice to observe, that let society only give fair play at one and the same time, as I flatter myself it is inclined to do, to your system of morals, and my system of metaphysics, and Scythrop's system of politics, and Mr Listless's system of manners, and Mr Toobad's system of religion, and the result will be as fine a mental chaos as even the immortal Kant himself could ever have hoped to see; in the prospect of which I rejoice.[5]

Peacock, by means of his caricature of Coleridge in Mr Flosky, succeeds in making three of the central Romantic poets into comic figures whose cherished ideas become pompous twaddle. Peacock's *Nightmare Abbey* is therefore comic satire, which is not mixed to any extent with other literary modes.

Women poets who used satire often targeted instances of vicious human behaviour of the day rather than individuals whom they knew. Towards the end of the eighteenth century, for example, Mary Robinson (1758–1800) published, under various pseudonyms, a number of striking satiric poems in quatrains; for example, 'The Birth-Day', which appeared in the *Morning*

Post on 21 January 1795, satirizes the public celebrations surrounding Queen Charlotte's birthday. The 'rich array' of the wealthy is contrasted ironically with the 'wretched poor' who are thrust out of the path of the celebratory procession. In a similar vein of satire, in 'January, 1795', published 10 days later in the *Morning Post*, allegorical abstractions are used to represent dominant contradictory modes in society:

> Taste and Talents quite deserted;
> All the Laws of Truth perverted;
> Arrogance o'er Merit soaring!
> Merit, silently deploring![6]

Steven Jones refers to Robinson merely as a Della Cruscan imitator,[7] but Robinson has various styles, which are signified by her use of different pseudonyms. Her Della Cruscan poems appeared under the name of 'Laura Maria', whereas these two satires of current late eighteenth-century class behaviour were published under the signature of 'Portia'. Robinson's later writing career demonstrates her versatility as well as her insights into society's range of hypocrisies.

William Blake (1757–1827) earned his living as an engraver,[8] but to some extent like Robinson he satirized – through the use of abstractions – aspects of established religious, legal, and governmental institutions and their various repressive and obstructive practices in society. Blake mixed the lyric mode with the satiric which combined to form poems of remarkable moral power. His *Songs of Innocence* (1789) and *Songs of Experience* (1794) were originally marketed for the moral education of children, but Blake's use of evocative and compelling symbolism ensured that readers of all ages formed an appreciative audience. W.H. Stevenson describes the origins of these two related works:

> The *Songs of Innocence* developed from a pastoral convention of children's verse which Blake at first sight seems to have accepted, not only in its form but also largely in its ideas. . . . Even as early as *Songs of Innocence*, however, his ideas and beliefs were quite radical. . . . The *Songs of Experience* arise from a desire to set the adult experience of real life against the innocent suppositions of children who have not experienced it – and against the less innocent indoctrination they receive from their parents. The collection is largely in parallel with the *Songs of Innocence*, each of these poems having a poem in *Innocence* to which it is more or less closely related.[9]

Blake's *Songs of Experience* often use irony in order to send up various institutions of Church, State, or monarchy. 'The Chimney Sweeper', for example, has two versions with the same title in each book. In the first version, the child speaker naively accepts the precept 'So if all do their duty they need not feel harm'. But the covert narrator shows us a boy who can only survive the death-dealing life of the chimney sweep by invoking his rich imaginative life – 'the angel told Tom, if he'd be a good boy,/He'd have God for his father and never want joy'. The narrator implies here that the boy must believe in this fiction in order to survive at all. The chimney sweeper in the later poem of *Songs of Experience* – in the form of a dialogue between an interlocutor and a chimney sweep boy – shows the boy is aware that his parents have injured his well-being, even if he manages to retain some of his child's vision of the world. His parents, as well as other members of the Established Church, are ridiculed in the boy's knowing comment 'They . . . are gone to praise God and his priest and king/Who make up a Heaven of our misery'.[10] Through the chimney sweeper's ironic conclusion, Blake makes the reader realize how the physical comfort of the churchgoers is dependent on the misery of the chimney sweeps, but these religious people do not realize their own lack of vision.

In *Songs of Experience*, however, Blake's satiric poem 'London' has no naive forerunner in *Songs of Innocence*, but stands alone as an indictment of eighteenth-century urban life. The oppressor and the oppressed are both party to 'mind-forged manacles', which pervade all areas of life, but particularly the sexual life. Blake's collocation links the ironic (who would make 'manacles' for him or herself?) with the symbolism of 'mind-forged', which suggests the power of mental imagery.

Blake's *Innocence* and *Experience* poems thus combine evocative symbolism with trenchant satire about society's repressive institutions and customary behaviour. His stylistically innovative prose poem *Marriage of Heaven and Hell* also combines symbolism with the use of paradox in order to criticize the oppressive nature of eighteenth-century social customs and laws. In his juxtaposition of prisons with brothels, for example, he satirizes, by means of an ironic statement, the damaging features of law and religion as instruments of repression: 'Prisons are built with stones of Law, brothels with bricks of Religion'. In his ironic aphorism, 'For man has closed himself up, till he sees all things through narrow chinks of his cavern',[11] the narrator implies that human beings, by not allowing themselves to see how institutional practices work towards the diminution of the personality, has locked himself into a 'cavern', from which his perceptions of truths are even more hampered. In other words, *inter alia*, society's supposedly charitable and benevolent institutions are hindrances to real charity.

Elizabeth Hands (*fl.* 1789), in *The Death of Amnon: A Poem with an Appendix Containing Pastorals and Other Poetical Pieces* (1789), employed satire to show up groups in established sections of society who had been born into social classes much above her own. She was a servant married to a blacksmith. Two of her poems – 'A Poem, on the Supposition of an Advertisement Appearing in a Morning Paper, of a Publication of a Volume of Poems, by a Servant-Maid' and 'A Poem, on the Supposition of the Book Having Been Published and Read' – imagine her audience's reception of her actual book of poems. In this pair of poems, she satirizes the philistinism of her upper- and middle-class putative audience. Through a skilful interplay of dialogue made up of rhyming couplets, she portrays these imaginary readers of her poems variously as ignorant, patronizing, snobbish, pretentious, censorious, and poorly equipped to appreciate any poetry of merit:

> 'A mad cow' – ha, ha, ha, ha,' returned half the room;
> 'What can y' expect better?' says Madam du Bloom.[12]

The poet implies, however, that these stereotypical members of the supposedly superior classes are out of touch with the poetic currents of their age, whereas she is able to articulate some of the contemporary questions about the role of the poet and the range of possible subjects for poetry.

Various authors of prose fiction in the Romantic period also at times satirized their readers, if not so straightforwardly as did Elizabeth Hands. It became almost commonplace for novelists from the 1780s onwards to mock their novel-reading heroine, a tendency which perhaps reached its zenith in Eaton Stannard Barrett's novel *The Heroine* (1814), in which the heroine models herself on a series of other heroines of novels. The moral lesson is that such mimicry of fictional characters might lead to disaster.

Both Jane Austen's *Northanger Abbey* (written in approximately 1798–99 but not published until 1818)[13] and Thomas Love Peacock's *Nightmare Abbey* (1818) are novels about the literary world and its authors. Austen's *Northanger Abbey* carries condensed allusions to and satirical pastiches of other popular novels, while the central characters of *Nightmare Abbey* are based on Peacock's satirical observations and caricatures of some of the leading figures of literary Romanticism – Byron, Coleridge and Shelley. These satiric send-ups of authors' sensational subject-matter and hyperbolic language might appear in the view of later critics to be atypical of the Romantic age. These satiric novels, however, serve to expose those who adopt manners and behaviour that mimic prevailing notions of moral worth at the expense of developing their own modes of behaviour and sense of self-worth. In mocking the follies of those who pretend to an excessive 'sensibility', for example, these authors reveal the absurdity of following exaggerated ideas about behaviour that readers might even have picked up from fictional characters.

Jane Austen began her writing career by satirizing the excesses, absurdities, and hyper-conventionality in some popular novels, particularly novels of sensibility. In her juvenilia of the late 1780s and early 1790s she parodies and burlesques conventional plots and linguistic clichés. An early work, *Love and Friendship* (?1793), consists of a fabricated collection of letters from Laura, an older mentor, to her friend Isabel's daughter, Marianne. These letters are constructed ostensibly to warn of the dangers of an excess of 'sensibility', but the actual effect is that of satirizing authors who contrive exaggerated plots and characters who are endowed with an unusual tendency towards fine feeling. In her letters, Laura extols the superiority of those who are possessed of excessive sensibility, and censures those who are merely 'good-tempered, civil, and obliging' as lacking feeling. Laura and her friend Sophia 'faint' at every instance of exaggerated feeling to which they are exposed, such as when their lovers, Edward and Augustus, meet:

> Never did I see such an affecting Scene as was the meeting of Edward and Augustus.
> 'My Life! My Soul!' (exclaimed the former). 'My Adorable Angel!' (replied the latter) as they flew into each other's arms. It was too pathetic for the feelings of Sophia and myself – We fainted alternately on a Sofa.

Austen subsequently deconstructs this literary cliché by means of Laura's epistolary account of how such an exaggerated sensibility might become a psychological weakness. Sophia dies, and Laura reports her friend's final words to Marianne :

> 'One fatal swoon has cost me my Life ... Beware of swoons, Dear Laura ... A frenzy fit is not one quarter so pernicious; it is an exercise to the Body and if not too violent, is, I dare say conducive to Health in its consequences – Run mad as often as you choose; but do not faint – .'[14]

Austen's satiric construction of the moral warnings of Laura's friend, Sophia, which falls into bathos, evokes humour at the expense of those who pride themselves on depth of feeling.

Austen's novel *Northanger Abbey* combines satiric social comedy with extended burlesque of Gothic fiction such as Ann Radcliffe's *The Mysteries of Udolpho* (1794) and Charlotte Smith's *Emmeline* (1788). But the novel can also be read as a complex satire of novels and their readers. The heroine, Catherine Morland, is a parody of the ideal heroine, exemplified in Charlotte Smith's *Emmeline*, in which the heroine had 'of every useful and ornamental feminine employment ... long since made herself mistress without any instruction'. Catherine, on the other hand, 'never could learn or understand any thing before she was taught; and sometimes not even then, for she was often inattentive, and occasionally stupid'. Whereas Emmeline 'had learned to play on the harp, by being present when Mrs Ashwood had lessons', Catherine has only progressed far enough to be able to 'listen to other people's performances with very little fatigue'.[15] While all of Austen's novels place great value on the ability of characters and readers to 'read' situations, other characters, and themselves, it is evident that in *Northanger Abbey* the heroine's reading and mis-reading of herself and other characters serve to form part of Austen's satire of novels and their readers.

Byron is not only a satirist of other authors, their imitators who form 'schools', and their readers, but, in a similar vein to that of Peacock, he also satirizes poetic evocations of what purports to be 'sublime'. Initially, Byron used various forms such as heroic couplets or quatrains in order to satirize writers whom he considered foolish. In an early poem, 'To the Author of a Sonnet' (1807), which was published posthumously, he mocks these lines on the grounds that they are neither comic nor tragic, but merely boring:

> Thy rhymes, without the aid of magic,
> May *once* be read – but never after:
> Yet their effect's by no means tragic,
> Although by far too dull for laughter.[16]

In fact, Byron asserts, if the author wishes to make the reader 'weep', he has only to make the reader hear his sonnet once again. In his later poem, 'English Bards and Scotch Reviewers' (1809), which consists of heroic couplets, Byron uses much the same kind of cutting mockery in a more sustained manner.

Byron's *The Vision of Judgement* (*The Liberal*, 1822), however, which is a burlesque of Southey's ode on the death of George III – *A Vision of Judgement* (1821) – had a serious political target. Byron's motives in writing this satire might nevertheless have been mainly personal: Byron and Southey had been enemies for some time. Byron objected to what he thought was Southey's reneging on his support for the French Revolution of 1789 by his later calls for the execution of those who were in favour of the Revolution. Southey had also attacked what he termed 'the Satanic school' of poetry of which Byron was supposed to form a part. Moreover, Southey's imputation that Byron had committed incest was a further factor behind Byron's malicious attack on Southey's *A Vision of Judgement.*

In *Don Juan* (1819–24), Byron takes on wider issues by satirizing some of the modes of writing as well as modes of thought of his age. Claude Rawson argues that Byron's *Don Juan* should be treated as belonging to the 'tradition of epic and mock-heroic'.[17] Initially, Byron employs a metafictive device, which demonstrates to the reader that writing is a process and not a result of a moment of inspiration:

> I want a hero, an uncommon want,
> When every year and month sends forth a new one,
> Till, after cloying the gazettes with cant,
> The age discovers he is not the true one.
> Of such as these I should not care to vaunt;
> I'll therefore take our ancient friend Don Juan –
> We have all seen him in the pantomime,
> Sent to the devil somewhat ere his time.[18]

The narrator implies that the acts of actual heroes are prone to being fictionalized (in 'cant' by journalists) in a way that is similar to the invention of heroes in stage drama (signified by 'pantomime'). In subsequent cantos, the narrator explains how fashionable society admires one popular hero after another, such as British or French military heroes of land or sea. From the narrator's viewpoint, the public is fickle in its admiration, and, when the military leader whom the people acclaim turns out to have flaws, they discover another one. Perhaps Byron is indirectly alluding here to his own sudden rise to and fall from popularity as a writer, when his actual self-destructive behaviour was confused in the minds of his readers with his self-constructions in his poetry. It is in these self-constructions that Byron is often said to be quintessentially 'Romantic', since one of the main characteristics of 'Romantic' writing is the use of the self-reflexive 'I' in order to demonstrate the author's success or otherwise in following the path of the cultivation of the self.

Robert Burns had already contrived a mock-heroic burlesque in his satiric narrative 'Tam o' Shanter, A Tale' (1791), in which the third-person narrator comments ironically both on the lack of enlightenment of various kinds in the anti-hero, Tam, as well as on his 'heroic' action. The narrator sets a scene in which drunken Tam is bound to be taken in by sight of 'the Deil':

> There sat auld Nick, in shape o'beast;
> A towzie tyke, black, grim and large,
> To gie them music was his charge:
> . . . .
> Coffins stood round, like open presses,
> That shaw'd the dead in their last dresses;

And so on. The narrator implies that Tam is so drunk that, in his own fantastic creations, he is incapable of distinguishing between the sublime and ludicrous:

> But wither'd beldams, auld and droll,
> Rigwoodie hags wad spean a foal,
> Lowping and flinging on a crummock,
> I wonder didna turn thy stomach.

The narrator's latter comment undercuts his protagonist's over-the-top fantasies, but to no avail. Tam is determined to discover a 'winsome wench' among the 'Deil's' crowd. When he discovers a suitable female to admire, the narrator claims ironically that his poetic 'Muse' cannot handle such desire. Nevertheless, the narrator recounts how Tam comes out of his dream by singing out 'Weel done, Cutty-sark!' to the witch he yearns for. But it is Tam's mare, Maggie, that suffers in the race to escape these witches, who, in Tam's fantasy, have become aware of an intruder. The vengeful witch tries to grab Tam, but succeeds only in breaking off Maggie's tail. The narrator mocks Tam's credulity in his own visions, as well as his cowardice, in his mock note:

> It is a well-known fact that witches, or any evil spirits, have no power to follow a poor wight any farther than the middle of the next running

> stream. – It may be proper likewise to mention to the benighted traveller, that when he falls in with *bogles*, whatever danger may be in his going forward, there is much more hazard in turning back.

Burns is here mocking also those antiquarians who provided footnotes in order to authenticate their work. In using the form of rhyming tetrameters, Burns can lightly ridicule those credulous readers who wish to believe in witches and warlocks. The notion of the male hero – who in drunkenness can imagine any descent into lust – is also mocked in the story's outcome.

The first canto of *Don Juan* seems to be partly, if not wholly, a vehicle in which Byron can express his own psychosocial problems and discontents. In this first section, the narrator satirizes supposedly intellectual women of the 'Bluestocking' type; the moral education of children and young people through censorship; heterosexual and platonic relationships; and the 'cuckold' in adultery. In the first Canto, the narrator is presented as a character in his own right and therefore independent of Byron. The narrator states, for example, 'I never married' (Stanza 53) but subsequently the first-person speaker of the story of the poem reveals himself as Byron. Towards the close of this first Canto, he suggests that 'whether/I shall proceed with his [Juan's] adventures is/Dependent on the public altogether' (Stanza 199). Byron's implication that if the public does not like this poem he will not continue to write Juan's story breaks the codes on which suspension of disbelief depends as well as mocks those readers who need to experience fictional events as if these had actually happened outside the author's imagination.

Jones suggests that Byron's source for his transformations of narrator and storyline was the pantomime, a popular form of low art in the Romantic period, which derived from the Italian *commedia dell'arte* and was attended by Byron as well as Shelley and Keats. According to this point of view:

> The poem [*Don Juan*] is about its own machinery, the trapdoors of comic rhymes giving way, the masks and improbable costumes being put on and stripped away, the picaresque mobility of characters quickly transported from Spain to Greece to Turkey to Russia to England, like the rolling of a panoramic backdrop.[19]

Jones' metaphors here draw attention to the structure of *Don Juan*, showing how the work is not flawed by being haphazard, but rather it is a highly contrived representation of the Romantic world delivered with panache and linguistic virtuosity.

In sections of Canto 1 of *Don Juan*, some of Byron's targets anticipate those of his satiric poem 'The Blues'. In many allusions to his former wife, Anne Isabella Milbanke, Byron introduces a direct personal element. In describing Donna Inez, Byron satirizes his 'Bluestocking' former wife:

In short, she was a walking calculation,
Miss Edgeworth's novels stepping from their covers,
Or Mrs Trimmer's books on education,
Or '*Coelebs' Wife*' set out in quest of lovers,
Morality's prim personification,
In which not Envy's self a flaw discovers;
To others' share let 'female errors fall',
For she had not even one – the worst of all.[20]

The narrator/Byron here suggests that Inez/Milbanke lacks passion in her cold decisiveness, and has learned her superhuman morality from educational primers and mechanistic works of fiction such as Hannah More's *Coelebs in Search of a Wife* (1809). Byron incidentally also makes light of three of the leading female educational authors of his day – Maria Edgeworth (1768–1849), Sarah Trimmer (1741–1810), and Hannah More (1745–1833). He portrays his former wife as ironically having the problem of being perfect in her goodness, whereas others, in reference to their marriage, have criticized Byron's behaviour. Joanna Baillie, for example, in her poem to Lady Byron, praises her fortitude in the face of her marriage to 'the moody lord'.[21] Byron's *Journal* (30 November 1813), however, shows that, prior to their marriage, he admired Anne Milbanke:

> She is a very superior woman, and very little spoiled, which is strange in an heiress – a girl of twenty – a peeress that is to be, in her own right – an only child, and a *savante*, who has always had her own way. She is a poetess – a mathematician – a metaphysician, and yet, withal, very kind, generous, and gentle, with very little pretension.[22]

To his aunt, Lady Melbourne, in whom he confided to some extent, and who urged his marriage with Anne Milbanke, he had earlier described Anne as 'Princess of Parallelograms' (letter to Lady Melbourne, 18 October 1812).[23] This reference mildly satirizes her mathematical abilities, and foreshadows his later poetic satires of her intellectual gifts.

Byron's attitude was bound to alter towards his wife after she requested a legal marital separation soon after their child, Augusta, was born. This breakdown of his relationship with his wife is satirized extensively in the first Canto of *Don Juan*:

For Inez called some druggists and physician,
And tried to prove her loving lord was *mad*,
But as he had some lucid intermissions,
She next decided he was only *bad*;
Yet when they asked her for her depositions,
No sort of explanation could be had,
Save that her duty both to man and God
Required this conduct – which seemed very odd.[24]

In this stanza, the narrator/Byron implies that Inez/Milbanke had only some spurious motivation, when he probably understood secretly that if he could be shown to be insane Milbanke might be able to get her fortune returned to her through the courts. Here Byron is using his semi-fiction in order to comment mockingly on his former wife's ineffectual attempts to use the law in her favour.

In *Don Juan*, the narrator/Byron portrays himself as a knowing man of the world, who is aware of society's follies, whether these follies are embodied in zealous females or immoral men. Byron's satire arises partly from his demonstrating that neither stereotypical figure has control over his or her behaviour, but is merely living out various ideologies of the day. His portrait of Don Jose, Donna Inez' husband, for example, reveals a man of 'careless' morality:

> He was a mortal of the careless kind,
> With no great love of learning or the learned,
> Who chose to go where'er he had a mind,
> And never dreamed his lady was concerned . . .

Byron not only revels in satirizing current stereotypes of his day; he also expresses his general misogyny at the same time as his malice towards his former wife: 'But – Oh! ye lords of ladies intellectual,/Inform us truly have they not hen-pecked you all?'[25] The virtuosity of Byron's rhyme here might encourage other misogynist readers to laugh at intellectual women who compete with men. Arthur Pollard refers to 'the attraction of Byron's outrageous rhymes',[26] but these rhymes cloak with humour Byron's just as outrageous misogyny, which, if you laugh with him, make you complicit in this misogyny.

In *Don Juan*, Byron not only targeted heterosexual shibboleths and minor subversions of heterosexuality, such as 'cross-dressing' and 'transvestite' behaviour.[27] He also drew readers' attention to some of the evils in militarism and warfare. Throughout this mock-epic poem, the narrator questions the moral values of international warfare with its accompanying constructions of military honour and glory.[28] Rawson comments on how, by the beginning of the nineteenth century, the conventional Augustan epic that was modelled on Homeric predecessors could no longer be written because of its outmoded conventions such as its questionable 'military morality'.[29] Byron uses the form of mock epic to subtly ridicule those militaristic readers who continued to feed on notions of heroic valour and deeds whatever the war and whatever the cost in human losses.

In 'The Blues: A Literary Eclogue' (1821), Byron draws on material that he had already used in the first two cantos of *Don Juan* (1819), a fact which suggests that perhaps 'The Blues' was drafted earlier than 1821. His use of the device of a mini-drama in heroic couplets involving a range of characters, from Tracy and Inkel to Sir Richard and Lady Bluebottle, allows him to represent – through dialogue – some conflicting aspects of his subject. The poem consists of two eclogues, which are modelled on Virgil's pastoral eclogues, but with an urban setting. Two scenes are represented, one of which takes place in front of the door of a lecture room, and the second at a 'Bluestocking' conversazione in a London salon, hosted by Sir Richard and Lady Bluebottle. In his use of these two scenes, Byron touches upon two of the important literary venues of his day: the lecture room, to which the literati and intellectuals could pay to gain entrance, and the literary salon, which only those invited could attend. Tracy seems to be a caricature of Byron himself in that this character is in pursuit of the hand of the wealthy Miss Lilac, one of the leading 'Blues' at both the lecture and the subsequent luncheon party at Lady Bluebottle's mansion. Inkel advises Tracy to extricate himself from her grasp:

> Pray get out of this hobble as fast as you can.
> You *wed* with Miss Lilac! 'twould be your perdition:
> She's a poet, a chymist, a mathematician.

The reader might infer from these lines that Inkel believes that education for women renders them unmarriageable. It might be considered theoretically unsound to impute these ideas to Byron, if it were not for the fact that his former wife, who abruptly left him, was also a poet, a mathematician and knowledgeable about scientific matters. Tracy reveals that he is partly after her for her dowry because her mother is wealthy:

> You forget Lady Lilac's as rich as a Jew.[30]

Byron might be also be referring again here to his wooing of and marriage to Anne Milbanke, who came from a wealthy family. But her family was not Jewish, and Byron appears to be using non-critically this racial stereotype in order to achieve a rhyme for 'pursue'.

The second eclogue opens with a monologue by Sir Richard Bluebottle, the 'lord' of the Bluestocking salon that is hosted by his wife. Sir Richard has no liking for the 'Blues' who intrude on him:

> But the thing of all things which distresses me more
> Than the bills of the week (though they trouble me sore)
> Is the numerous, humorous, backbiting crew
> Of scribblers, wits, lecturers, white, black, and blue,
> Who are brought to my house as an inn, to my cost –
> For the bill here, it seems, is defray'd by the host –
> No pleasure! No leisure! no thought for my pains,
> But to hear a vile jargon which addles my brains;
> A smatter and chatter, glean'd out of reviews,
> By the rag, tag, and bobtail, of those they call 'BLUES'.[31]

The portrait of the 'Blues' here is a negative one, and the eclogue concludes with Sir Richard comically wishing that all those at his wife's luncheon party should also suffer his miserable marriage.

The main target of Byron's satiric attack, however, is to be found in references to 'the sublime', which is portrayed as a pretentious and somewhat pointless abstraction. In 'The Blues', Inkel, for example, is shocked when Tracy requires him to write a love poem that expresses either admiration for Miss Lilac's 'sublime' beauty or Tracy's proxy love in 'sublime' language. Whichever meaning is taken from Tracy's use of the word 'sublime', Inkel resents the idea that he might be considered to be a poet of the 'sublime'. Later, when Botherby enthuses in an affected manner over supposed feelings of awe at the 'sublime', Inkel implies that he is drunk. Sentimentality in relation to feelings of the 'sublime' is consistently ridiculed – mainly in male characters – throughout 'The Blues'. As well as mocking pretentious notions of the 'sublime', Byron also ridicules his favourite targets – intellectual women of the 'Bluestocking' movement who seem to invite his invective because they remind him of his wife, and the 'Lakers' school of poetry of Wordsworth, Coleridge, and Southey, who are his main rivals for such honours as society might award its poets.

Satire as a mode of writing in the Romantic period has received an increasing amount of critical attention over the last 25 years. From Marilyn Butler's *Peacock Displayed: A Satirist in His Context* (1979) to Frederick L. Beaty's *Byron the Satirist* (1985) and Jonathan Bate's 'Apeing Romanticism' (1994), critics have shown a renewed interest in how some of the authors contemporaneous with Wordsworth, Coleridge and others mocked some of the aspects of life and literature in the Romantic age. Bate, for example, in his discussion of satiric works by Peacock, Hazlitt, and Byron, writes 'how easy it is to render the Romantic sublime ludicrous' and suggests that '*Don Juan* is among many other things an anti-Romantic manifesto'.[32] Satire is one of the important modes of the Romantic age that deserves our consideration, because some of the satiric works of that age, such as 'Tam o' Shanter', *Don Juan*, *Nightmare Abbey*, or *Northanger Abbey*, stand out as highly skilled and astute pieces of writing. Moreover, an appreciation of these works furthers the reader's understanding of the nature of the 'Romantic' then and now.

Notes

1 Arthur Pollard, *Satire* (London, 1970), p. 3.
2 Steven Jones, 'Introduction', *Satire and Romanticism* (London, 2000), pp. 1 and 16.
3 Thomas Love Peacock, *Nightmare Abbey* (London, 1818; new edn, Harmondsworth, 1969, repr. 1986), p. 48 and pp. 46–7. All further page references are to this edition.
4 *Nightmare Abbey*, p. 68.
5 *Nightmare Abbey*, p. 100.
6 Mary Robinson, *Selected Poems*, ed. Judith Pascoe (Ontario, Canada, 2000), p. 357. All further page references to Robinson's poems are to this edition.

7 See Jones, *Satire and Romanticism*, pp. 118 and 133. The Della Cruscans were named after Robert Merry (1755–98), who used the pseudonym of Della Crusca. His poems were noted for overwrought diction and emotionalism. See Robinson's 'Ode to Della Crusca', *Selected Poems*, pp. 85–7).
8 David Punter, 'Introduction, *William Blake: Selected Poetry and Prose* (London, 1988), pp. 1–3.
9 W.H. Stevenson, ed., *The Poems of William Blake* (London, 1971), p. 208. All further page references to Blake's poems are to this edition.
10 *The Poems of William Blake*, pp. 68–9 and 218–19.
11 *Ibid.*, pp. 109 and 114.
12 See *Women Romantic Poets, 1785–1832: An Anthology*, ed. Jennifer Breen (London, 1992; new edn, 1994), p. 30.
13 See Marilyn Butler, 'Introduction', *Northanger Abbey* (1818; Harmondsworth, 1995), p. xi.
14 Jane Austen, *Catharine and Other Writings*, ed. Margaret Anne Doody and Douglas Murray (Oxford, 1993; reissued 1998), pp. 84 and 99.
15 Quoted in Mary Lascelles, *Jane Austen and Her Art* (Oxford, 1939; repr. 1995), p. 60.
16 Lord Byron, *Poetical Works*, ed. Frederick Page, rev. John Jump (Oxford, 1904; 1970), p. 50. All further references are to this edition.
17 Claude Rawson, *Satire and Sentiment, 1660–1830: Stress Points in the English Augustan Tradition* (Cambridge, 1994; New Haven and New York, 2000), p. 99.
18 Lord Byron, *Don Juan*, ed. T.G. Steffan, E. Steffan, and W.W. Pratt (Harmondsworth, 1973; repr. 1984), p. 46. All further references to this epic are to this edition.
19 *Satire and Romanticism*, p. 192.
20 *Don Juan*, p. 50.
21 'Recollections of a Dear and Steady Friend', in *The Selected Poems of Joanna Baillie*, ed. Jennifer Breen (Manchester, 1999), p. 138.
22 Lord Byron, *A Self-Portrait: Letters and Diaries, 1798 to* 1824, ed. Peter Quennell (London, 1950), p.228.
23 Byron, *A Self-Portrait*, p. 154.
24 *Don Juan*, p. 52.
25 *Don Juan*, pp. 50 and 51.
26 Pollard, *Satire*, p. 64.
27 See, for example, Susan J. Wolfson, '"Their She Condition": Cross-Dressing and the Politics of Gender in *Don Juan*', in *Byron*, ed. Jane Stabler (London and New York, 1998), pp. 94–109.
28 See *Don Juan*, Canto VII, pp. 298–316.
29 Rawson, *Satire and Sentiment*, p. 100.
30 Byron, *Poetical Works*, p. 151.
31 Byron, *Poetical Works*, p. 155.
32 Jonathan Bate, 'Apeing Romanticism', in *English Comedy*, ed. Michael Cordner, Peter Holland, and John Kerrigan (Cambridge, 1994), pp. 225 and 228.

7

Science and literature in the Romantic age

In the late eighteenth century, the split between the literary arts and the sciences that became the norm in the twentieth century had only just begun, and, in the earlier period, the two forms of knowledge were still seen as compatible. Literary authors of various kinds often had some knowledge of one or other of the newly developing branches of science such as botany or chemistry. Radical scientists such as Humphrey Davy (1778–1829) and Joseph Priestley (1733–1804) were also well acquainted with, if not practitioners of, one or more of the literary modes of expression.[1] Poets and scientists generally could be said to share at times a similar sense of wonder and spirit of enquiry about actions in and attributes of the natural physical world.

Between 1770 and 1830, the study of natural history and natural philosophy was gradually transformed into what we now call 'science' with its various branches of knowledge. In 1765, *A General Dictionary of the Arts and Sciences* defined 'natural philosophy' as the study of 'the powers and properties of natural bodies, and their mutual actions on one another'. But soon this study began to include all the then established sciences; for example, the *Encyclopaedia Britannica* related the term 'natural philosophy' to astronomy, botany, chemistry, mechanics, and optics. By the beginning of the nineteenth century, according to Richard Yeo:

> natural philosophy was no longer a generic term for scientific knowledge of nature; instead, it more usually referred to the core Newtonian sciences – mechanics, optics, electricity, and magnetism – later known collectively as 'physics' . . . by 1800 they [encyclopedias] were breaking 'natural history' into biology, zoology, physiology, geology, and comparative anatomy.[2]

The term 'science' became more or less official in 1831 with the establishment of the British Association for the Advancement of Science. Before then, the sciences were called either 'natural philosophy', which generally indicated what we now regard as physics, and 'natural history', which included the biological and chemical sciences.

A few of the leading critics and poets in the Romantic age were aware of some of the advancements in natural philosophy and natural history that originated in the period of eighteenth-century Enlightenment. One of the foremost of these was Samuel Taylor Coleridge (1772–1834), who in his philosophical prose writings tried to keep abreast of all areas of natural philosophy and natural history in an attempt to pre-empt what he saw as a systematic breakdown of scientific knowledge into separate specialisms. In *Biographia Literaria* (1817), he criticized his contemporaries who seemed to him to dismiss 'system' as well as 'logical connection' because, he thought, these pseudo-theorists 'pick and choose whatever is most plausible and showy . . . [and] select whatever words can have some semblance of sense attached to them without the least expenditure of thought. . . .'[3] In 1798–99, at the universities of Hamburg and Gottingen, Coleridge had studied both physiology and natural history (that is, the biological and chemical sciences), as well as German language and literature, and had received a thorough grounding in philosophy as well as other aspects of objective scientific thought. His studies at greater depth than most of the amateur natural philosophers of that day encouraged him to criticize the weaknesses of the so-called 'enlightenment' of the general populace.[4]

In his revised 'Preface' to the third edition of *Lyrical Ballads* (1802) William Wordsworth (1770–1850) attempted, in two central areas, to define the relationship between poetry and science. His first area for discussion involved a consideration of the similarity between these two forms of representation of knowledge. Both the poet and the scientist study nature, according to Wordsworth, but the difference in their studies lies in the method of acquisition of this knowledge. The knowledge of the scientist is more arduously won in that scientific thinking does not come naturally to him, even if, like the experience of poetry, it gives the scientist pleasure:

> He [the poet] considers man and nature as essentially adapted to each other, and the mind of man as naturally the mirror of the fairest and most interesting qualities of nature. And thus the Poet, prompted by this feeling of pleasure which accompanies him through the whole course of his studies, converses with general nature with affections akin to those, which, through labour and length of time, the Man of Science has raised up in himself, by conversing with those particular parts of nature which are the objects of his studies. The knowledge of both the Poet and the Man of Science is pleasure; but the knowledge of the one [poetry] cleaves to us as a necessary part of our existence, our natural and unalienable inheritance; the other [science] is a personal and individual acquisition, slow to come to us, and by no habitual and direct sympathy connecting us with our fellow beings.

This somewhat tenuous argument about the habitual necessity of the poetic mode of thought which Wordsworth claims contrasts with the more self imposed scientific mode of thought does not lead anywhere very much.

Wordsworth's second area of contention, that is, scientific applications as a subject or theme of poems, is more pragmatic:

> If the labours of men of Science should ever create any material revolution, direct or indirect, in our condition, and in the impressions which we habitually receive, the Poet will sleep then no more than at present, but he will be ready to follow the footsteps of the Man of Science, not only in those general indirect effects, but he will be at his side, carrying sensation into the midst of the objects of Science itself. The remotest discoveries of the Chemist, the Botanist, or Mineralogist, will be as proper objects of the Poet's art as any upon which it can be employed, if the time should ever come when these things shall be familiar to us, and the relations under which they are contemplated by the followers of these respective Sciences shall be manifestly and palpably material to us as enjoying and suffering beings.[5]

Wordsworth seems to be here alluding indirectly to the vitalist-materialist debate, of which he would have been aware through, among others, his contact with John Thelwall (1764–1834), a poet and radical reformer, who published his controversial lecture *An Essay Towards a Definition of Animal Vitality* in 1793, after he had attended lectures at Guy's and St Thomas's hospitals in anatomy, physiology, chemistry, and *materia medica*. Thelwall argued in favour of a materialist view of human beings who he thought were animated by means of their physiology, which, even if it included a 'vital principle', need not be of divine origin. Thelwall tried to demonstrate that the 'vital principle' that animated humans was some kind of material and identifiable electrical fluid intrinsic to the blood.[6]

To some extent, Percy Bysshe Shelley seems to have later followed Wordsworth's ideas about a putative relationship between poetry and science, although Shelley's views in *A Defence of Poetry* (1821), which was written as a direct response to Thomas Love Peacock's satiric essay *The Four Ages of Poetry* (1820), are more extreme than are Wordsworth's. Shelley postulated that poetry 'is as it were the interpenetration of a diviner nature through our own', and, as such, poetry:

> is at once the centre and circumference of knowledge; it is that which comprehends all science, and that to which all science must be referred. It is at the same time the root and blossom of all other systems of thought; it is that from which all spring, and that which adorns all; and that which, if blighted, denies the fruit and the seed, and withholds from the barren world the nourishment and the succession of the scions of the tree of life. It is the perfect and consummate surface and bloom of all things; it is as the odour and the colour of the rose to the texture of the elements which compose it, as the form and splendour of unfaded beauty to the secrets of anatomy and corruption.[7]

Shelley's metaphor, in which he compares poetry to the intangible immanence of the unique tint and perfume of the rose, imaginatively conjures up a poetic essence that exists in all matter, but which cannot be studied or quantified by scientists. Science, however, might itself be imbued with some of the elements of the poetic because poetry is the expression of the imagination, and the imagination lies behind creative thinking of any kind, whether it is literary, scientific, or philosophic. Shelley here metaphorically shows how poetry is immanent in all things as colour and perfume are the intangible but distinguishing characteristics of a rose, or as beauty can only exist with the possibility of its decay. All forms of thought, according to Shelley, including science and philosophy, are imbued with the poetry of the creative imagination – the 'root and blossom of all other systems of thought'.

Shelley's ideas about the creative imagination possibly also owe something to his reading of the work of Samuel Taylor Coleridge, particularly a few of his early poems, which reveal how a sense of childlike wonder is at the root of poetic revelation and scientific knowledge. In his blank verse conversational poem 'Frost At Midnight' (February, 1798), which he wrote just prior to his studies in Germany, Coleridge celebrated – in both himself and in his infant son, Hartley – a sense of wonder in response to the physical world. He imaginatively reconstructs Hartley's waking to see the 'secret ministry' of the frost's icicles which, his father postulates:

> Will catch thine eye, and with their novelty
> Suspend thy little soul; and then make thee shout
> And stretch and flutter forth from thy mother's arms
> As thou would'st fly for very eagerness.[8]

In these lines, Coleridge captures the spirit of infant wonder, which stimulates the child to discover causes of natural phenomena and to experience the world in a tactile manner. As a Unitarian, Coleridge shares the Dissenters' interest in fostering the moral and spiritual development of children. At the same time, Coleridge identifies in his child one of the originating motives of all science, that is, a desire to investigate the operations of the world of nature.

In another meditative blank verse poem, 'The Nightingale', written two months later, Coleridge again celebrates a sense of wonder in his first-born, this time in relation to his catching sight of the moon for the first time:

> . . . once when he awoke
> In a most distressful mood (some inward pain
> Had made up that strange thing, an infant's dream –)
> I hurried with him to our orchard-plot,
> And he beheld the moon, and hushed at once
> Suspends his sobs, and laughs most silently,
> While his fair eyes that swam with undropped tears
> Did glitter in the yellow moonbeam! . . .[9]

The poet here inadvertently demonstrates the difference between scientific study of a natural phenomenon, which is objective and non-sentimental, and the feelings of awe at one of the glories of the universe, experienced by the poet, or, in this case, the incipient poet. Coleridge, the father and poet, is awed by his experience of watching his infant son catch his first sight of the moon, an experience which to the observer is arresting enough to stop his crying, whatever the baby might have actually felt. A scientist might study an emotion of awe as an experience of the sublime, but usually scientists do not seek to express such emotions in subjective language.

Coleridge's ideas about the imagination and creativity were influenced by his study of German literature and philosophy, particularly that of Immanuel Kant, who postulated that the perception of objects is partly subjective. In relation to the 'beautiful', for example, the mind responds to an object by means of concepts of beauty that the given person has already established. The apperception of the 'sublime', according to Kant, is even more likely to represent an individual response to a given object or scene. In Britain, late eighteenth-century philosophical studies were based on John Locke's much earlier *An Essay Concerning Human Understanding* (1690), in which he emphasized the role of experience in developing knowledge. The 'Enlightenment' in Britain can be seen as a major development in ways of investigating both the physical and mental worlds, from examining fossils to reporting the effects of nitrous oxide on the behaviour of humans and to studying the impact of depriving a mouse of oxygen. Any factual knowledge about the nature of the material world, however, might not lead to a concomitant illumination of the mind in relation to the non-material world of feeling and emotion, or what was then termed 'sensibility'.

Wordsworth, like Coleridge, explored in poems the experience of childhood, but, rather than looking at his own children and fathering, he represented in passages in his blank verse poem *The Prelude*, and other lyric poems, his own intuitive responses to his early experiences. Both he and Coleridge initially subscribed to David Hartley's theories of 'association of ideas' related to unspecified nerve endings, but as a theory of understanding the mind it was never very tenable.[10] Wordsworth's coining of the phrase 'shadowy recollections', however, in relation to memories of infantile experience has been reified into twentieth-century dogmas of psychoanalysis. In his lyric poem 'Intimations of Immortality' (1807), Wordsworth celebrates his infantile experience as a source of poetic inspiration:

> But for those first affections,
> Those shadowy recollections,
> Which, be they what they may,
> Are yet the fountain-light of all our day,
> Are yet the master-light of all our seeing;
> Uphold us, cherish and have power to make
> Our noisy years seem moments in the being

> Of the eternal Silence: truths that wake,
> To perish never:
> Which neither listlessness, nor mad endeavour,
> Nor man nor boy,
> Nor all that is at enmity with joy,
> Can utterly abolish or destroy! [11]

In these lines, as in other stanzas of this poem, Wordsworth suggests that self-understanding can only be discovered by taking note of those moments – in *The Prelude* he alluded to them evocatively as 'spots of time' – when the mind is illuminated by sudden memories of childhood experiences. Wordsworth's poetic description of inner responses to memories of early infancy is akin to twentieth-century psychoanalytic treatment in which the analyst relied on his patient to tell his past history in the form of 'free association', that is, recalling intuitively and spontaneously the highlights of his life without recourse to rationality or logic. But psychoanalysis and psychotherapy have been criticized because of this bias towards the subjective study of the patient. Poetry, on the other hand, as T.S. Eliot declared, works by means of 'the logic of the imagination', and is as valid a way of understanding human beings as any social or other applied science.

Many poets of the Romantic age – from Wordsworth and Coleridge to Shelley and Keats – were initially influenced by the botanical poetry in heroic couplets of Erasmus Darwin (1731–1802), a medical practitioner and poet, who combined botany and biology in descriptions of plants and flowers. Darwin translated Linnaeus's classification of plants and used this system in his poem in heroic couplets *The Loves of Plants* (1789). He then wrote a successor, *The Economy of Vegetation* (1791), which he published together with *The Loves of Plants* in *The Botanic Garden* (1791). His later prose poem, *Zoonomia* (1774–76) described human diseases and psychosomatic illnesses.[12]

In her blank verse poem *Beachy Head* (1807), which is a meditation on the geography of a headland on the southern English coast, Charlotte Smith, as Judith Pascoe notes in her seminal article, followed Erasmus Darwin in attempting to merge science with poetry. Her description of flowers, plants, animals and birds owes much to her interest in botany:

> Some pensive lover of uncultur'd flowers,
> Who, from the tumps with bright green mosses clad,
> Plucks the wood sorrel, with its light thin leaves,
> Heart-shaped, and triply folded; and its root
> Gathers, the copse's pride, anemones,
> With rays like golden studs on ivory laid
> Most delicate: but touched with purple clouds . . .[13]

In footnotes, Smith gives the Latin names, following Linnaeus's classification, for each plant. In the illustrative excerpt above, her diction is essentially poetic, particularly in the simile of anemones 'like golden studs on ivory'. Charlotte Smith's quasi-botanic descriptions are of interest in demonstrating how women poets developed a scientific interest in botany as well as a literary interest in poetry.[14] In *Beachy Head*, the poet gives the significance of this promontory in English history and pre-history, as well as detailing the types of flora and fauna that abound on this geological outcrop. Readers can thus visualize the terrain at the same time as engage in contemplation of much earlier European incursions into England, from Roman times to the early nineteenth century. Smith's form is also of interest in that within her blank verse she includes an imaginary love lyric that might have been addressed by a shepherd to his beloved. In *Beachy Head*, the narrator subsumes a quasi-scientific depiction of the terrain into an historical overview of mankind in Europe, concluding with a narrative of the life of a hermit who drowned at Beachy Head while engaged in the voluntary task of rescuing wrecked mariners from the sea.

Shelley's interest in and learning about scientific matters and technology was sporadic and non-systematic, but his poetry, as Desmond King-Hele demonstrates, was influenced by the poetry and theories about plant-life of Darwin.[15] 'To a Skylark' (1820) shows evidence of close observation of the skylark's flight, which is reflected in the rise and fall of the stanza's form. In a series of similes, the poet compares the skylark to animate and inanimate objects in the natural world – the glow-worm, the rose and rainfall. In his comparison of the skylark's song to a rose and its scent, Shelley echoes Darwin's attribution, in *The Botanic Garden*, of sexuality to plants:

> Like a rose embowered
>   In its own green leaves,
> By warm winds deflowered,
>   Till the scent it gives
> Makes faint with too much sweet those heavy-winged thieves . . .

The rose is 'deflowered' by the 'warm winds', which scatter its petals and seeds in the process of dissemination. The poet envies the bird his joyous song at the same time as he acknowledges that humans cannot appreciate the beauty of the birdsong without having experienced the pains and trials of life. Paradoxically, without such knowledge, human auditors would not appreciate the bird's song. Moreover, the skylark's song is effortless because it is instinctive, but a poet's song is the outcome of experience and understanding of the world. 'To A Skylark' replicates the flight of the bird, and, at the same time, attempts to attain in language the quality of its rapturous song. To the poet, the 'rapture' that the bird expresses in its song seems unattainable via the comparable art of poetry:

> Teach me half the gladness
>   That thy brain must know,
> Such harmonious madness
>   From my lips would flow,
> The world should listen then – as I am listening now.[16]

It is the poet's recognition of his inability to capture the effortless harmony of the skylark's song that suggests that neither poetry nor science can achieve in language an aesthetically satisfying representation of the natural world.

Shelley's poetry, however, can be shown to have reflected a wider scientific knowledge than that of botany and biology. His 'Ode to the West Wind' (wr. 1819; pub. 1820), for example, is imbued with an understanding of geology and meteorology. By means of a footnote, which gives the source of this ode, Shelley links his imagery to an actual experience of thunder and lightning at Arno, near Florence, Italy. Shelley, however, personifies the four elements of medieval philosophy – earth, air, water, and fire – and assimilates these into imagery of Greek mythologies of rebirth and factual images of the wind's role in scattering seeds over the ground for germination in spring. The poem concludes on a peculiarly evocative piece of rhetoric, which implies the possibility of social progress through the poet's prophetic powers: 'If Winter comes, can Spring be far behind?'[17]

Shelley's verse letter in heroic couplets 'Letter to Maria Gisborne' (1820), which initially was not intended for publication, satirizes Henry Raveley's efforts to construct a steamship, a scheme for which Shelley provided some of the money. In his workshop, Raveley attempted to build a prototype, which Shelley compares to the magical constructions of Proteus, the Greek god who was reputed to be able to escape by transforming himself into any shape he wanted:

> Proteus transformed to metal did not make
> More figures or more strange; nor did he take
> Such shapes of unintelligible brass,
> Or heap himself in such a horrid mass
> Of tin and iron not to be understood,
> And forms of unimaginable wood . . .

Shelley not only mocks his friend, but he also makes fun of the new technology of his day, which he pretends to find incomprehensible. Shelley had scientific mentors throughout his brief life, as Desmond King-Hele has discovered, but his interest in science appeared to take second place to his literary leanings. In his poems such as 'Ode to the West Wind' and 'To A Skylark', Shelley demonstrates his awareness of scientific theories of, for example, cloud formation or seed germination, but he expresses this knowledge in language that is rooted in metaphor, particularly in his allusions to Greek mythologies. In his 'Letter to Maria Gisborne', Shelley claims that his main bent is towards the philosophical and political:

> And here like some weird Archimage sit I,
> Plotting dark spells and devilish enginery,
> The self-impelling steam wheels of the mind
> Which pump up oaths from clergymen, and grind

> The gentle spirit of our meek reviews
> Into a powdery foam of salt abuse,
> Ruffling the dull wave of their self-content . . .[18]

In these lines, he uses to good effect imagery that is culled from possible applications of steam power in order to satirize reviewers' discomforted reactions to his radical opinions about the 'engines' of society. Shelley's ideas about science and poetry might seem in *A Defence of Poetry* to be idealized, but in 'A Letter to Maria Gisborne' he demonstrates a more pragmatic view of poetry and a more ironic approach to science and technology.

John Keats (1793–1821), by virtue of his training in the practice and theory of medicine, developed a more disciplined understanding of science than either Percy Bysshe Shelley or Charlotte Smith. In fact, Keats resembled Erasmus Darwin in being as knowledgeable about poetry as about the application of science to medicine. Darwin had studied medicine at Cambridge University and had qualified as a medical practitioner after two years at the University of Edinburgh,[19] whereas Keats obtained his Licentiate of the Society of Apothecaries in 1816 after a more extensive practical training in medicine. In order to obtain this certificate, Keats's guardian, Richard Abbey, had apprenticed him for five years to Thomas Hammond, a practising apothecary and surgeon. After these five obligatory years of assisting Hammond in his medical practice, Keats completed his medical training by attending lectures and working as a 'dresser' at Guy's Hospital. In his employment as 'dresser', Keats assisted at operations, or conducted minor ones himself. The lectures he attended were in anatomy and physiology, chemistry, and the theory and practice of medicine, as well as the dissection of human corpses. He also attended classes in *materia medica* which included the study of botany.[20] Donald Goellnicht notes that knowledge of medicines and drugs was at that time founded on botanical studies: 'the study of botany was an extremely important aspect of medical training when Keats attended Guy's in 1815. . . . As an apothecary, Keats would be expected to compound medicines for his patients, mainly from botanic ingredients.' At Guy's, Keats went on botanical field trips with William Salisbury, the botany lecturer, collecting specimens and identifying them.[21]

Keats's work in medicine during his formative years as a young adult progressed side by side with his interest in poetry, but critics have tended to emphasize the importance of his weekly excursions to read poetry with Charles Cowden Clarke during those years rather than to recognize the significance of Keats's training in the newly developing profession of scientific medicine. Keats's appreciation of poetry progressed at a similar pace to his study of medicine, so that it is not surprising that his letters and poems are studded with metaphors and analogies that originate in his formal scientific studies.

In 'Ode to a Nightingale', for example, Keats alludes to the rudiments of pharmacology, which he understood through the minor operations that he had performed as an assistant to Hammond and as a dresser at Guy's Hospital. In this ode, the poet compares some of the effects of hearing the nightingale's song with the soporific state which sedatives from hemlock or other opiates induce in those who take them:

> My heart aches, and a drowsy numbness pains
> My sense, as though of hemlock I had drunk,
> Or emptied some dull opiate to the drains
> One minute past, and Lethe-wards had sunk . . .

Paradoxically, the poet's feelings of half-relieved pain are brought about, not by 'envy' of the nightingale and her song, but by 'being too happy' at the sound of the birdsong. The term 'Lethe-wards' alludes to the Greek myth of Lethe, about souls who await rebirth by drinking the waters of the river Lethe in order to annihilate the past. The poet implies that pain-inhibiting drugs not only block out physical pain, but also impose a state of temporary memory loss. These drugs – like hearing the song of the nightingale – induce a trance-like state, which aids the taker to transcend ordinary existence and to acquire a consequent receptivity to the intuitive and the numinous. Even if Keats took no drugs himself, he would have often observed the effects of sedatives on his patients. Moreover, the narcotic drug opium was often prescribed for the treatment of symptoms that were accompanied by pain.

In the second stanza, Keats proposes alcohol as a more enjoyable means of escaping life's sorrows, personifying wine from southern Europe in the memorable phrasing of 'the blushful Hippocrene,/With beaded bubbles winking at the brim,/And purple-stained mouth'. In the third stanza, the poet describes his experience of the world, from which he wants to disappear:

> Fade far away, dissolve, and quite forget
> What thou among the leaves hast never known,
> The weariness, the fever, and the fret
> Here, where men sit and hear each other groan;
> Where palsy shakes a few, sad, last grey hairs,
> Where youth grows pale, and spectre-thin, and dies;
> Where but to think is to be full of sorrow
> And leaden-eyed despairs; . . .

These lines probably allude to scenes of approaching death that Keats witnessed either when, as an apprentice, he accompanied Hammond on his rounds, or the surgical rounds in the hospital wards at Guy's. Some critics, as John Barnard notes,[22] have suggested that Keats's portrayal of the inevitable mortality of human beings refers mainly to the death from tuberculosis of Keats's brother, Tom, but in the line 'Here, where men sit and hear each other groan' Keats's sympathies extend to humanity generally, and possibly imply the sounds he heard in hospital wards among the sick and dying. In his work as a 'dresser' at Guy's, Keats worked constantly in the wards where he would have often encountered the last stages of illness followed by death.

'Ode to A Nightingale' might be read as an allegorical expression of the poet's dilemma between the choices available to him for his life's work – medicine or poetry. The nightingale's song symbolizes the escapist world of the poetic, which nevertheless for him is not continuously enrapturing. Once the nightingale and her music are 'fled', so is his inspiring moment, and he is left to philosophize on the nature of reality. Is the intangible beauty of poetry the dream, or is actual life, with its pains and sorrows, unreal? This question remains a rhetorical one for Keats, and in part paradoxically forms the inspiration for his poetry, as does his somewhat melancholic disposition, which leads him to the utterance of his half-concealed wish 'to cease upon the midnight with no pain', thus avoiding life's miseries any further.

Keats's 'Ode on a Grecian Urn' (1820) also might appear rhetorically to describe the paradoxical nature of artistic creation in which transient beauty is captured more or less permanently, or at least as long as the artistic object continues to exist. Yet also inherent in this poem are implications of human mortality with its physical pains and sorrows:

> When old age shall this generation waste,
> Thou shalt remain, in midst of other woe
> Than ours, a friend to man, to whom thou sayst,
> 'Beauty is truth, truth beauty, – that is all
> Ye know on earth, and all ye need to know.'

In these lines, the poet poses an answer to the rhetorical question as to whether the work of art – song, artefact or poem – is a more truthful and more permanent account of actuality than the experience of, for example, 'human passion . . . That leaves a heart high-sorrowful and cloyed,/A burning forehead and a parching tongue'.[23] Here Keats the trained physician seems to be aware of the psyche-soma relationship, which even at that time could be seen to be related to mysterious fevers and illnesses. Moreover, Keats's summation of life as 'woe' is possibly connected in part to his years of treating illnesses by means of what medical practitioners now consider to be inadequate or partial forms of cure.

Mary Shelley's work of science fiction, *Frankenstein* (1818), might be now regarded as one of the most searching and comprehensive literary explorations of scientific experimentation and its effects on society. In this account of a man who tries to understand the secret of engendering life outside sexual procreation, and puts into practice what he discovers, Mary Shelley highlights the possibly adverse consequences of the late eighteenth- and early nineteenth-century obsessive drive towards mastery of the physical world. This world-view, which encouraged specialists to think that the material world could be completely understood, dominated the *modus operandi* of the middle and upper classes at that time. The eighteenth century had seen a ferment of activity related to discovering how the natural world operated, and to communicating with others these discoveries through lectures and discussion as well as by means of the written word.

During the period in which Mary Shelley wrote *Frankenstein,* scientific lectures at the newly established Royal Institution of Science were highly popular among fashionable intellectuals. One of these lecturers, William Lawrence (1783–1865), who was a medical reformer as well as anatomist and anthropologist, was also P.B. Shelley's physician. Mary Shelley was thus probably aware of the scientific dispute that arose between Lawrence and John Abernethy (1764–1831), President of the Royal College of Surgeons. In his Hunterian lectures of 1814, in relation to the nature and origin of a postulated life principle, Abernethy tried to suggest that, even if life evolved from matter, man was nevertheless imbued with some kind of divine essence. On the other hand, Lawrence in his Hunterian lectures of 1816 argued against any form of divine intervention in the organization of the material from which life was formed. When Mary Shelley constructed the character of Frankenstein, who thought he could discover the secrets of creating human life and apply this knowledge, she was partly reflecting a scientific controversy of her day.[24] Her protagonist, Frankenstein, resembled the men of the social and intellectual world in which she had grown up as the daughter of Mary Wollstonecraft and William Godwin. The cultivated men – literary, scientific, and historical of this world – travelled, studied at European universities, or developed their interests in politics and the world at large. And, like Frankenstein, they thought that their new discoveries, in whatever field, could make a difference to their world and to humankind. But Frankenstein brings to birth a 'monster' who, partly because of his lack of early nurture in family life, brings havoc to his creator's own existence.

Mary Shelley's epistolary novel, *Frankenstein*, is both a story of 'Gothic' horror and a moral tale. Her construction of the characters of both the anti-hero, Frankenstein, and Walton, the Arctic explorer to whom Frankenstein narrates his story of the 'monster', centres on one of the significant motifs of her age: an obsession with discovering, through scientific study, a means of a rational understanding and control of aspects of the universe. In Walton's case, he sought to meet his thirst for knowledge by means of the exploration of unknown territory. Walton is saved from death because he turns back for the sake of his crew from his disastrous exploratory voyage to the Arctic. Frankenstein, however, dies in his pursuit of revenge on the 'monster' he brought to life. In *Frankenstein*, Mary Shelley's knowledge of some of the scientific controversies of the day in relation to man's desire to discover the origins of forms of life is imaginatively represented in her work of science fiction.

'Science' in its nomenclature was only disentangled from 'natural philosophy' at the end of the Romantic age, so that any discussion of science in relation to literature of that age is inevitably linked to philosophical theories about life and art. What is distinctive about some of the Romantic literary authors' approaches to science and art is their use of their art to encapsulate in metaphor theories of sensation and perception, as well as theories about the relationship between conscious and unconscious aspects of mental behaviour. In their art, a few of these authors, such as Coleridge, Wordsworth, Keats and Percy Bysshe Shelley, explore some of the complex links between psyche and soma, and, in Mary Shelley's case, more general sociological and ethical questions about the scientific engendering of life.

Notes

1 Humphrey Davy 'had written poetry in the 1790s and helped Wordsworth edit the second edition of *Lyrical Ballads* in 1800' (*An Oxford Companion to the Romantic Age*, ed. Iain McCalman, Oxford, 1999).
2 *Ibid*, p. 326.
3 S.T. Coleridge, *Biographia Literaria*, ed. Nigel Leask (London, 1999), p. 167.
4 For an account of 'popular Enlightenment', see Lorraine Daston, 'The Ethos of Enlightenment', *The Sciences in Enlightened Europe*, ed. William Clark, Jan Golinski, and Simon Schaffer (Chicago, 2000), p. 500.
5 *Lyrical Ballads*, ed. R.L. Brett and A.R. Jones (London, 1963; 2nd edn, 1991), pp. 259–60.
6 See Nicholas Roe, *John Keats and the Culture of Dissent* (Oxford, 1997), pp. 176–9.
7 P.B. Shelley, *A Defence of Poetry* in *Selected Poetry and Prose*, ed. Alasdair D.F. Macrae (London, 1991), pp. 227–8.
8 Samuel Taylor Coleridge, *The Complete Poems*, ed. William Keach (Harmondsworth, 1997), pp. 231–3 and 517.
9 S.T. Coleridge, *The Complete Poems*, p. 247.
10 David Hartley (1705–57) was the author of *Observations on Man* (1749). See S.T. Coleridge, *Biographia Literaria*, ed. Nigel Leask, for Coleridge's deconstruction of Hartley's theories about how the nerves operated (pp. 67–70).
11 William Wordsworth, *Poetical Works*, ed. Thomas Hutchinson (London, 1904; new edn, rev. Ernest de Selincourt, 1936, repr. 1966), p. 461.
12 See Desmond King-Hele, *Erasmus Darwin and the Romantic Poets* (Basingstoke, 1986), pp. 11–13.
13 *The Poems of Charlotte Smith*, ed. Stuart Curran (New York, 1993), p. 177.
14 Judith Pascoe concludes from women poets' interest in Erasmus Darwin's *The Botanic Garden*: 'They embroidered numerous poetic variations of the work and credited Darwin as a kind of poetic mentor' (see Judith Pascoe, 'Female Botanists and the Poetry of Charlotte Smith', in *Re-Visioning Romanticism: British Women Writers, 1776–1837*, ed. Carol Shiner Wilson and Joel Haefner, Philadelphia, 1994, pp. 199–200).
15 Desmond King-Hele, *Erasmus Darwin and the Romantic Poets*, pp. 191–233.
16 Percy Bysshe Shelley, *Selected Poems* (London, 1977, repr. 1983), pp. 104–6.
17 Shelley, *Selected Poems*, p. 78.
18 Shelley, *Selected Poems*, ll. 45–50 and 106–112, pp. 108 and 109.
19 Desmond King-Hele, *Erasmus Darwin and the Romantic Poets*, p. 5.
20 Robert Gittings, *A Biography of John Keats* (Harmondsworth, 1988), pp. 61, 82–3, and 215–16.

21 Donald Goellnicht, *The Poet-Physician: Keats and Medical Science* (Pittsburgh, Pa., 1984), pp. 85–6.
22 John Barnard, ed., *John Keats: The Complete Poems* (Harmondsworth, 3rd edn, 1988), p. 679.
23 *Ibid.*, pp. 345–6.
24 See Marilyn Butler, '*Frankenstein* and Radical Science', *Times Literary Supplement*, 4 April 1993, repr. in *Frankenstein*, ed. J. Paul Hunter (New York, 1996), pp. 302–13.

8

British literary responses to the French Revolution

Edmund Burke's *Reflections on the French Revolution* (1790) and Thomas Paine's riposte to Burke, *The Rights of Man, Part I* (1791), possibly influenced – in different and opposing ways – the British political climate in the Romantic age more than any other works, in that between them they provoked a strengthening of a democratic movement that worked towards political equality among classes. William Doyle, in *The Oxford History of the French Revolution*, summarizes the sales in Britain of these two political tracts:

> Burke's *Reflections* were a best seller (30,000 in two years) but were easily outstripped by sales totalling about 200,000 for *Rights of Man* as hitherto moribund reform societies revitalized themselves to promote its diffusion in London, the provinces, and Scotland and Ireland too.[1]

The first literary responses to the fall of the Bastille, signifier of the opening days of the French Revolution, acclaimed what was at the time often seen by middle-class British radicals as a triumph of rationalism. E.P. Thompson describes how 'the welcome to the first stages of the French Revolution came largely from middle-class and dissenting groups. It was not until 1792 that these ideas gained a wide popular following, mainly through the agency of Paine's *Rights of Man*.' As Doyle points out, however, the British government did not take long to bring in legislation that aimed at the suppression of any *sans culotte* movement in Britain, such as the London Corresponding Society, which sprang up in January 1792 more in response to Paine's *Rights of Man* than to the French Revolution itself. E.P. Thompson sees the circulation of Paine's *Rights of Man* as inaugurating 'a new democratic consciousness', which the middle-class bourgeois tried to defeat by means of 'Church and King' mobs that were 'employed from 1792 onwards to terrorize the English Jacobins'.[2]

In fear of the incitement of a revolution, a Royal Proclamation Against Seditious Writings and Publications was passed in May 1792:

> The second anniversary of the Bastille's fall, in contrast to the previous year, was marked with banquets in major provincial towns throughout the British Isles. ... But not all of England was radicalised. In Birmingham, a 'Bastille dinner' in July 1791 led to a riot against the dissenters who had been its leading attenders. Crowds cheering for Church and King sacked chapels, meetinghouses, and the home of the Unitarian scientist Joseph Priestley, while local magistrates stood obligingly aside. Decades of fruitless effort to launch 'God Save the King' as a national song were suddenly crowned with success as respectable people reflected on the flight to Varennes; and in May 1792, the government issued a proclamation against seditious writings and opened proceedings against Paine.[3]

Although this proclamation was possibly intended more to prevent the popular press from printing further anti-royalist and pro-parliamentary reform chapbooks, handbills, ballads, and songs, literary artists appeared to be afraid to come out openly in favour of the French Revolution or of radical reform in Britain. Nevertheless, this action against seditious or inflammatory writing did not prevent novelists from expressing views about the necessity for political reform in their fictional works, and the 'Jacobin novel' emerged at the turn of the eighteenth century. Gary Kelly describes these English Jacobin novelists as:

> a number of intellectuals and miscellaneous writers of liberal social views who were deeply indebted to the Enlightenment and to Sensibility and who, inspired by revolution abroad and political protest in Britain, gave a much sharper edge to the social criticism usually found in Enlightenment and Sentimental fiction. These writers included Thomas Holcroft, William Godwin, and Mary Wollstonecraft.[4]

From the commencement of the French Revolution, British writers through poetry and prose attempted to convey to the British public the significance of this sudden and dramatic change in French political and social life and, at times, its repercussions on English political life. David Bindman notes that artistic renderings of the fall of the Bastille form:

> a well-established genre, encompassing dramas, operas (Beethoven's *Fidelio* being the best-known example), and even paintings, produced mainly, though not exclusively, in the years immediately following the prison's destruction. The Bastille genre depends upon an absolute contrast between 'despotism', represented by a luridly imaginative picture of the Bastille as a place of hideous cruelty towards the innocent, and a vision of 'liberty' in which man may reach joy and perfection after his release from the prison.

As Bindman recounts, William Blake was among those authors in the early days of the French Revolution who attempted to represent symbolically the fall of the Bastille and its after-effects. The radical publisher Joseph Johnson had initially commissioned a longer poem, but Blake only drafted the first book, which was set up in print to appear in 1791, but was not published at that time, nor, indeed, during Blake's lifetime. Bindman concludes that the 'reasons for its failure to be published are not known'.[5]

Blake's poem *The French Revolution* begins with reflections on the violent overthrow of the Constitution and the institutions of the monarchy and established religion in France:

> The dead brood over Europe, the cloud and vision descends
> over cheerful France.
> O cloud well appointed! Sick, sick, the Prince on his couch,
> wreathed in dim
> And appalling mist, his strong hand outstretched, from his
> shoulder down the bone,
> Runs aching cold into the sceptre too heavy for mortal grasp.
> No more
> To be swayed by visible hand, nor in cruelty bruise the mild
> flourishing mountains.[6]

These lines dramatize through visual imagery the relations between powerful men in authority ('the cloud') and revolutionaries who might have the 'vision' by which to improve society partly through the overthrow of those in control of the state. Louis XVI is depicted with a misted vision that prevents his restoration of his 'sceptre' to his 'cruel' grasp: Blake, even though he had not visited France, shows the ambivalent and contradictory aspects of the revolutionary forces in conflict there. These five introductory unrhymed octameters are an evocation of a portentous event for European history, the violent possibilities of which filled many Europeans with dread.

The uncertain beginnings in 1789–90 of the French Revolution are represented in complex metaphors, such as the alternating 'cloud and vision' of participants or the depiction of an unusable royal 'sceptre' which has become 'too heavy for mortal grasp'. The image of the 'mild flourishing mountains', which might stand for French idealism, or for the French people themselves, implies the poet's empathy with the people's cause.

Blake's symbolic if lurid representation of the destruction of the Bastille carries an apocalyptic and millennial note, even though the victory seems a Pyrrhic one in view of the fact that the Bastille at that time only held seven prisoners. The poet here alludes to the murdered governor of the Bastille as a prisoner of his overweening desire for power over helpless men:

> . . . in his soul stood the purple plague,
> Tugging his iron manacles, and piercing through the seven towers
> dark and sickly,
> Panting over the prisoners like a wolf gorged; . . .[7]

Blake portrays in biblical imagery of fire and brimstone the actions of some of the main participants in the French Revolution, such as this exchange between Louis XVI and the then financial minister Necker, who has fallen out of favour:

> '. . . Necker rise. Leave the kingdom; thy life is
> surrounded with snares;
> We have called an Assembly, but not to destroy; we have given
> gifts, not to the weak;
> I hear rustle of muskets, and brightening of swords, and visages
> reddening with war,
> Frowning and looking up from brooding villages and every
> darkening city;
> Ancient wonders frown over the kingdom, and cries of women
> and babes are heard,
> And tempests of doubt roll around me, and fierce sorrows,
> because of the nobles of France;
> Depart, answer not, for the tempest must fall, as in years that
> are passed away.'

Blake's characterization of Necker and Louis XVI bears some relation to the facts of events of the early days of the Revolution; for example, Necker's resignation and flight to Geneva is represented by Blake as 'Dropping a tear, the old man his place left, and when he was gone out/He set his face towards Geneva to flee.'[8] Necker was known for his emotional responses in crises. William Doyle, the historian, describes more prosaically Necker's resignation from the revolutionary government: 'Hounded ever since October 1789 by radical journalists like Marat, spurned and despised by leading deputies like Mirabeau, and forced by the Assembly to carry out policies he had no faith in, on 3 September 1790 he resigned.'[9]

Bindman argues that Blake's approach to the French Revolution is couched in the 'terms of the Burke–Paine controversy' in a similar a way to his later poem *America* (1793):

> With the hindsight given by the French Revolution, the American Revolution was, if one were a Painite, the opening of a redemptive process which might culminate in universal revolution. If one were a Burkean, on the other hand, it was nothing less than a plague which threatened to engulf the world.

Later, Bindman remarks on Paine's part in the American Revolution: 'The publication of Paine's pamphlet *Common Sense* in 1776 played a major part in the American colonists' decision to seek full independence from Britain.'[10] Throughout this essay, Bindman discusses Blake's work in terms of his anti-materialist and visionary political and religious beliefs in relation to his reading of Paine and Burke.

Helen Maria Williams, an English author who visited France in 1790, and remained there more or less permanently, also contributed to the Bastille genre, choosing the epistolary form as a means of conveying the immediacy of events of the Revolution and their aftermath. Her first volume, *Letters Written from France in the Summer of 1790* (1790) was followed by a sequential one, *Letters from France, 1792–6* (1796). Her other works include *Letters Containing a Sketch of the Politics of France* (1794) and *Sketches of the State of Manners and Opinions in the French Republic towards the Close of the Eighteenth Century* (1801).[11] In Paris in 1790, she visited the Bastille after the prison had been sacked in 1789:

> After having visited the Bastille, we may indeed be surprised, that a nation so enlightened as the French, submitted so long to the oppression of their government; but we must cease to wonder that their indignant spirits at length shook off the galling yoke. . . .
>
> As the heroes of the Bastille passed along the streets after its surrender, the citizens stood at the doors of their houses, loaded with wine, brandy, and other refreshments, which they offered to these deliverers of their country; but they unanimously refused to taste any strong liquors, considering the great work they had undertaken as not yet accomplished, and being determined to watch the whole night in case of any surprise.

In this letter, and the subsequent volumes of letters she produced in relation to the Revolution and its aftermath, Williams used to good effect the eighteenth-century genre of the literary epistle, a form that allowed an informality that ensured a note of authenticity.

In this same letter, Williams revealed her antipathy to authoritarian rule and her support for the abolition of the monarchy:

> Those who have contemplated the dungeons of the Bastille, without rejoicing in the French Revolution, may, for aught I know, be very respectable persons, and very agreeable companions in the hours of prosperity; but, if my heart were sinking with anguish, I should not fly to those persons for consolation. . . . If the splendour of a despotic throne can only shine like the radiance of lightning, while all around is involved in gloom and horror, in the name of heaven let its baleful lustre be extinguished forever. May no such strong contrast of light and shade again exist in the political system of France! But may the beams of liberty, like the beams of day, shed their benign influence on the cottage of the peasant, as well as on the place of the monarch! My Liberty, which for so many ages past has taken pleasure in softening the evils of the bleak and rugged climates of the North, in fertilizing a barren soil, in clearing the swamp, in lifting mounds against the inundations of the tempest, diffuse her blessings also on the genial

> lands of France, and bid the husbandman rejoice under the shade of the olive and the vine![12]

In her later epistolary poem in the eighteenth-century form of heroic couplets to a friend, Dr Moore, which was published in 1792, Williams again celebrated the early days of the French Revolution:

> For now on Gallia's plains the peasant knows
> Those equal rights impartial heaven bestows.
> He now, by freedom's ray illumined, taught
> Some self-respect, some energy of thought,
> Discerns the blessings that to all belong,
> And lives to guard his humble shed from wrong.[13]

These lines reveal that Williams' philosophical welcome of the Revolution was not modified by subsequent cataclysmic events of which she must have been aware, since she lived in France – mainly in Paris – from 1791 onwards. Even though by 1792 French supporters and opponents of the Revolution had split into warring and murderous factions, Williams still maintained the same political attitude to the commandeering of the Legislative Assembly and subsequent plotting towards the overthrow of the monarchy in France that she had had in 1790.

As a Dissenter, she welcomed the fact that Protestants had had all civil disabilities removed at the onset of the Revolution. It is not surprising that a conservative element in England, who were at first eager to read her first-hand accounts of revolutionary ferment in Paris, disapproved of her siding – intellectually at least – with the Girondins, along with her Paris sponsor, Madame du Fosse, wife of a French aristocrat. The Girondins were a political group who, led by Brissot, supported the National Convention, which was elected to replace the Legislative Assembly, and went along with the abolition of the monarchy in the shape of Louis XVI, but who did not favour the execution of the King.[14] In September 1793, the Jacobins[15] in Paris defeated the Girondins, and many of Williams' Girondin friends were guillotined. Williams herself was imprisoned in Paris because she supported the Girondins, but she, as well as her mother and sister, were freed a few months later through the influence of a relation of Madame du Fosse. Williams, unlike other radical English poets of the 1790s, apart from William Blake, continued to support the spirit of the French principles of 'liberty, equality, fraternity' throughout this imprisonment and later experiences of French bloodthirsty fervour. At times, she sought refuge in Switzerland.

Mary Wollstonecraft, who was acquainted with Blake through the publisher Joseph Johnson, lived in Paris between 1792 and 1794. Joseph Johnson commissioned Wollstonecraft's *An Historical and Moral View of the Origin and Progress of the French Revolution; and the Effect It Has Produced in Europe* (1794) which she introduced as the first volume of two or three, but no further volumes or drafts of volumes appeared during her lifetime or posthumously. In her Preface to this work, Wollstonecraft uncompromisingly concludes that the French Revolution emerged as a fruit of the philosophical enlightenment in France during the eighteenth century:

> we shall be able to discern clearly that the revolution was neither produced by the abilities or intrigues of a few individuals; nor was the effect of sudden or short-lived enthusiasm; but the natural consequence of intellectual improvement, gradually proceeding to perfection in the advancement of communities, from a state of barbarism to that of polished society, till now arrived at the point when sincerity of principles seems to be hastening the overthrow of the tremendous empire of superstition and hypocrisy, erected upon the ruins of gothic brutality and ignorance.[16]

Here Wollstonecraft demonstrates her belief in the perfectibility of human beings, which pre-dates Godwin's ideas about the perfectibility of man that he sets out in *Political Justice* (1795).[17] Wollstonecraft, in contrast with William Blake, takes a rationalist approach to the French Revolution, and, like other Dissenters and free thinkers at that time, celebrates the overthrow of a corrupt system of authoritarian power backed by a religious institution, which she refers to metaphorically as a 'tremendous empire of superstition and hypocrisy'.

Wollstonecraft's letter to Joseph Johnson that she wrote on the day of the execution of Louis XVI – 26 December 1792 – shows her mastery of the epistolary style. In this personal letter to her publisher, she also demonstrates a 'radical Sensibility', that is, she trusted her 'innate emotional response to provide the basis of a beneficial social order' and embracing 'a philosophy which proposed to liberate individual energies'.[18] Even though she did not witness the execution of the King of France, she conveys its onerous impact:

> About nine o'clock this morning, the king passed by my window, moving silently along (excepting now and then a few strokes on the drum, which rendered the stillness more awful) through empty streets, surrounded by the national guards, who, clustering round the carriage, seemed to deserve their name. The inhabitants flocked to their windows, but the casements were all shut, not a voice was heard, nor did I see any thing like an insulting gesture. – For the first time since I entered France, I bowed to the majesty of the people, and respected the propriety of behaviour so perfectly in unison with my own feelings. I can scarcely tell you why, but an association of ideas made the tears flow insensibly from my eyes, when I saw Louis sitting, with more dignity that I expected from his character, in a hackney coach, going to meet death, where so many of his race have triumphed.[19]

Wollstonecraft emphasizes the silence that accompanied the King's last journey in a manner which magnifies the impact on herself and thus on the reader. She uses a brief reference to her own response in the face of this tragedy so that her 'tears' become an expression of sensibility of which, as an objective reporter, she claims that she is 'insensible'. She also sets Louis' execution in the context of what she knows about his earlier behaviour (however accurate she might be), which she implies has been less 'dignified' than is his comportment now in the face of death by the guillotine.

William Wordsworth also visited France during the early days of the French Revolution and wrote about these experiences in his blank verse autobiographical poem *The Prelude*. This poem was to lead into another philosophical poem, *The Recluse*, but Wordsworth never completed the latter work. In 1790, he went on a walking tour of the French Alps with Robert Jones, a fellow student at Cambridge University. They reached Calais on 13 July 1790, the eve of the fall of the Bastille on 14 July 1789, a victory that the inhabitants of Calais were about to celebrate. Nicholas Roe considers that 'it was a moment Wordsworth remembered for the rest of his life'.[20] Wordsworth recalled this moment in *The Prelude*, of which the first 13-book draft was completed in 1805, but not published in his lifetime. His aim at that time was to enjoy contact with nature in the French Alps, but he could not help but notice the feeling of excitement in the populace on the eve of the first anniversary of the fall of the Bastille:

> . . . Europe at that time was thrilled with joy,
> France standing on the top of golden hours,
> And human nature seeming born again.
> . . . we chanced
> To land at Calais on the very eve
> Of that great federal day; and there we saw,
> In a mean city, and among a few,
> How bright a face is worn when joy of one
> Is joy for tens of millions.[21]

By the time Wordsworth next visited France in 1791, he was more politically informed, in that he had read 'the master-pamphlets of the day' of, *inter alia*, Edmund Burke and Thomas Paine. Duncan Wu agrees with Roe that Wordsworth probably read Burke's *Reflections on the French Revolution* (1790) in the spring of 1791 and the first part of Paine's *The Rights of Man* at about the same time.

Wordsworth was in France in 1792 and, according to Wu, he probably read the second part of *The Rights of Man* 'in a French edition some time during the spring or summer'. Paine's *The Rights of Man*, Parts I and II, was banned in England in May 1792, and Paine was charged with sedition. Wu states, 'He was tried and sentenced to death *in absentia*, 18 December, at about the time Wordsworth returned to England'.[22]

In Books IX and X of *The Prelude*, Wordsworth recounts his experiences in France immediately after the fall of the Bastille. His main aim in *The Prelude* is the exploration of his poetic selfhood, an exploration that he addressed to his friend, S.T. Coleridge, and his sister, Dorothy. Such an approach at self-explanation resembles a self-analysis, which is unreliable because the subject and the analysing subject constitute the same person. Objectivity about the behaviour of oneself and others is bound to be inaccurate because it is impossible to obviate the subjective element of the observer. The resulting work is bound to be impressionistic since there are few workable or reliable methods of measuring the accuracy of a person's own self-assessment, except those of comparing statements with those of others as well as referring to the external facts of social history. In France in 1790, Wordsworth was a young man of 20, but when he wrote Book IX of *The Prelude* in which he describes these experiences in Paris and Orleans in 1790 and 1791–92 he was 34, and had achieved a certain fame from the publication of the *Lyrical Ballads* in its second edition with its explanatory Preface. In *The Prelude*, Wordsworth concealed relationships which might compromise him; for example, Wordsworth relates that he became a 'patriot' after becoming friendly with a French officer in the revolutionary army, Michel Beaupuy, who sympathized with the republican aims. Wordsworth does not reveal also that he had become intimate with a civilian, Annette Vallon, who at first supported the aims of the Revolution, and later became a royalist. He and Annette Vallon had a child, Caroline, in December 1792, but he omitted from *The Prelude* any direct poetic representation of these episodes.[23]

Wordsworth shows, however, that he later recognized that the forces of revolutionary activity did not represent the 'golden hour' that he had imagined in 1790, but:

> . . . 'Twas in truth an hour
> Of universal ferment; mildest men
> Were agitated; and commotions, strife
> Of passions and opinions, filled the walls
> Of peaceful houses with unquiet sounds.
> The soil of common life, was, at that time,
> Too hot to tread upon.

At first, Wordsworth describes how he mixed socially with officers who were royalists and 'defenders of the Crown' and who tried 'to persuade him to their cause'. But he explains that he was already Republican in sympathy, because of his upbringing in the north of England:

> For, born in a poor district, and which yet
> Retaineth more of ancient homeliness,
> Than any other nook of English ground,
> It was my fortune scarcely to have seen,

Through the whole tenour of my schoolday time,
The face of one, who, whether boy or man,
Was vested with attention or respect
Through claims of wealth or blood; nor was it least
Of many benefits, in later years
Derived from academic institutes
And rules, that they held something up to view
Of a Republic, where all stood thus far
Upon equal ground; that we were brothers all
In honour, as in one community,
Scholars and gentlemen; where, furthermore,
Distinction open lay to all that came,
And wealth and title were in less esteem
Than talents, worth, and prosperous industry.
. . . It could not be
But that one tutored thus should look with awe
Upon the faculties of man, receive
Gladly the highest promises, and hail,
At best, the government of equal rights
And individual worth.[24]

Wordsworth's representation of the development of his republican sympathies, however, was reflected through his maturation and through his later knowledge of what had taken place in France and Europe after 1793: the wars with England and much of Europe, and the rise and fall of Napoleon.

Wordsworth gives an account of his reaction at that time to the 'September massacres', which took place when he was staying at Blois on the Loire river:

The State, as if to stamp the final seal
On her security, and to the world
Show what she was, a high and fearless soul,
Exulting in defiance, or heart-stung
By sharp resentment, or belike to taunt
With spiteful gratitude the baffled League,
That had stirred up her slackening faculties
To a new transition, when the King was crushed,
Spared not the empty throne, and in proud haste
Assumed the body and venerable name
Of a republic. Lamentable crimes,
'Tis true, had gone before this hour, dire work
Of massacre, in which the senseless sword
Was prayed to as a judge; but these were past . . .[25]

The Jacobin faction in Paris had not yet reached their decision to execute King Louis XVI and Queen Marie Antoinette. In fact, these executions of royalty occurred after Wordsworth had returned to England. His uncles would not fund his stay in France any longer.[26] Wordsworth subsequently thanked Providence for forcing him to return to England, thus avoiding the harsh life of a Republican in France at that time:

> . . . In this frame of mind
> Dragged by a chain of harsh necessity,
> So seemed it, – now I thankfully acknowledge,
> Forced by the gracious providence of Heaven, –
> To England I returned, else (though assured
> That I both was and must be of small weight,
> No better than a landsman on the deck
> Of a ship struggling with a hideous storm)
> Doubtless, I should then have made common cause
> With some who perished; haply perished too,
> A poor mistaken and bewildered offering, –
> Should to the breast of Nature have gone back,
> With all my resolutions, all my hopes,
> A Poet only to myself, to men
> Useless, and even, beloved Friend! A soul
> To thee unknown![27]

Nigel Leask suggests that Book X of *The Prelude*:

> tells us how meeting Coleridge had restored Wordsworth's confidence in the republican ideas that he had imbibed from Michael Beaupuy and other Girondins, and which had been so badly shaken by the rise of Robespierre and the outbreak of war between England and the young French republic.[28]

In 1793, when Wordsworth heard that Britain had declared war on France after the execution of Louis XVI in December 1792, he was dismayed – first, because for him England's attempted dismantling of the principles of the French Revolution through invasion and conquest was a betrayal; and, second, his return to France was officially forbidden, and to return clandestinely would be extremely dangerous. What can be established from both *The Prelude* and Wordsworth's *Letter to the Bishop of Llandaff* (composed February–March 1793, but published posthumously) was that Wordsworth in 1792 still held radical political views. In this letter, which is a reply to an anti-revolutionary Appendix affixed to a sermon preached by Richard Watson, Bishop of Llandaff, and published in pamphlet form in early 1793, Wordsworth shows support for the guillotining of Louis XVI, even though 'the blind fondness of his people had placed a human being in that monstrous situation which rendered him unaccountable before a human tribunal'. In other words, there was no mechanism in the French Constitution whereby he might be tried and convicted. Wordsworth nevertheless concludes that the majority of the French population were convinced of their King's crimes committed under tyranny:

> A bishop [M. Gregoire], a man of philosophy and humanity as distinguished as your Lordship, declared at the opening of the national convention, and twenty-five millions of men were convinced of the truth of the assertion, that there was not a citizen on the tenth of August who, if he could have dragged before the eyes of Louis the corse of one of his murdered brothers, might not have exclaimed to him, Tyran, voila ton ouvrage . . . a time of revolution is not the season of true Liberty. Alas! the obstinacy & perversion of men is such that she is too often obliged to borrow the very arms of despotism to overthrow him, and in order to reign in peace must establish herself by violence. She deplores such stern necessity, but the safety of the people, her supreme law, is her consolation. This apparent contradiction between the principles of liberty and the march of revolution, this spirit of jealousy, of severity, of disquietude, of vexation, indispensable from a state of war between the oppressors and oppressed, must of necessity confuse the ideas of morality and contract the benign exertion of the best affections of the human heart.

In this letter, Wordsworth also espoused the fight of the ordinary man for suffrage and equal treatment in law:

> Setting aside the idea of a peasant or mechanic being a legislator, what vast education is requisite to enable him to judge amongst his neighbours which is most qualified by his industry and integrity to be intrusted with the care of the interests of himself and his fellow citizens? . . . Equality, without which liberty cannot exist, is to be met with in perfection in that state in which no distinctions are admitted but such as have evidently for their object the general good. The end of government cannot be attained without authorising some members of society to command, and, of course, without imposing on the rest the necessity of obedience.[29]

As Owen and Smyser remark in their commentary on this latter passage, Wordsworth is partly reflecting ideas in the revolutionary *Droits de L'Homme et du Citoyen* and partly assimilating ideas from Rousseau's *Du Contrat Social.* In 1793, Wordsworth demonstrated that he was still a Republican, but, as Brett and Jones suggest, Wordsworth was also mentally unbalanced, and so might have become enthusiastic about political philosophies from psychological need. Brett and Jones explain his attachment to Godwin's theories in *Political Justice* (1793) in this light, but, when he had recovered his mental stability, 'by 1798 Wordsworth had rejected Godwin's dichotomy of reason and emotion'.[30] Through Coleridge, Wordsworth adopted Hartley's ideas about experience of sensations being at the base of personal development, including the development of morality.

We might, however, trace a connection between the republican outlook that Wordsworth portrays in his 'Letter to the Bishop of Llandaff' and his approach to the poetic treatment of the worst-off, which he expresses in the *Lyrical Ballads* of 1798, and about which he proselytizes in his 'Preface' to the second edition of *Lyrical Ballads* of 1800. In reference to his choice of poetic subject matter, for example, he writes:

> Low and rustic life was generally chosen because in that situation the essential passions of the heart find a better soil in which they can attain their maturity, are less under restraint, and speak a plainer and more emphatic language; because in that situation our elementary feelings exist in a state of greater simplicity and consequently may be more accurately contemplated and more forcibly communicated; because the manners of rural life germinate from those elementary feelings; and from the necessary character of rural occupations are more easily comprehended; and are more durable; and lastly, because in that situation the passions of men are incorporated with the beautiful and permanent forms of nature. The language too of these men is adopted (purified indeed from what appears to be its real defects, from all lasting and rational causes of dislike or disgust) because such men hourly communicate with the best objects from which the best part of language is originally derived; and because, from their rank in society and the sameness and narrow circle of their intercourse, being less under the action of social vanity they convey their feelings and notions in simple and unelaborated expressions. Accordingly, such a language arising out of repeated experience and regular feelings is a more permanent and a far more philosophical language than that which is frequently substituted for it by Poets, who think that they are conferring honour upon themselves and their art in proportion as they separate themselves from the sympathies of men, and indulge in arbitrary and capricious habits of expression in order to furnish food for fickle tastes and fickle appetites of their own creation.[31]

Wordsworth has transferred French ideals of *l'égalité* to the composition of English poetry in that his approach to the representation in poetry of aspects of the lives of the lower classes reflects his democratic sympathies in relation to the new French Republic. His 'lyrical ballads' and other poems of 1798 epitomize his new-found interest in the worst-off and give imaginative expression to his later theory that feeling is more spontaneous in the lower classes than in the upper classes. Leask, however, links Wordsworth's attitude to 'low and rustic life' to his discovery of Pantisocracy through Coleridge's plan to set up a colony with equal land rights on the banks of the Susquehannah river. Leask postulates that Wordsworth found a modified Pantisocratic society in the Lake District. He cites Wordsworth's poem 'Home at Grasmere' in order to show:

> the extent to which the idea of Pantisocracy as emigration from a hopelessly corrupt Europe dominated by a surplus rather than a subsistence economy, division of labour and antagonistic class interests affected Wordsworth's 'rediscovery' of the virtues of the Lakeland peasants.

Leask adds that Wordsworth's 1801 letter to Charles Fox reiterates how Wordsworth has found a 'civic ideal' in England, and not in America, as Coleridge and the Pantisocrats had hoped.[32]

Wordsworth's relationship with Coleridge, according to Roe, began in 1795 when they first met, 'but they had no obvious mutual influence until two years later. Nevertheless, Wordsworth deliberately presents Coleridge as a redeeming figure in Book Ten.'[33] Leask suggests that Coleridge turned to Pantisocracy 'as a radical alternative to [Godwin's] *Political Justice* (1793)' in that Coleridge's attitude to small landholders challenged Godwin's approach:

> whereas Godwin appealed to man as he *ought* to be, basing virtue solely on an appeal to reason, he rather addressed him as he *was*, grounding virtue on the habits of moral responsibility and the domestic affections which he associated with the proprietorship of small shares of equally distributed land.[34]

Leask also shows how Coleridge's egalitarian approach, based on property rights, influenced Wordsworth's 'Preface' of 1800 to their joint *Lyrical Ballads*. By 1805, Wordsworth had concluded that he could contribute more to society if he followed the vocation of poet rather than that of patriot, a plan that he forged with Coleridge.

Prior to Wordsworth's first drafts of *The Prelude* in 1805, Coleridge, in 'Fears in Solitude' (1798), a meditative poem in blank verse, ranged discursively from the topic of spring in Somerset to his own radical youth to current threats of social disorder and invasion by France. The 'action' of this poem takes place in an idyllic setting in which the protagonist is swept up in solitary musings of an optimistic kind:

> Here he might lie on fern or withered heath,
> While from the singing lark (that sings unseen
> The minstrelsy that solitude loves best),
> And from the sun, and from the breezy air,
> Sweet influences trembled o'er his frame;
> And he, with many feelings, many thoughts,
> Made up a meditative joy, and found
> Religious meanings in the forms of Nature!

To Coleridge, the influence of the natural world is not sufficient to keep out the political and social fears that are partly self-created by what he refers to initially as 'youthful . . . folly'. In this ode, Coleridge rehearses the states of mind of the adherents of the two forms of fanaticism – those who want to bring about constitutional reform peacefully and those who want to bring about a republic through infiltration from France. This subject develops into his own love of country and his religious feeling, both of which have emerged in his early life in England. This poem evolves organically from a delight in nature to an exploration of his own and society's 'folly and rank wickedness' which bring about disorder to a renewal of a recognition of nature's power and a concomitant redemptive power of human love:

> . . . that by nature's quietness
> And solitary musings, all my heart
> Is softened, and made worthy to indulge
> Love, and the thoughts that yearn for human kind.[35]

This topographical and meditative poem shows a similar kind of movement to his 'Frost at Midnight' (1798), except that the latter is confined to themes of religion, domesticity and human love. 'France: An Ode' (published in the same pamphlet as 'Fears in Solitude' and 'Frost at Midnight'), might have appealed to his publisher, Joseph Johnson, because of its address to the abstraction 'Liberty', but this 'ode' is more conventional in form and less compelling in its use of language than the other two innovatory blank verse poems in that same pamphlet.

Literary responses in Britain to the early days of the French Revolution flourished throughout the 1790s, and revolutionary France continued to interest British writers well into the nineteenth century. As Alison Yarrington and Kelvin Everest point out:

> reactions [to the French Revolution], for example of first generation poets [Wordsworth, Coleridge and Blake], became part of an intellectual development with major importance for the second generation such as Shelley and Byron; so that the apostasy of their literary forerunners itself became a part of the Revolutionary impact, and helped to shape and alter its meaning for a new generation.[36]

In a letter of 17 May 1816 about their arrival in Paris, that was perhaps addressed to Fanny Imlay, and which Mary and P.B. Shelley published later in *History of a Six Weeks' Tour* (1817), Mary Shelley comments on the attitude of the French to English 'subjects' in 1816. After the English government had persisted in a war against France and Napoleon that resulted in their 1815 defeat, French resentment against touring English visitors was strong. Shelley writes:

> Nor is it wonderful that they should regard the subjects of a government which fills their country with hostile garrisons, and sustains a detested dynasty on the throne, with an acrimony and indignation of which that government alone is the proper object.

Shelley, in a further letter of 1 June 1816, from Coligny, near Geneva, refers to 'a small obelisk . . . erected to the glory of Rousseau' whose writing she describes as having 'mainly contributed to mature' the Revolution in France. She adds her judgement of that Revolution, 'which, notwithstanding the temporary bloodshed and injustice with which it was polluted, has produced enduring benefits to mankind, which all the chicanery of statesmen, nor even the great conspiracy of kings, can entirely render vain'.[37] In this percipient observation, not long after the event, Mary Shelley puts the French Revolution into a historical perspective that most writers or readers would accept today.

Notes

1 William Doyle, *The Oxford History of the French Revolution* (Oxford, 1989), p. 169.
2 E.P. Thompson, *The Making of the English Working Class* (London, 1963; repr. 1968, 1980), pp. 80 and 82.
3 Doyle, *The Oxford History of the French Revolution*, p. 170.
4 Gary Kelly, *English Fiction of the Romantic Period* (London and New York, 1989), p. 26.
5 David Bindman, '"My own mind is my own church": Blake, Paine and the French Revolution' in *Reflections of Revolution: Images of Romanticism*, ed. Alison Yarrington and Kelvin Everest (London and New York, 1993), p. 113.
6 William Blake, *Poems*, ed. W.H. Stevenson, text by David Erdman (London, 1971), ll. 1–5, p. 125. All further references to Blake's poems are to this edition.
7 *Ibid.*, ll. 24–5, p.127.
8 *Ibid.*, ll. 109–15 and 121–2, p. 132.
9 William Doyle, *The Oxford History of the French Revolution*, p. 134.
10 Bindman, '"My own mind is my own church": Blake, Paine and the French Revolution', pp. 115 and122.
11 See Janet Todd, 'Introduction', *Letters from France: 1792–6* (New York, facsimile edn, 1975).
12 Helen Maria Williams, *Letters Written from France in the Summer of 1790*, repr. in *Women Romantics 1785–1832: Writing in Prose*, ed. Jennifer Breen (London, 1996), pp. 71–4.
13 'To Dr Moore, In Answer to a Poetical Epistle written by Him in Wales', ll. 37–42, *Women Romantic Poets, 1785–1832: An Anthology*, ed. Jennifer Breen (London, 2nd edn, 1994), p. 60.
14 See Doyle, *The Oxford History of the French Revolution*, p. 195.
15 The Jacobins in France were a political faction that opposed another mainly Parisian political group, the Girondins. English Jacobins tended to be either middle-class authors and others with liberal views in relation to democracy, or artisans who might belong to the London Corresponding Society or other societies of a similar kind. These societies sprang up in response to Paine's *The Rights of Man*. Anti-Jacobins in England were those who were against any movement towards increased democracy in Britain. See Kelly, *English Fiction of the Romantic Period*, pp. 26 and 30.
16 *The Works of Mary Wollstonecraft*, ed. Marilyn Butler and Janet Todd, Vol. 6 (London, 1989), pp. 6–7.

17 See William Godwin, *Enquiry Concerning Political Justice With Selections from Godwin's Other Writings*, ed. K. Codell Carter (Oxford, 1971), Book I, Ch. V, pp. 58–59.
18 I am using Chris Jones's definition of a 'radical Sensibility' in 'Radical Sensibility in the 1790s' in *Reflections of Revolution*, ed. A. Yarrington and K. Everest (London and New York, 1993), p. 69.
19 In *Women Romantics, 1785–1832: Writing in Prose*, ed. Jennifer Breen (London, 1996), p. 19.
20 Nicholas Roe, *Wordsworth and Coleridge: The Radical Years* (Oxford, 1988), p. 20.
21 William Wordsworth, *Poetical Works*, ed. Thomas Hutchinson (London, 1904; new edn rev. Ernest de Selincourt, 1936, repr. 1966), *The Prelude*, VI, ll. 339–49, p. 532. All further page references to Wordsworth's poems are to this edition.
22 Duncan Wu, *Wordsworth's Reading, 1770–1779* (Cambridge, 1993), pp. 22 and 109.
23 See Kenneth R. Johnston, *The Hidden Wordsworth* (New York, 1998), p. 299.
24 *The Prelude,* Book IX, ll. 215–43, pp.557–8.
25 *The Prelude,* Book X, ll. 31–44, p. 562.
26 Johnston, *The Hidden Wordsworth*, p. 312.
27 *The Prelude*, Book X, ll. 221–36, p. 565.
28 Nigel Leask, 'Pantisocracy and the Politics of the "Preface" to *Lyrical Ballads*', in *Reflections of Revolution*, ed. A. Yarrington and K. Everest (London and New York, 1993), pp. 42–3.
29 'A Letter to the Bishop of Llandaff', in *The Prose Works of William Wordsworth*, edited W.J.B. Owen and Jane Worthington Smyser (Oxford, 1974), pp. 32–4, and 38–42. Wordsworth's reply to the Bishop was probably composed in February or March 1793 (see Owen and Symser, p. 20).
30 William Wordsworth and S.T. Coleridge, *Lyrical Ballads*, ed. R.L. Brett and A.R. Jones, (London, 1963, 2nd edn, 1991), p. xxxiv.
31 *Ibid.*, pp. 245–6.
32 Leask, 'Pantisocracy', pp. 54–5.
33 Roe, *Wordsworth and Coleridge*, p. 200. He states that Coleridge was involved in movements against the war with France as well as with constitutional reform movements of 1794–5, but two Acts of Parliament – Grenville's 'Treasonable Practices' Bill and Pitt's 'Seditious Meetings' Bill – induced caution in both Coleridge and Wordsworth about expressing their republican sympathies (pp. 148–54).
34 Leask, 'Pantisocracy', p. 46.
35 Samuel Taylor Coleridge, *Poems*, ed. John Beer (London and Vermont, 1993; repr. 2000), pp. 284 and 289.
36 Alison Yarrington and Kelvin Everest, 'Introduction', in *Reflections of Revolution*, ed. A. Yarrington and K. Everest (London and New York, 1993), p. 3.
37 Mary Shelley and P.B. Shelley, *History of A Six Weeks' Tour*, repr. in *Women Romantics, 1785–1832: Writing in Prose*, ed. Jennifer Breen (London, 1996), pp. 214 and 218.

9

The 'canon' of British Romantic literature

The term 'canon' originally meant either the list of genuine (as opposed to spurious) books of the Christian Bible, or those works that can be attributed definitively to one author; but the word 'canon' has also come to mean a list of all the books that are thought to be worth reading in a literary period, or in an area or region, or in the whole of literature. In relation to Romanticism, critics often discuss the 'canon' of 'Romantic' literature in terms of genre, so that drama, poetry, essays, and the novel are treated separately. Poetry has usually been regarded as the most significant of the genres that flourished during the age of Romanticism. However much this assumption has appeared to be unfair to some of the novelists and even essayists of the Romantic age, the writing of poetry in Britain between 1785 and 1832 was extraordinarily innovative and wide-ranging. In his essay 'Wordsworth', which was first published in *Tait's Magazine* in 1839, Thomas de Quincey referred to the work of the 'Lake poets' – especially that of Coleridge and Wordsworth – as 'this regeneration of our national poetry'.[1]

The two most important 'Lake poets', William Wordsworth and Samuel Taylor Coleridge, gradually attracted a contemporary readership after the publication of their *Lyrical Ballads* in 1798, which was followed by a second edition in 1800 with an additional prefatory essay. Wordsworth and Coleridge favoured the practice of writing criticism to back up their poetry. Coleridge in *Biographia Literaria*, for example, discussed his own development as critic and poet partly in relation to Wordsworth's poetry. Keats and Shelley also, through letters and essays, projected themselves as major poets.

Wordsworth and Coleridge, Shelley, and Keats – both in their poetry and their writing about poetry – seemed to get to the heart of literary creation, and posterity has mostly accorded to them their abrogation of a central position in the Romantic canon as well as in the literary canon overall. It is not a matter of enquiring into whether these poets deserve this position – since they evidently do – but rather it is a matter of enquiring as to whether more poets of the Romantic age also deserve recognition as the authors of aesthetically outstanding poems.

The recognition of a 'canon' of works in British literature that came to be regarded as aesthetically and culturally valuable began in the mid-eighteenth century with the publication of various anthologies of oral ballads and poems that had usually been published previously. One of the most influential anthologies was Thomas Percy's *Reliques of Ancient Poetry* in 1765. Percy in his selection of English poetry not only printed his choice of 'improved' ballads but also reprinted his preferred poems from among Elizabethan songs and his contemporaries' poems, such as one by William Shenstone.

The editor, Roger Lonsdale, in his scholarly and influential anthology *The New Oxford Book of Eighteenth-Century Verse* (1984), outlined some of the ways in which a canon of eighteenth- and early nineteenth-century poetry came to be formed. He noted, first, 'Dodsley's *Collection of Poems* (1748–58), invariably trusted as definitively representative of the mid-century' and, second, Robert Anderson's *Works of the British Poets* (Edinburgh, 1792–95), followed by Alexander Chalmers' *Works of the English Poets* (1810). These anthologists used principles of selection that excluded anonymous authors, women, poets of single volumes who never collected their poetry, and living poets. Lonsdale added that 'these compilations were calculated to appeal to a respectable readership at a precise historical moment'.[2] If we are to judge by later collections and selections of British poets, however, it can be seen that these early vast collections were drawn on by later anthologists, and it was probably Lonsdale himself who made the first large break from the traditional 'canon' of eighteenth-century poetry by reverting to all the original volumes of poetry that had been published in that century and making a new anthology of poems which included many hitherto forgotten poems of some significance.

Not only anthologists and antiquarian collectors established this 'canon'. Thomas Warton and Dr Samuel Johnson, in their works of early literary criticism and biography, elevated certain writers above others: Warton's *History of English Poetry* was published between 1774 and 1781; Johnson's *Lives of the Poets* came out between 1779 and 1781; and Joseph Ritson's *Bibliographia Poetica*, a bibliography of poets between the twelfth and the sixteenth centuries, was printed in 1802. These attempts at establishing important poets of earlier periods formed an outline of literary history that came more or less to be accepted as the 'tradition' of English poetry.

After 1800, reviewers in monthly journals were among the important canon-making influences of the day. Marilyn Butler has documented the rise of the influential *Edinburgh Review* (1802) and the *Quarterly Review* (1809) and the effects of these two journals on political and literary culture at the beginning of the nineteenth century. Both journals proselytized in favour of the war against Napoleonic France, which did not come to an end until 1815. And, as Butler demonstrates, these two journals, based in Scotland, set out to shape literary culture through assessment reviews of creative writing:

> just as Jeffrey [editor of the *Edinburgh Review*] had invented the myth of a Lake school, so the *Quarterly* team identified, in order to 'demonise', an entire Satanic school of Byron camp-followers, to which Shelley, C.R. Maturin and the anonymous author of *Frankenstein* were all recruited. At about the same time the *Quarterly* and *Blackwood's* established the profile of a middle-class Cockney School, headed by Leigh Hunt and including Keats, which was held to subvert morals through promoting sexual licentiousness.[3]

Apart from noting this tendency of these journals to create 'schools' of poetry, Butler also identifies – in *Blackwood's Edinburgh Magazine* (1817) and the *London Magazine* (1820) – a new trend of literary gossip and the creation of a new breed of literary celebrities who were prominent reviewers or journalists. Hazlitt was one of these newly celebrated 'stars', and editors vied with each other to obtain his services as a writer of literary gossip and literary essays.

If we examine how Hazlitt profiled and reviewed some of the writers whom he regarded as expressing the 'spirit of the age', we might ascertain how one of the star reviewers of the Romantic age affected the position in the canon of those he chose to write about. Hazlitt's criticism of Coleridge's and Wordsworth's self-reported alteration from radicalism to conservatism first appeared as journalism before these pieces were republished in *The Spirit of the Age* (1824; 2nd edn, 1825). Hazlitt had originally trained as a pictorial artist, especially of portraits, so that his sketches of authors and other notable men are often expressed in visual imagery. Additionally, he developed a technique of seemingly praising his subject only to diminish him. His portrait of Coleridge in an essay, 'My First Acquaintance with Poets', which appeared in *The Liberal* (April, 1823), sets up an underlying comparison between the inspirational radical poet of 1798 and what Hazlitt regarded as the apostate of 1823. On the surface, this piece is suffused with Hazlitt's admiration for S.T. Coleridge, an admiration that he did not lose completely, despite Coleridge's subtle derogation of him as a friend after Hazlitt had displeased both Coleridge and Wordsworth during a visit to the Lake District in 1803. Hazlitt had become overly familiar with a young woman who had had to discourage him; and he had consequently incurred the wrath of the young woman's friends, so much so that Wordsworth and Coleridge felt it incumbent on them to help Hazlitt make an *incognito* escape.

Hazlitt begins 'My First Acquaintance with Poets' (1823) with an account of his first meeting – at the age of 20 – with Coleridge on the occasion of Coleridge's inaugural sermon at a Unitarian church at Shrewsbury in Shropshire, when Hazlitt's father had a living as a Dissenting Minister at nearby Wem. He briefly compares Coleridge with his own father who was faithful to 'the cause of civil and religious liberty' throughout his life. Hazlitt points out how Coleridge gave up his aim of becoming a

Unitarian minister as soon as Thomas Wedgwood offered him an annuity of £150 a year 'if he chose to waive his present pursuit, and devote himself entirely to the study of poetry and philosophy. Coleridge seemed to make up his mind to close with this proposal in the act of tying on one of his shoes.' This precise description of what seems to the young Hazlitt to be Coleridge's sudden change in vocation is seen from the dual point of view of the young enthusiastic Hazlitt and the older cynical man.

The purport of 'My First Acquaintance with Poets' is not the act of hero worship that it at first seems, as we can see from this humorous description of the conduct of a naive hero-worshipper, Chester, who 'kept on a sort of trot by the side of Coleridge, like a running footman by a state coach, that he might not lose a syllable or sound that fell from Coleridge's lips.' Elsewhere in this essay, Hazlitt is more direct in his views about flaws at the heart of 'Romantic' idolatry; for example, he describes a breakfast that is in harmony with the natural world: 'on the second day, we breakfasted luxuriously in an old-fashioned parlour on tea, toast, eggs and honey, in the very sight of the bee-hives from which it had been taken, and a garden full of thyme and wild flowers that had produced it.' This moment of natural enjoyment is also a moment that calls forth remarks on representations of nature: 'on this occasion, Coleridge spoke of Virgil's *Georgics*, but not well. I do not think he had much feeling for the classical or elegant.' Hazlitt here subtly mocks Coleridge's attempt to inform his breakfast auditors with a classical account of bee-keeping and honey.

On Hazlitt's first visit to Coleridge at Nether Stowey, Coleridge took him to meet Wordsworth at Alfoxden, and Coleridge described to him the background of the unpublished *Lyrical Ballads*:

> He [Coleridge] said the *Lyrical Ballads* were an experiment about to be tried by him and Wordsworth, to see how far the public taste would endure poetry written in a more natural and simple style than had hitherto been attempted; totally discarding the artifices of poetical diction, and making use of only such words as had probably been common in the most ordinary language since the days of Henry II.[4]

Hazlitt's nostalgic recollections of Coleridge's writing of the poems for which he is most famed – 'The Ancient Mariner', 'Frost at Midnight', and 'The Aolean Lyre', for example – indicate how Hazlitt at the age of 20 approached the new quality of the poetry that his mentor wrote early in his career. It seems to have been Coleridge's abandonment of poetry that Hazlitt, in his subsequent essay 'Coleridge' (1825), most regretted:

> If Mr Coleridge had not been the most impressive talker of his age, he would probably have been the finest writer; but he lays down his pen to make sure of an auditor, and mortgages the admiration of posterity for the stare of an idler. If he had not been a poet, he would have been a powerful logician; if he had not dipped his wing in the Unitarian

> controversy, he might have soared to the very summit of fancy. But, in writing verse, he is trying to subject the Muse to *transcendental* theories: in his abstract reasoning, he misses his way by strewing it with flowers.
>
> All that he has done of moment, he had done twenty years ago: since then, he may be said to have lived on the sound of his own voice.[5]

Hazlitt's satiric criticism here of the later Coleridge was based on his dislike of what he saw as the forsaking of genuine poetry, such as in the *Lyrical Ballads*, in favour of philosophical abstractions. The effect of Hazlitt's influential essay about Coleridge seemed to help consolidate Coleridge's permanent position in the canon of Romantic poetry, and these essays seemed to help to establish the still-held consensus that Coleridge as well as Wordsworth wrote their more effective poetry in 1797 to 1804, at the beginning of their writing careers.

Another essayist of the Romantic age, Thomas de Quincey, not only helped to establish Wordsworth in the canon permanently, but also began to draw attention to the principal qualities which readers internationally have subsequently been taught to appreciate in Wordsworth:

> Wordsworth is peculiarly the poet for the solitary and the meditative; and, throughout the countless myriads of future America and future Australia, no less than Polynesia and Southern Africa, there will be situations without end fitted by their loneliness to favour his influence for centuries to come.[6]

It is interesting to note, in relation to de Quincey's prediction, that the twentieth-century specialisms of psychology, psychoanalysis and psychiatry have taken up some of Wordsworth's lines, such as 'The child is father to the man', as catchphrases, which are used to support one or other theory of human mental processes. Wordsworth's experience of transcendence, which he expressed in poems such as 'Intimations of Immortality from Recollections of Early Childhood' (1807), continue to be read in this way, for example, by the developmental psychologist Margaret Donaldson in her *Human Minds: An Exploration* (1992) in which she cites Wordsworth's poetic vision as an example of an emotional transcendent mode in which 'the soul . . . retains an obscure sense of possible sublimity'.[7] A poetic replication of feelings of transcendence is a quality that dominates much of Wordsworth's and Coleridge's, as well as Shelley's and Keats's, poetry, appealing to our interest in their poetic renderings of their inner experiences.

It is ironic that William Hazlitt, whose writings put the works of others such as Wordsworth and Coleridge on the literary historical map, has not become a central figure himself in the English literary canon. Various attempts have been made to restore Hazlitt to the leading position that he held in his own time; for example, Thomas McFarland in 1987 argued that

Charles Lamb, William Hazlitt, and Thomas de Quincey should be restored to the canon of Romanticism:

> Lamb, Hazlitt, de Quincey, each was a figure deeply embattled amid the convulsive disruptions and accumulating stresses that defined Romanticism. Each must be seen against the background of the spirit of the age. Each projected his personality and experience into idiosyncratic statement.[8]

But is that sufficient? Restoration to the canon, at least in the case of Hazlitt, does not seem to have taken place. Instead, of late he has received critical attention of a somewhat negative kind in relation to his treatment of women, including his attempt, by means of a mock adultery, to divorce his wife, Sarah, in Scotland.

Charles Lamb's *Essays of Elia* and Thomas de Quincey's *Confessions of an Opium Eater*, however, have recently received attention in relation to a late twentieth-century interest in Orientalism.[9] An interest in Lamb's and de Quincey's 'confessional' writing might also have been stimulated by the twenty-first-century demand for increased revelation of the self in both journalism and autobiography. Lamb turns self-revelation into an art rather than an act of confession and self-abasement. Coleridge's *Biographia Literaria* is primarily a record of his literary development, particularly in connection with his relationship with William Wordsworth, and has been seen by one critic as emulating the essay style of Lamb, his friend and predecessor. Lamb, however, employs the first-person occasional essay as a 'confessional' form in which he reveals, for example, the depths of his own degradation in alcoholism:

> I have known one . . . when he has tried to abstain but for one evening, – though the poisonous potion had long since ceased to bring back its first enchantments, though he was sure it would rather deepen his gloom than brighten it, – in the violence of the struggle, and the necessity he has felt of getting rid of the present sensation at any rate, I have known him to scream out, to cry aloud, for the anguish and pain of the strife within him.
>
> Why should I hesitate to declare, that the man of whom I speak is myself? I have no puling apology to make to mankind. I see them all in one way or another deviating from the pure reason. It is to my own nature alone I am accountable for the woe that I have brought upon it.[10]

The reader's curiosity is aroused when at first Lamb preserves the anonymity of the drunkard. When the revelation is made that the alcoholic is Lamb himself, the reader is forced to admire Lamb's honesty, and at the same time to divest him or herself of any moralism, because Lamb adds that he is harming no one but himself. This is a clever piece of writing, because the reader at that point is obliged to accept as 'truth' Lamb's further self-revelation, which includes an account of his addiction to tobacco, as well as the effects on his constitution and his psyche of 12 years of over-indulgence in alcohol. Lamb's account – which he finally suggests is to serve as a warning to others – of why he became drunk, as well the effects of his drunkenness on his family and friends, is as psychologically accurate now as it was at the time of writing.

Through the aegis of the publisher M.J. Godwin, the second wife of William Godwin, Charles and Mary Lamb were commissioned to write poetry and prose for children. The Romantic age is notable for its innovatory writing for children, which seems to have stemmed from the interest of Dissenting educationists in the moral development, through literature, of young people. Some of this poetry, especially by William Blake, Charles and Mary Lamb, Jane Taylor, and Dorothy Wordsworth, is highly original, although none of these authors had children of their own. Mary Lamb is usually seen as a minor part of a not very important collaboration with her brother, Charles, in the writing of *Poetry for Children* (1809). Although this work was not reprinted until 1903 in its self-contained form,[11] M.J. Godwin subsequently anthologized regularly a selection of their poems. The Lambs' poems, of which Mary wrote two-thirds, should be read in contrast with William Blake's *Songs of Innocence* (1789), a work that was also originally published for children.

Thus, despite a resurgence of critical interest in authors such as Charles Lamb and Thomas de Quincey, four major poets of the Romantic age – Wordsworth, Coleridge, Shelley, and Keats – still stand foremost in the Romantic canon. Wordsworth and Coleridge in particular – the 'elders' of Romanticism – have maintained this position partly because of the critical interest taken in them during their own time and later in the Victorian period, particularly by the essayist and poet Matthew Arnold (1822–88). Apart from these four poets, the Romantic canon has undergone a few changes, and today some critics are advocating further changes.

The critic Marilyn Butler, in 'Repossessing the Past: the Case for an Open Literary History', recently made some pertinent observations in relation to the Romantic 'canon' in Britain and in America, suggesting that academic literary interests should become broader. She suggests that our traditional notions of literature that have come down to us from the nineteenth century need to be revised: 'The consequences of shirking a revision are great, for the opportunity facing teachers of literature in our lifetime may not recur in the next generation. Should millions of potential readers of great literature, in all parts of the world, be welcomed or repelled, given access to the past or in effect denied it?'[12] Butler's rhetorical question, however, leads to a specific question: *which* neglected past literature should be reprinted and prescribed on university courses?

With regard to revising the 'canon', Thomas Love Peacock, in *The Four Ages of Poetry* (1820), made a prediction which does not flatter critics of later ages in relation to their abilities in recognizing worthwhile poetry:

> the poetical audience will not only continually diminish in the proportion of its number to that of the rest of the reading public, but will also sink lower and lower in the comparison of intellectual acquirement.

To this prediction, Peacock adds that the 'drivellers' [feeble poets] and the 'mountebanks' [academic critics] 'are contending for the poetical palm and the critical chair'.[13] Peacock's caustic satire here, however, seems to have been forgotten.

If we move forward 100 years to a time when poetry was still seen as important to society, Virginia Woolf adumbrated ways of avoiding the admission to the canon of what she termed 'rubbish-reading':

> Every literature, as it grows old, has its rubbish-heap, its record of vanished moments and forgotten lives told in faltering and feeble accents that have perished . . . we can compare book with book as we compare building with building. . . . Let us then be severe in our judgements; let us compare each book with the greatest of its kind. . . . To carry out this part of a reader's duty needs such imagination, insight, and learning that it is hard to conceive any one mind sufficiently endowed. . . . Would it not be wiser, then, to remit this part of reading to the critics, the gowned and furred authorities of the library to decide the question of the book's absolute value for us? Yet how impossible? . . . But as time goes on perhaps we can train our taste.[14]

Woolf's essay as well as Peacock's prophecy are particularly relevant to us today, when we read not only authors from the established canon but also various novelists, dramatists, and poets from earlier centuries who have been rediscovered and edited by 'gowned and furred authorities' who wish to extend the canon of so-called 'great works' of the past.

Attempts to extend the canon are sometimes based on a scholarly find, such as Roger Lonsdale's rediscovery of Joanna Baillie's anonymously published first book of poetry; or on a newly developed historical emphasis, such as Marilyn Butler's re-evaluation of Robert Southey's work. At other times, an attempt to extend the canon occurs because an assessment is made that is based on subjective ideology, taste or whim and which cannot claim objectivity. Satire, for example, was once seen as an anathema to 'Romanticism'. Sir Walter Scott's 'hybrid' novels, which mix realism with historical romance, after years of critical neglect are now being reprinted with up-to-date editing in the Edinburgh Edition of the Waverley Novels, a project which is due to be completed in 2003. Jane Austen also, who was once treated as a 'classical' writer, has been restored to the Romantic canon, along with other important male and female novelists who are discussed in Chapter 2.

One area that is gradually being reassessed by academic critics is that of women's lyric poetry. In my earlier *The Selected Poems of Joanna Baillie*

(1999), I made a case for including in the canon some of her major poems such as 'A Disappointment', 'A Winter Day' and 'A Summer Day', as well as her songs in Scots English. In fact, in relation to my own anthologies of forgotten women poets and critics of the Romantic age, I reprinted only authors of that period who wrote on interesting subjects in a competent manner. All the poems in my anthology were selected because of their artistic merit rather than because these poems are representative of a historical age or an ideology. Readers might therefore consider any of these poems for inclusion in the canon, such as Anna Barbauld's blank verse poem 'Washing Day' (1797). Barbauld imagines the toils of domesticity as a suitable subject for poetry, a theme that later poets, particularly in the twentieth century, have also adopted. The poet unites classical learning with vivid perceptions in a manner that satirizes reverence for classical symbols as well as obsessive housekeeping: the 'Muses' have lost the 'language of gods' and unmended stockings have 'yawning rents' that 'Gape as wide as Erebus'. At the conclusion of this poem, the story is resolved in an autobiographical fragment in which the first-person speaker recalls her childhood delight in blowing soap-bubbles, which she transmutes into an image of late eighteenth-century hot-air ballooning. The phenomenal achievement in 1782 of the Montgolfier brothers in sending hot-air balloons 'buoyant through the clouds' stands as a symbol of sublime possibilities for men and women in any field of creative endeavour, which, for the first-person speaker, includes poetry:

> Earth, air, and sky, and ocean hath its bubbles,
> And verse is one of them – this most of all.[15]

We might simply associate 'bubbles' with the evanescent, and conclude with Andrew Bennett that the narrator implies that poetry (including 'Washing Day') is an ephemeral art.[16]

Barbauld, however, equates the blowing of soap bubbles ('the sports of children') with both hot-air ballooning ('the toils of men') and with the writing of poetry, which suggests that a more complex reading must be made. Barbauld might not have foreseen twenty-first-century space travel, but she sees that the magic of imaginative acts is epitomized in images of creating a hot-air balloon that can float through the sky, or of creating a 'bubble' of significant poetry. She recognizes in this complex metaphor that all art in one sense is merely an attempt to encapsulate an event or a moment. Such moments *are* evanescent, since the language that is used in order to transcend the passing moment and to leave a record for posterity is not the event itself – whether it is the feat of the Montgolfier brothers or the magic of blowing soap bubbles. What Barbauld seems to have expressed in these lines is a recognition that posthumous appreciation of art is not guaranteed, but that men and women will nevertheless still dream and imagine new possibilities for humankind, whether it be in art or science. In 'Washing Day', Barbauld imagines the toils of domesticity as a suitable subject for poetry, a theme that later poets, particularly in the twentieth century, have adopted.

These attempts to place women in a central canon of poetry, including that of the Romantic age, are, however, not new. As early as 1848, Frederic Rowton edited *The Female Poets of Great Britain, Chronologically Arranged: with Copious Selections and Critical Remarks*, beginning with Juliana Berners (*fl.* 1460), who published tracts on hawking, hunting, and armoury, and included some poetry in these tracts. His selection includes 94 poets, and ends with early poems by Elizabeth Barrett Browning. He reprinted poems by many of the women poets who published in the Romantic age – Joanna Baillie, Anna Letitia Barbauld, Mary Robinson, Charlotte Smith, and others who were even more popular in their own time, such as Felicia Hemans and Letitia Elisabeth Landon. His introduction, in which he expresses received opinions of his day about the reciprocal roles of men and women, nevertheless makes the point that:

> the fact that this is almost the first book expressly devoted to the poetical productions of the British Female mind, tends strongly to prove that woman's intellect has been overlooked, if not despised by us hitherto; and that it is high time we should awake to a sense of our own folly and injustice.[17]

His anthology was well received at the time of publication, but did not make much impact in relation to placing these women poets in poetry anthologies generally. In 1928, for example, Humphrey Milford included very few women writers in his influential anthology *The Oxford Book of English Verse of the Romantic Period: 1798–1837*. These poets – who were represented by one or two poems each – were Joanna Baillie, Anna Barbauld, Anna Seward, Carolina Nairne, and Felicia Hemans. The fact that 150 years passed before Anna Barbauld's or Joanna Baillie's innovative poetry has been given posthumous recognition in edited hardback editions demonstrates that, even though the process is a slow and difficult one, the Romantic canon is still open to change.

The critical reception accorded posthumously to some male authors of the Romantic age might be seen as just as unpromising as that received by the women poets of that period. It has been claimed recently[18] that John Clare has been more or less neglected, at least by critics, even if a good selection of his poetry has been published in anthologies for schools and undergraduates throughout the nineteenth and twentieth centuries. Is regular publication in anthologies each century enough to assure a posthumous reputation? One of Clare's editors, Geoffrey Summerfield, suggests that acclaim of Clare as a poet was not sustained:

> Clare's reputation during his lifetime flared briefly like a shooting star, waned and disappeared into a limbo of neglect. Posthumously, it has progressed in fits and starts; but in every generation since his death he has been briefly rediscovered. . . . His critical reputation has always

> been problematical; academics have tended to cling to received opinion: romantic poetry had achieved a kind of definition by the mid-nineteenth century, and was known to comprise Wordsworth, Coleridge, Keats, Byron and Shelley.[19]

Criticism of John Clare's poetry has increased in the 10 years since Summerfield made this assessment, however, partly because theorists began to examine the subjective nature of critical opinion and to reassess the grounds on which they made literary critical judgements.

A consensus thus seems to have been reached about treating writers from the lower class without special pleading or different criteria from those used in assessing writers from the middle and upper classes. This move to encourage critical appraisal of working- or labouring-class poets has recently led to a more wide-ranging interest in John Clare, a farm labourer turned poet, and much debate has occurred about how to present Clare's poems to the reader in the light of his irregular punctuation. P.M.S. Dawson comments on the practice of editorial interference in the publication of Clare's work, suggesting that 'good editorial practice is now seen as an exact reproduction of what the poet wrote, with minimal correction of obvious errors'.[20] In addition, John Lucas has drawn attention to the possibility of identifying a 'popular radicalism', particularly in Clare's poem 'The Mores', as well as in several other poems.[21]

John Clare's poetic descriptions of the natural world can be seen to advantage in the context of marginalized women's poetry,[22] as well as in comparison with some of the 'canonized' male poets, such as John Keats. Merryn and Raymond Williams report Clare's response to John Keats's descriptions of rural scenes:

> His descriptions of scenery are often very fine but as it is the case with other inhabitants of great citys he often described nature as she appeared to his fancys & not as he would have described her had he witnessed the things he describes ... what appear as beautys in the eyes of a pent up citizen are looked upon as conceits by those who live in the country.[23]

Although neither Hampstead nor Enfield – places which Keats frequented – were not yet urbanized in the way these suburbs are today, Clare was possibly indirectly referring to his own experience of the countryside as a farm labourer, which contrasted with Keats's work as an apothecary. In one of several of Clare's poems to autumn, for example, he visualizes the country terrain in the light of his own experience of working on the land in a dry summer followed by autumn:

> The ground parched and cracked is Like overbaked bread
> The greensward all wrecked is Bents dried up and dead
> The fallow fields glitter Like water indeed
> And gossamers twitter Flung from weed unto weed[24]

The absence of punctuation, the varied use of anapaestic metre, and the doubling up of lines combine to suggest a seasonal climatic change that perhaps mirrors Clare's feelings about his social situation. The image of 'overbaked bread' with its cracks and dry rifts aptly describes water-deprived soil after harvest. But Clare's image here suggests that he and the poet John Keats might have imaginatively inhabited different countries, since Keats, in 'To Autumn' (1820), described the fallow fields not as shimmering in heat but mellowed, to the observer, by the evening sunset: 'barred clouds bloom the soft-dying day,/And touch the stubble-plains with rosy hue'.[25] In contrast, Clare's final stanza holds an apocalyptic note of hellish doom:

> Hill-tops like hot iron Glitter hot i' the sun
> And the Rivers we're eyeing Burn to gold as they run
> Burning hot is the ground Liquid gold is the air
> Whoever looks round Sees Eternity there[26]

Clare's vision of autumn is in part naturalistic and in part symbolic. The hot sun produces a chimera of fields that resemble gleaming water, and the river water itself glows golden in the sun. But, the poet claims, those who are willing to contemplate the natural world in all its burning glory will find a symbolic 'Eternity', which is Hell.

Keats's vision of autumn is also symbolic, but more conventional. The image of sunset in the phrase 'the soft-dying day', and the allusion to a requiem in the metaphoric line 'Then in a wailful choir the small gnats mourn', carry connotations of death, but Keats's language here is more melancholic and less direct than is Clare's. Clare seems – as he claims – to be 'eyeing' realistically what he sees, whereas Keats gives his vision of autumn a linguistic resonance which has been deservedly celebrated, but which is nevertheless less precise than Clare's straightforward similes and metaphors such as 'overbaked bread' and 'hot iron'. My implication here is not that one poet is superior to the other, but that an analysis of some of the differences between the two poets highlights their individual qualities. Such comparisons are not often made in critical accounts of Romanticism because four or five authors have been placed at a pinnacle of achievement, and others are grouped far below, if they are grouped at all.

The works of William Hazlitt, Thomas de Quincey, the Lambs, and John Clare are after all but a few examples of the rich literary output of the Romantic age. Critics need to use their various skills and techniques of historical and literary aesthetic assessment in order to revive the riches of the writings of that age, from the hieratic to the demotic. Towards the close of the eighteenth century, print publications increased:

> The eighteenth century had witnessed an unprecedented rate of growth in demand for the printed word, and had seen the beginnings of the final stages of the transformation of Britain into a print-dependent

> society. ... The development of the provincial trade, and of more efficient mechanisms of supply and distribution of London books throughout the country, both exploited and helped to create a market.[27]

Many kinds of authors found new opportunities to publish in response to market demands, and it is surprising that so few of these authors – of the hundreds who were published – are not given the opportunity of finding a new readership today.

Notes

1 Thomas de Quincey, *Reminiscences of the English Lake Poets*, ed. John E. Jordan (London, 1961), p. 88.
2 *The New Oxford Book of Eighteenth-Century Verse* (Oxford, 1984), p. xxxvi.
3 Marilyn Butler, 'Culture's Medium: the Role of the Review', in *The Cambridge Companion to British Romanticism*, ed. Stuart Curran (Cambridge, 1993), pp. 141–2.
4 My First Acquaintance with Poets', repr. in William Hazlitt, *Selected Writings*, ed. Jon Cook (Oxford, 1991), pp. 508, 518 and 227–8.
5 William Hazlitt, *The Spirit of the Age*, ed. E.D. Mackerness (Plymouth, 1969; 2nd edn, 1991), pp. 55–6.
6 Thomas de Quincey, *Reminiscences of the English Lake Poets*, p. 108.
7 Margaret Donaldson, *Human Minds: An Exploration* (Harmondsworth, 1992).
8 Thomas McFarland, 'Preface', *Romantic Cruxes: the English Essayists and the Spirit of the Age* (Oxford, 1987), p. 1.
9 See, for example, Nigel Leask, *British Romantic Writers and the East: Anxieties of Empire* (Cambridge, 1992).
10 Charles Lamb, 'Confessions of A Drunkard' (1813), in *The Works in Prose and Verse of Charles and Mary Lamb*, Vol. I, *Miscellaneous Prose*, *Elia, Last Essays of Elia*, ed. Thomas Hutchinson (Oxford, 1908), pp. 169–70.
11 In 1903, E.V. Lucas edited the works of Charles and Mary Lamb in a definitive edition: *The Works of Charles and Mary Lamb* (5 vols, London, 1903). Subsequently, he edited their correspondence: *The Letters of Charles and Mary Lamb* (3 vols, London, 1935).
12 Marilyn Butler, 'Repossessing the Past: the Case for an Open Literary History', in *Rethinking Historicism: Critical Readings in Romantic History*, ed. Marjorie Levinson (Oxford, 1989), 64–84.
13 T.L. Peacock, *The Four Ages of Poetry* (1820), ed. H.F.B. Brett-Smith (Oxford, 1921), p. 19.
14 Virginia Woolf, 'How Should One Read A Book?', *The Common Reader* (London, 1932), pp. 27 and 32–3.
15 See *Women Romantic Poets, 1785–1832: An Anthology*, ed. Jennifer Breen (London, 1992; 2nd edn, 1994), p. 83.
16 See Andrew Bennett, *Romantic Poets and the Culture of Posterity* (Cambridge, 1999), p. 69.
17 Frederic Rowton, *The Female Poets of Great Britain, Chronologically Arranged: with Copious Selections and Critical Remarks* (London, 1848), 'Introductory Chapter', p. xvii.
18 P.M.S. Dawson states that John Clare 'can still justly be considered as neglected' in *Literature of the Romantic Period: A Bibliographical Guide*, ed. Michael O'Neill (Oxford, 1998), p. 170.

19 John Clare, *Selected Poetry*, ed. and introd. Geoffrey Summerfield (Harmondsworth, 1990), pp. 21–2.
20 P.M.S. Dawson, 'John Clare' in *Literature of the Romantic Period: A Bibliographical Guide*, p. 167.
21 John Lucas, *John Clare* (Plymouth, 1994), p. 40.
22 See Clare MacDonald Shaw, 'Some Contemporary Women Poets in Clare's Library', in *The Independent Spirit: John Clare and the Self-Taught Tradition*, ed. John Goodridge (Helpston, 1994), pp. 87–124.
23 'Introduction', *John Clare: Selected Poetry and Prose*, ed. Merryn and Raymond Williams (London, 1986) p. 17.
24 John Clare, *Selected Poetry*, ed. and introd. Geoffrey Summerfield, p. 345.
25 John Keats, *The Complete Poems*, ed. John Barnard (Harmondsworth, 3rd edn, 1988), p. 435.
26 John Clare, *Selected Poetry*, ed. and introd. Geoffrey Summerfield, p. 345.
27 John Feather, *A History of British Publishing* (London, 1988), p. 129.

Chronology of authors of the Romantic age

Year	Artistic context	Historical events
1784	Clara Reeve, *The Progress of Romance*	
1785	Boswell, *Journal of a Tour of The Hebrides* Cowper, *Poems* Gainsborough, *Mrs Siddons* (portrait) Elisabeth Vigee-Lebrun, *Bacchante* (painting) Ann Yearsley, *Poems on Several Occasions*	Bill for Parliamentary Reform collapses; Edmund Cartwright patents the power loom; first Channel crossing made by balloon
1786	Burns, *Poems* Reynolds, *The Duchess of Devonshire and her Small Daughter* (portrait) Beckford, *Vathek*	Financial reforms; commercial treaty with France
1787	Mary Wollstonecraft, *Thoughts on the Education of Daughters* Charlotte Smith, *Elegiac Sonnets* Elisabeth Vigee-Lebrun, *Marie Antoinette and Her Children* (portrait)	American Constitution signed
1788	Hannah More, *Slavery: A Poem* Charlotte Smith, *Emmeline* Mary Wollstonecraft, *Original Stories from Real Life*; *Mary* Adelaide Labille-Guiard, *Louise Elisabeth de France* (painting)	Australia settled by British; *Times* founded; trial of Warren Hastings begins; William Wilberforce's first motion to abolish slave trade

1789	Blake, *Songs of Innocence; Book of Thel* Philip, *The Voyage of Governor Philip to Botany Bay* Elizabeth Hands, *The Death of Amnon*	French Revolution, Fall of Bastille (July); Declaration of Rights of Man and the Citizen (August); Washington is US President; first cotton textiles factory in Manchester
1790	Joanna Baillie, *Poems* Burke, *Reflections on the French Revolution* Helen Maria Williams, *Julia; Letters Written from France* Blake, *Marriage of Heaven and Hell*	Lavoisier publishes a table of chemical elements
1791	Burns, *Tam o' Shanter* Paine, *The Rights of Man* Anna Barbauld, *Epistle to William Wilberforce*	
1792	Robert Anderson, ed., *Poets of Great Britain* Mary Wollstonecraft, *A Vindication of the Rights of Woman* Helen Maria Williams, *Letters from France*	Pitt's attack on slave trade; September Massacres in Paris; Republic proclaimed in France; first successful use of coal gas in lighting
1793	Jane Austen, *Love and Friendship* Burns, *Songs* Wordsworth, *An Evening Walk* Godwin, *Political Justice* Mary Hays, *Letters and Essays* Mary Robinson, *Poems, 1791–3*	Washington's second term as President; execution of Louis XVI (June); execution of Marie-Antoinette (October); France at war with Britain
1794	Blake, *Songs of Experience* Ann Radcliffe, *Mysteries of Udolpho* Godwin, *Caleb Williams* Southey, *Poems*	Execution of Lavoisier in France; Habeus Corpus Act suspended in Britain until 1801
1795	Maria Edgeworth, *Letters for Literary Ladies*	Treason and Sedition acts; acquittal of Warren Hastings; first settlement of New Zealand
1796	Wordsworth, *The Borderers* Ann Yearsley, *The Rural Lyre* Mary Wollstonecraft, *Letters Written . . . Sweden, Norway, And Denmark* Frances Burney, *Camilla* Lewis, *The Monk*	War between Spain and Britain; Royal Technical College founded in Glasgow

1797	Coleridge, *The Ancient Mariner* Southey, *Poems* Charlotte Smith, *Elegiac Sonnets*, Vol. 2	*Journal of Natural Philosophy, Chemistry and Other Arts* founded
1798	Joanna Baillie, *Plays on the Passions*, Vol. 1 Malthus, *Principles of Population* Mary Wollstonecraft, *Maria, or the Wrongs of Woman* Wordsworth and Coleridge, *Lyrical Ballads*	
1799	Blake, *The Adoration of the Magi* (tempera) Hannah More, *Strictures on the Modern System of Female Education*	Napoleon is First Consul; Religious Tract Society is founded; Treason and Sedition Acts
1800	Maria Edgeworth, *Castle Rackrent* Wordsworth, *Michael* Marie-Guihelmine Benoist, *Portrait of a Negress* (painting)	Jefferson is US President; Royal Institution of Science founded
1801	Maria Edgeworth, *Belinda* Amelia Opie, *The Father and Daughter; Memoirs of Mary Robinson*	First Census (pop. 9,168,000) General Enclosure Act
1802	Joanna Baillie, *Plays on the Passions*, Vol. 2 Amelia Opie, *Poems*	Peace of Amiens, Health and Morals of Apprentices Act; beginnings of photography
1803	Mme. De Staël, *Delphine* Turner, *Calais Pier* (painting)	War with France renewed; John Dalton establishes atomic theory
1804	Joanna Baillie, *Miscellaneous Plays* Matilda Betham, *Biographical Dictionary of Celebrated Women* Blake, *Jerusalem; Milton*	Thomas Telford commences construction of Caledonian Canal
1805	Milne, *Simple Poems on Simple Subjects* Scott, *Lay of the Last Minstrel* Jane and Ann Taylor, *Original Poems for Infant Minds* Wordsworth completes *The Prelude* (published in 1850) Turner, *Shipwreck* (painting)	Battle of Trafalgar; London Docks opened; first factory lit by gas at Manchester

Year	Works	Events
1806	Byron, *Fugitive Pieces* Charlotte Richardson, *Poems Written on Different Occasions* Mary Robinson, *Poetical Works* Charlotte Smith, *Beachy Head and other Poems* Sydney Owenson, *The Wild Irish Girl*	Bill for the Abolition of the Slave Trade passed in Parliament; East India Docks open in London
1807	Byron, *Hours of Idleness* Charles and Mary Lamb, *Tales from Shakespeare* Mme. De Staël, *Corinne* Turner, *The Sun Rising through Vapour* (painting) Wordsworth, *Poems in Two Volumes*	Air pump for mines introduced
1808	Anne Grant, *The Highlanders* Felicia Hemans, *Poems* Amelia Opie, *The Warrior's Return* Leigh Hunt founds *Examiner*	Peninsular War begins
1809	Charles and Mary Lamb, *Poetry for Children* *Quarterly Review* founded	
1810	Alexander Chalmers, *English Poets* Coleridge lectures on Shakespeare Anna Seward, *Poetical Works*	Durham Miners' Strike; method of preserving food in cans is discovered
1811	Jane Austen, *Sense and Sensibility* Scott, *The Lady of the Lake* Shelley, *The Necessity of Atheism*	Princes of Wales is Regent; Shelley is expelled from Oxford
1812	Joanna Baillie, *Plays on the Passions,* Vol. 3 Byron, *Childe Harold* (Cantos 1 and 2) Maria Edgeworth, *The Absentee* Felicia Hemans, *The Domestic Affections*	French retreat from Moscow; Elgin Marbles brought to England; 'Luddite Riots' commence; John Common invents a reaping machine
1813	Jane Austen, *Pride and Prejudice* Byron, *The Bride of Abydos* Shelley, *Queen Mab* Blake, *Day of Judgement* (drawings)	

1814	Jane Austen, *Mansfield Park* Frances Burney, *The Wanderer* Byron, *The Corsair* Anne Grant, *Eighteen Hundred And Thirteen* Wordsworth, *The Excursion* Scott, *Waverley* Turner, *The Frosty Morning* (painting)	Napoleon abdicates; first Treaty of Paris between Allies and France; invention of cylinder-press printing; Corn Law passed by Parliament
1815	Constable, *Boat Building* (painting)	Battle of Waterloo; Stephenson patents the steam engine
1816	Jane Austen, *Emma* Byron, *Poems on His Domestic Circumstances* Coleridge, *Christabel; Kubla Khan; Pains of Sleep* Hannah More, *Poems* Peacock, *Headlong Hall* Shelley, *Alastor and Other Poems* Jane Taylor, *Essays in Rhyme on Morals and Manners* *Blackwood's* magazine founded	End of twenty years' war leaves acute distress in England; Robert Owen opens up school in cotton mill
1817	Coleridge, *Biographia Literaria* Hazlitt, *The Round Table* Keats, *Poems* Constable, *Flatford Mill* (painting) M. and P.B. Shelley, *History of a Six Weeks' Tour*	Habeus Corpus suspended
1818	Jane Austen, *Northanger Abbey* Keats, *Endymion* Peacock, *Nightmare Abbey* Mary Shelley, *Frankenstein*	First passenger ship made of iron; Institute of Civil Engineers founded
1819	Byron, *Don Juan* (two cantos) Hazlitt, *Political Essays* Scott, *The Heart of Midlothian* Shelley, *The Cenci*	Peterloo Massacre; first Macadam roads laid
1820	Clare, *Poems* Anna Barbauld, *The British Novelists* Keats, *La Belle Dame Sans Merci; Lamia; Isabella; Eve of St Agnes; Hyperion and Other Poems* Lamb, *Essays of Elia* Peacock, *Four Ages of Poetry*	Accession of George IV; Royal Astronomical Society founded; opening of Regent's Canal, London

1820	Shelley, *Prometheus Unbound* Southey, *Vision of Judgement* Wordsworth, *The River Duddon, a Series of Sonnets*	
1821	Joanna Baillie, *Metrical Legends* Clare, *The Village Minstrel* De Quincey, *Confessions of an Opium Eater* Letitia E. Landon, *The Fate of Adelaide* Constable, *The Hay Wain* (painting) Shelley, *Adonais; Epipsychidion*	London Co-operative Society founded; Michael Faraday expounds the principle of the electric motor
1822	Byron, *The Vision of Judgment* Shelley, *Hellas* Wordsworth, *Ecclesiastical Sketches*	Royal Academy of Music founded in London
1823	Helen Maria Williams, *Poems On Various Subjects* Felicia Hemans, *The Siege of Valencia* Lamb, *Essays of Elia* Hazlitt, *Libor Amoris* Shelley, *Poetical Pieces*	Peel's penal reforms begin; Birkbeck College founded; Charles Babbage works on a calculating machine; *The Lancet* founded; Mechanics Institutes founded
1824	Letitia E. Landon, *The Improvisatrice* M.R. Mitford, *Our Village* Hogg, *Confessions of a Justified Sinner* Shelley, *Posthumous Poems*, ed. Mary Shelley	Repeal of 1662 Poor Law Act; Repeal of Combination Laws of 1799 and 1801; establishment of National Gallery
1825	Anna Barbauld, *Works* Hazlitt, *Spirit of the Age* Felicia Hemans, *The Forest Sanctuary* Letitia E. Landon, *The Troubadour*	First passenger train in Britain (Stockton–Darlington); commercial crisis in England
1826	Elizabeth Barrett, *An Essay on Mind with Other Poems* Mary Shelley, *The Last Man*	Anti-Power Loom Riots in Lancashire
1827	Clare, *The Shepherd's Calendar* Fenimore Cooper, *The Prairie* Letitia E. Landon, *The Golden Violet* Keble, *The Christian Year*	University of London founded

1828	Felicia Hemans, *Records of Women* Carlyle, *Essay on Burns* Constable, *Salisbury Cathedral* (painting)	Wellington is Prime Minister; repeal of Test and Corporation Act
1829	Letitia E. Landon, *The Venetian Bracelet* James Mill, *Analysis of the Human Mind* Tennyson, *Timbuctoo*	Catholic Emancipation Act; Metropolitan Police Force established by Peel
1830	Cobbett, *Rural Rides* Felicia Hemans, *Songs of the Affections* Mary Shelley, *Perkin Warbeck* Tennyson, *Poems*	Accession of William IV; resignation of Wellington; Earl Grey is Prime Minister; agricultural labourers' riots in South England; Royal Geographical Society founded

Suggestions for further reading

Primary works

Anthologies

Breen, Jennifer, ed., *Women Romantic Poets, 1785–1832: An Anthology* (London, 1992; new edn, 1994).

Breen, Jennifer, ed., *Women Romantics, 1785–1832: Writing in Prose* (London, 1996).

Feldman, Paula and Daniel Robinson, eds, *A Century of Sonnets, 1750–1850* (New York, 1999).

Lonsdale, Roger, *The New Oxford Book of Eighteenth-Century Verse* (Oxford, 1984).

McGann, Jerome, ed., *The New Oxford Book of Romantic Period Verse* (Oxford, 1993).

Percy, Thomas, *Reliques of Ancient English Poetry* (Edinburgh, 1765; repr. 1864).

Milford, Humphrey, ed., *The Oxford Book of Romantic Verse* (London, 1901).

Wu, Duncan, ed., *Romantic Woman Poets: An Anthology* (Oxford, 1997).

Novels

Austen, Jane, *Love and Friendship* (c. 1793); repr. in *Catharine and Other Writings*, ed. Margaret Anne Doody and Douglas Murray (Oxford, 1993; reissued 1998).

Austen, Jane, *Sense and Sensibility* (1811; Harmondsworth, 1995).

Austen, Jane, *Pride and Prejudice* (1813; Harmondsworth, 1997).

Austen, Jane, *Mansfield Park* (1814; Harmondsworth, 1996).

Austen, Jane, *Emma* (1816; Harmondsworth, 1997).

Austen, Jane, *Northanger Abbey* (1818; Harmondsworth, 1995).

Austen, Jane, *Persuasion* (1818; Harmondsworth, 1985).
Beckford, William, *Vathek* (1786; Oxford, 1999).
Burney, Frances, *Evelina* (1778; Oxford, 1998).
Burney, Frances, *Cecilia* (1782; Oxford, 1999).
Burney, Frances, *Camilla* (1796; Oxford, 1999).
Burney, Frances, *The Wanderer* (1814; Oxford, 1991).
Edgeworth, Maria, *Castle Rackrent* (1800; Harmondsworth, 1992).
Edgeworth, Maria, *Belinda* (1801; Oxford, 1999).
Godwin, William, *Caleb Williams* (1794; Harmondsworth, 1987).
Hamilton, Elizabeth, *Memoirs of Modern Philosophers* (1800; Ontario, 2000).
Hays, Mary, *Memoirs of Emma Courtney* (1796; Ontario, 2000).
Hogg, James, *Private Memoirs and Confessions of a Justified Sinner* (1824; Harmondsworth, 1983).
Lewis, Matthew, *The Monk* (1796; Oxford, 1996).
Mackenzie, Henry, *The Man of Feeling* (1771; Oxford, 2001).
Maturin, Charles, *Melmoth the Wanderer* (1826; Harmondsworth, 2000).
Owenson, Sydney, Lady Morgan, *The Wild Irish Girl* (1806; Oxford, 1999).
Peacock, Thomas Love, *Nightmare Abbey*, ed. Raymond Wright (London, 1818; Harmondsworth, 1969, repr. 1986).
Peacock, Thomas Love, *Nightmare Abbey* (1818), *Crotchet Castle* (1831) (Harmondsworth, 1982).
Radcliffe, Ann, *A Sicilian* Romance (1791; Oxford, 1998).
Radcliffe, Ann, *The Romance of the Forest* (1792; Oxford, 1998).
Radcliffe, Ann, *The Mysteries of Udolpho* (1794; Oxford, 1998).
Radcliffe, Ann, *The Italian* (1797; Oxford, 1998).
Reeve, Clara, *The Progress of Romance* (1785; New York, 1970).
Rousseau, Jean-Jacques, *Emile* (1762; London, 1993).
Scott, Sir Walter, *Waverley* (1814; Harmondsworth, 1986)
Scott, Sir Walter, *The Heart of Midlothian* (1818–19; Oxford, 1999).
Shelley, Mary Godwin, *Frankenstein* (1818; New York, 1996).
Smith, Charlotte, *Emmeline* (1788; out of print).
Sterne, Lawrence, *A Sentimental Journey* (1768; Oxford, 1998).
Von Goethe, Johann Wolfgang, *The Sorrows of Young Werther*, trans. Michael Hulse (1774; Harmondsworth, 1989).
Walpole, Horace, *The Castle of Otranto* (1765; Oxford, 1998).
Wollstonecraft, Mary, *Mary* (1788); *Maria, or the Wrongs of Women* (1798; Harmondsworth, 1992).

Poetry

Baillie, Joanna, *Selected Poems*, ed. Jennifer Breen (Manchester, 1999).
Barbauld, Anna, *The Poems*, ed. William McCarthy and Elizabeth Kraft (Athens, Georgia, 1994).

Blake, William, *Selected Poetry and Prose*, ed. David Punter (London, 1988).

The Poems and Songs of Robert Burns, ed. James Kinsley (3 vols, London, 1968).

Lord Byron, *Poetical Works*, ed. Frederick Page (Harmondsworth, 1904; rev. John Jump, 1970).

Lord Byron, *Don Juan*, ed. T.G. Steffan, E. Steffan and W.W. Pratt (Harmondsworth, 1973; repr. 1984).

Clare, John, *Selected Poetry and Prose*, ed. Merryn and Raymond Williams (London, 1986).

Clare, John, *Selected Poetry*, ed. and introd. Geoffrey Summerfield (Harmondsworth, 1990).

Coleridge, Samuel Taylor, *Poems*, ed. John Beer (London and Vermont, 1963; new edn, 1993).

Keats, John, *The Complete Poems*, ed. John Barnard (1973; 3rd edn, Harmondsworth, 1988).

Keats, John, *Selected Poems*, ed. Nicholas Roe (London and Vermont, 1995).

The Works of Charles and Mary Lamb, ed. Lucas, E.V. (5 vols, London, 1903).

Robinson, Mary, *Selected Poems*, ed. Judith Pascoe (Ontario, Canada, 2000).

Tottel's Miscellany, ed. Hyder Rollin (2 vols, Cambridge, 1965).

Shelley, P.B., *Selected Poems*, ed. Timothy Webb (London, 1977; repr. 1983).

The Poems of Charlotte Smith, ed. Stuart Curran (New York, 1993).

Wordsworth, William and S.T. Coleridge, *Lyrical Ballads*, ed. R.L. Brett and A.R. Jones (1798; repr. London, 1963; 2nd edn, 1991).

Wordsworth, William, *Poetical Works*, ed. Thomas Hutchinson (London, 1904; new edn. rev. Ernest de Selincourt, 1936; repr. 1966).

Essays, memoirs, letters and reviews

The Collected Letters of Joanna Baillie, ed. Judith Bailey Slagle (2 vols, Madison, USA, 1999).

Burke, Edmund, *A Philosophical Enquiry into the Origin of Our Ideas of the Sublime and Beautiful* (2nd edn, 1757; Oxford, 1990).

The Letters of Robert Burns, ed. G. Ross Roy (2 vols, Oxford, 1985).

Coleridge, S.T., *Biographia Literaria*, ed. Nigel Leask (London and Vermont, 1997).

De Quincey, Thomas, *Reminiscences of the English Lake Poets*, ed. John E. Jordan (London, 1961).

Godwin, William, *Enquiry Concerning Political Justice* (1793; Harmondsworth, 1985).

Hazlitt, William, *Selected Writings*, ed. Jon Cook (Oxford, 1991).
Hazlitt, William, *The Spirit of the Age*, ed. E.D. Mackerness (Plymouth, 1969; 2nd edn, 1991).
Letters of John Keats: A Selection, ed. Gittings, Robert (London, 1970; repr. 1982).
Lamb, Charles, 'Confessions of A Drunkard' (1813), in *The Works in Prose and Verse of Charles and Mary Lamb*, Vol. I, *Miscellaneous Prose, Elia, Last Essays of Elia*, ed. Thomas Hutchinson (Oxford, 1908).
The Letters of Charles and Mary Lamb, ed. Lucas, E.V. (3 vols, London, 1935).
Peacock, Thomas Love, *The Four Ages of Poetry; Shelley's Defence of Poetry; Browning's Essay on Shelley*, ed. H.F.B. Brett-Smith (Oxford, 1821).
Shelley, Percy Bysshe, *A Defence of Poetry* (London, 1840).
The Works of Mary Wollstonecraft, Vol. 7, *Contributions to the Analytical Review*, ed. Marilyn Butler and Janet Todd (London, 1989).
The Letters of William and Dorothy Wordsworth, ed. Ernest de Selincourt (London, 2nd edn, rev. Alan G. Hill, 1967–93).

Secondary works

Biographies, memoirs, essays, social history, criticism

Barker-Benfield, G., *The Culture of Sensibility: Sex and Society in Eighteenth-Century Britain* (Chicago and London, 1992).
Beer, Gillian, *The Romance* (London, 1970).
Beer, John, *Questioning Romanticism* (Baltimore, Maryland, 1995).
Benis, Toby R., *Romanticism on the Road: The Marginal Gains of Wordsworth's Homeless* (Cambridge, 2000).
Bennett, Andrew, *Romantic Poets and the Culture of Posterity* (Cambridge, 1999).
Bold, Alan, *The Ballad* (London, 1979).
Botting, Fred, *Gothic* (London and New York, 1996).
Butler, Marilyn, *Romantics, Rebels and Reactionaries: English Literature and Its Background, 1760–1830* (Oxford, 1981; repr. 1992).
Butler, Marilyn, *Jane Austen and the War of Ideas* (Oxford, 1988).
Carhart, Margaret, *The Life and Work of Joanna Baillie* (New Haven, USA; London, 1923).
Clark, Timothy, 'Crisis in the Concept of the University', in *The Arts and Sciences of Criticism*, ed. David Fuller and Patricia Waugh (Oxford, 1999).
Clark, William, Jan Golinski and Simon Schaffer, eds, *The Sciences in Enlightened Europe* (Chicago, 1999).
Crawford, Robert, *Devolving English Literature* (Oxford, 1992).

Crawford, Robert, ed., *Robert Burns and Cultural Authority* (Edinburgh, 1997).

Curran, Stuart, ed., *The Cambridge Companion to Romanticism* (Cambridge, 1993).

De Almeida, Hermione, *Romantic Medicine and John Keats* (Oxford, 1991).

Doody, Margaret Anne, *Frances Burney: The Life in the Works* (New Brunswick, 1988).

Doody, Margaret Anne, *The True Story of the Novel* (New Brunswick, 1996).

Doyle, William, *The Oxford History of the French Revolution* (Oxford, 1989).

Favret, Mary A. and Nicola J. Watson, eds, *At the Limits of Romanticism* (Bloomington, Indiana, 1994).

Feldman, Paula R. and Theresa M. Kelley, eds, *Romantic Women Writers: Voices and Countervoices* (Hanover and London, 1995).

Fuller, John, *The Sonnet* (London, 1972; repr. 1978).

Goodridge, John, ed., *The Independent Spirit: John Clare and the Self-Taught Tradition* (Helpston, 1994).

Groom, Nick, *The Making of Percy's Reliques* (Oxford, 1999).

Holmes, Richard, *Shelley: The Pursuit* (London, 1974).

Hunter, J. Paul, ed., *Frankenstein* (New York, 1996).

Johnson, Claudia, *Equivocal Beings: Politics, Gender, and Sentimentality in the 1790s* (Chicago, 1995).

Johnston, Kenneth, *The Hidden Wordsworth: Poet, Lover, Rebel, Spy* (New York and London, 1998).

Jones, Steven, *Shelley's Satire: Violence, Exhortation and Authority* (Illinois, USA, 1994).

Jones, Steven, *Satire and Romanticism* (Basingstoke, 2000).

Jost, Francois, 'Anatomy of an Ode: Shelley and the Sonnet Tradition', in *Comparative Literature*, 34 (1982).

Kelly, Gary, *The English Jacobin Novel 1780–1805* (London, 1976).

Kelly, Gary, *English Fiction of the Romantic Period 1789–1830* (London, 1989).

Kiely, Robert, *The Romantic Novel in England* (Boston, 1972).

Lascelles, Mary, *Jane Austen and Her Art* (Oxford, 1983).

Levinson, Marjorie, ed., *Rethinking Historicism: Critical Readings in Romantic History* (Oxford, 1989).

McFarland, Thomas, *Romantic Cruxes: the English Essayists and the Spirit of the Age* (Oxford, 1987).

McGann, Jerome, *The Romantic Ideology: A Critical Investigation* (Chicago, 1983).

McGann, Jerome, *The Poetics of Sensibility: A Revolution in Literary Style* (New York, 1996).

Mayo, Robert, 'The Contemporaneity of the *Lyrical Ballads*', *PMLA*, 69 (New York, 1954), 486–522.

Mellor, Anne K., ed., *Romanticism and Feminism* (Bloomington, Indiana, 1988).

Mellor, Anne K., *Mary Shelley* (London, 1988).

Newlyn, Lucy, *Coleridge, Wordsworth and the Language of Allusion* (Oxford, 1986).

O'Neill, Michael, *Shelley* (Harlow, 1993).

O'Neill, Michael, ed., *Literature of the Romantic Period: A Bibliographical Guide* (Oxford, 1998).

Oppenheimer, Paul, *The Birth of the Modern Mind: New Facts and a Theory* (New York, 1989).

Park, Roy, *Hazlitt and the Spirit of the Age: Abstraction and Critical Theory* (Oxford, 1971).

Pollard, Arthur, *Satire* (London, 1970; repr. 1977).

Porter, Roy, *English Society in the Eighteenth Century* (Harmondsworth, 1983; rev. edn, 1990).

Rawson, Claude, *Satire and Sentiment 1660–1830* (Cambridge, 1994; new edn, New Haven and London, 2000).

Ridenour, George M., *Shelley: A Collection of Critical Essays* (Englewood Cliffs, N.J., 1965).

Robertson, Fiona, 'Novels', in *An Oxford Companion to the Romantic Age: British Culture 1776–1832*, ed. Iain McCalman (Oxford, 1999).

Roe, Nicholas, *Wordsworth and Coleridge: The Radical Years* (Oxford, 1988).

St Clair, William, *The Godwins and the Shelleys* (Baltimore, 1989).

Spiller, Michael G., *The Development of the Sonnet: An Introduction* (London, 1992).

Thompson, E.P., *The Making of the English Working Class* (London, 1963; repr. 1968, 1980).

Wagner, Jennifer, *A Moment's Monument: Revisionary Poetics and the Nineteenth-Century English Sonnet* (N.J. and London, 1996).

Watson, Nicola J., *Revolution and the Form of the British Novel: 1790–1825* (Oxford, 1994).

Wilson, Carol, Shiner Wilson and Joel Haefner, eds, *Re-Visioning Romanticism: British Women Writers, 1776–1837* (Philadelphia, 1994).

Woodings, R.B., *Shelley* (London, 1968).

Wu, Duncan, *Wordsworth's Reading, 1770–1779* (Cambridge, 1993).

Yeo, Richard, 'Natural Philosophy (Science)', in *An Oxford Companion to the Romantic Age: British Culture 1776–1832* (New York, 1999).

Yarrington, Alison and Kelvin Everest, eds, *Reflections of Revolution: Images of Romanticism* (London and New York, 1993).

Index